CHANGE YOUR THINKING, CHANGE YOUR LIFE

CHANGE YOUR THINKING, CHANGE YOUR LIFE

How to Unlock Your Full Potential for Success and Achievement

BRIAN TRACY

WILEY

JOHN WILEY & SONS, INC.

Published by John Wiley & Sons, Inc., Hoboken, New Jersey.
Published simultaneously in Canada.

For general information on our other products and services, please contact our
Customer Care Department within the United States at (800) 762-2974, outside
the United States at (317) 572-3993 or fax (317) 572-4002.

Wiley also publishes its books in a variety of electronic formats. Some content that
appears in print may not be available in electronic books. For more information
about Wiley products, visit our web site at www.wiley.com.

Library of Congress Cataloging-in-Publication Data:
Tracy, Brian.
    Change your thinking, change your life : how to unlock your full
potential for success and achievement / Brian Tracy.
        p. cm.
    ISBN 0-471-44858-3 (alk. paper)
    1. Success—Psychological aspects. I. Title.
BF637.S8T634 2003
158.1—dc21   2003006625

Printed in the United States of America.

10 9 8 7 6 5 4 3 2 1

To my wife Barbara,
from whom I have learned so much
about the importance of love and family.
You are my mainstay
and my greatest inspiration.

Foreword

If you are ready to leverage yourself to greatness and achieve giant results, you have the right road map in your hands. You have before you the DNA of your future. All you need to create a wonderful future for yourself is to read this book, decide how you are going to apply it to your own life, write out a plan, and then go forth with enthusiasm and make it happen.

I have a confession to make. I am one of Brian's raving fans. I have studied him, his brilliant work, and the extraordinary results he has achieved. I am also one of his close colleagues and friends. We have worked together on many platforms, and met and talked with each other on numerous occasions.

Brian is one of the finest thinkers and writers on inner development and personal success in the world. I know; I have sold over 82 million books aimed at helping people get the most out of themselves.

Change Your Thinking, Change Your Life shows you how to discover your extraordinary inner resources and tap your incredible powers. You will learn how to attract into your life all the people and resources you need to achieve any goal you can set for yourself.

You will absolutely amaze yourself as you start to achieve new and better results by employing these concepts and ideas in everything you do. These are the same concepts used by all big-time winners, self-made millionaires, and leaders in every field.

In this book, you will learn a step-by-step process to great success that you will eventually implement, easily and effortlessly. This strategy for success is so logical, so inviting, and ultimately so fulfilling and omni-beneficial that it is virtually a breakthrough in personal performance.

As long as you are going to think anyway, why not think great thoughts and get great results?

Brian is a shining light in the speaking and writing world. He has done incredible thinking and achieved amazing results, for himself and many hundreds of thousands of other people. Brian's thinking in this book will inspire you to do the same or more.

Get ready for one of the great adventures and explorations into the last great frontier, and the first—your mind! You are about to have a wonderful experience.

MARK VICTOR HANSEN
Author, *Chicken Soup for the Soul*

Contents

Acknowledgments

The writing of this book has taken many years of work, reading, teaching, and experience. Many people have contributed to my thinking and have been invisible guides as these chapters came together. I would like to first thank my friend Mark Victor Hansen, who introduced me many years ago to Emmet Fox, perhaps the finest spiritual thinker of the twentieth century. Ernest Holmes, founder of Science of Mind, opened my eyes and heart to the incredible universe of potential contained within each person when they *changed their thinking and changed their lives*. Great spiritual teachers such as Charles Fillmore, Neville, Eric Butterworth, Wayne Dyer, and Roberto Assagioli have had a profound influence on my thinking.

I would also like to thank those great practical thinkers on success who have had such a wonderful influence on me—and on the world—such as Napoleon Hill, Maxwell Maltz, Claude Bristol, David Schwarz, W. Clement Stone, Earl Nightingale, Jim Rohn, Zig Ziglar, Dennis Waitley, and Charlie Jones.

Business thinkers such as Peter Drucker, Andrew Grove, Ken Blanchard, Warren Bennis, Tom Peters, Nido Qubein, and Marshall Goldsmith have greatly enriched me with their ideas and insights.

I would like to thank my editor, Matthew Holt of John Wiley & Sons, for his unflinching support of this book, and his constant encouragement over the many months that it has taken to write and edit.

Not least, I thank my wonderful wife Barbara and my fabulous children—Christina, Michael, David, and Catherine—for their support and patience during the long hours away from them to finish this book.

Introduction

There is nothing on earth that you cannot have—once you
have mentally accepted the fact that you can have it.

—Robert Collier

■ THE TRUTH ABOUT YOU

You are a thoroughly good person. You deserve a wonderful life, full
of success, happiness, joy, and excitement. You are entitled to have
happy relationships, excellent health, meaningful work, and financial independence. These are your birthright. This is what your life
is meant to include.

You are engineered for success and designed to have high levels
of self-esteem, self-respect, and personal pride. You are extraordinary; there has never been anyone exactly like you in all the history
of mankind on earth. You have absolutely amazing untapped talents
and abilities that, when properly unleashed and applied, can bring
you everything you could ever want in life.

You are living at the greatest time in all of human history. You
are surrounded by abundant opportunities that you can take advantage of to realize your dreams. The only real limits on what you can
be, do, or have are the limits you place on yourself by your own
thinking. Your future is virtually unlimited.

■ GET REAL!

How did you react to the preceding three paragraphs? You probably
had two responses. First, you liked what they said, and your fondest
wish was for them to be true for you. But your second response was
probably one of skepticism and disbelief. Even though you deeply

desire to live a wonderfully healthy, happy, prosperous life, when you read those words, your doubts and fears arose immediately to remind you of reasons why these dreams and goals may not be possible for you. Well, join the crowd!

This is exactly how I felt many years ago. Even though I wanted to be a big success in life, I was unskilled, uneducated, and unemployed. I had no idea what I could do to improve my situation. I felt trapped between big ideas on the one hand and limited resources and opportunities on the other. Then I discovered a series of remarkable principles that have been responsible for all the great successes and achievements of the ages, and my life changed forever.

After proving these laws and principles in my own life, I began speaking, and training others to apply the same ideas. Since then, I have given more than two thousand talks and seminars as long as four days in length, in 24 countries, to a total of more than two million participants. Most of them were also skeptical when they first heard these ideas of optimism and possibility, until they learned what you are going to learn in the pages ahead. It changed their lives, as it will change yours.

■ THE GREAT PRINCIPLE

Perhaps the most important mental and spiritual principle ever discovered is that *you become what you think about most of the time.* Your outer world is very much a mirror image of your inner world. What is going on *outside* of you is a reflection of what is going in *inside* of you. You can tell the inner condition of a person by looking at the outer conditions of his or her life. And it cannot be otherwise.

■ THOUGHTS ARE THINGS

Your mind is extraordinarily powerful. Your thoughts control and determine almost everything that happens to you. They can raise or lower your heart rate, improve or interfere with your digestion, change the chemical composition of your blood, and help you to sleep or keep you awake at night.

Your thoughts can make you happy or sad, sometimes in an instant. They can make you alert and aware, or distracted and depressed. They can make you popular or unpopular, confident or insecure, positive or negative. Your thoughts can make you feel powerful or powerless, a victim or a victor, a hero or a coward.

In your material life, your thoughts can make you a success or a failure, prosperous or poverty-stricken, respected or ignored. Your thoughts, and the actions that they trigger, determine your whole life. And the best news of all is that they are completely under your own control.

■ THOUGHTS, FEELINGS, AND DESIRES

You are a complex bundle of thoughts, feelings, attitudes, desires, images, fears, hopes, doubts, opinions, and ambitions, each of them constantly changing, sometimes from second to second. Each of these elements of your personality affects the others, sometimes in unpredictable ways. Your entire life is the result of the intertwining and interconnecting of these factors.

Your thoughts trigger images and pictures, and the emotions that go with them. These images and emotions trigger attitudes and actions. Your actions then have consequences and results that determine what happens to you.

If you think about success and confidence, you will feel strong and competent, and you will perform better at whatever you attempt. If you think about making mistakes or being embarrassed, you will perform poorly, no matter how good you really are.

Pictures and images, from your imagination or from the external influences, produce ideas, emotions, and attitudes that correspond to them. They then trigger actions that bring about certain results and outcomes. The *thought* of a person or situation can cause you to instantly feel happy or sad, elated or angry, loving or lonely.

■ ATTITUDES, ACTIONS, AND EMOTIONS

Your attitudes, positive or negative, constructive or destructive, lead to corresponding images, emotions, and actions that affect your life and relationships. Your attitudes, in turn, are based on your previous experiences and your basic premises about how things are supposed to be.

Your actions trigger the emotions and attitudes that go with them. By the Law of Reversibility, you can actually act your way into feeling in a manner consistent with the action. By acting as if you were already happy, positive, and confident, you soon begin to feel that way on the inside. And your actions are under your direct control, whereas your emotions are not.

In and of themselves, the outer aspects of your life are *neutral*. It is only the *meaning* that you give to them that determines your attitudes, opinions, emotions, and reactions to them. If you change your thinking about any part of your life, you will change how you feel and behave in that area. And since only you can decide what to think, you have the ability to take complete control over your life.

■ QUESTION YOUR BELIEFS

The Law of Belief says: *Whatever you believe, with conviction, becomes your reality.* You always act in a manner consistent with your deepest and most intensely held beliefs, whether they are true or not. And all your beliefs are learned. At one time, you did not have them.

Your beliefs largely determine your reality. You do not believe what you *see*; you rather *see* what you already believe. You can have life-enhancing beliefs that make you happy and optimistic, or you can have negative beliefs about yourself and your potential that act as roadblocks to the realization of everything that is truly possible for you.

The most harmful beliefs you can have are your *self-limiting beliefs*. These are beliefs about yourself and your potential that hold you back. Most of them are not true. Most of them are the result of information you have accepted without question, often from early childhood. Even if it is completely untrue, if you *believe* yourself to be limited in areas such as achieving wonderful health and happiness and earning a lot of money, that will become your truth. As the author Richard Bach in his book *Illusions* wrote, "Argue for your limitations and sure enough, they're yours."

■ YOU ARE A LIVING MAGNET

The Law of Attraction says that you are a "living magnet" and that *you invariably attract into your life the people, ideas, opportunities, and circumstances in harmony with your dominant thoughts.*

When you think positive, optimistic, loving, and successful thoughts, you create a *force field* of magnetism that attracts, like iron filings to a magnet, the very things you are thinking about. This law explains why it is that you don't have to be concerned where your good is going to come from. If you can keep your mind clearly focused on what you want, and refrain from thinking about what you *don't* want, you will *attract* everything you need to achieve your goals, exactly when you are ready. Change your thinking and you change your life.

■ THE ONLY REAL MEASURE

Bertrand Russell, the English philosopher, once said, "The very best proof that something can be done is that others have already done it." In the New Testament, Jesus taught the way to measure the truth of any principle: "By their fruits, ye shall know them."

In other words, the only question you need to ask about any idea is, "Does it work?" Does it bring about the results that you desire? Milton Friedman, the Nobel prizewinning economist, said, "The only true measure of a theory or idea is your ability to make accurate predictions of the future based on it."

The good news is that the ideas and principles you are about to learn have been tested and proven in the lives and experiences of millions of people. In themselves, like any principles of nature, they are *neutral*. Nature plays no favorites. Nature treats everyone alike. Whatever seed you plant in the ground, nature will grow. Whatever *thought seeds* you plant in your mind, nature will grow as well. It is entirely up to you.

■ CHOOSE YOUR THOUGHTS

Successful people are those who *think* more effectively than unsuccessful people. They approach their lives, relationships, goals, problems, and experiences differently from others. They sow better seeds, and as a result they reap better lives. If you learn to think and act like other successful, happy, healthy, and prosperous people, you will soon enjoy the kind of lives they do. When you change your thinking, you change your life.

> Nature understands no jesting. She is always true, always serious, always severe. She is always right, and the errors and faults are always those of man. The man incapable of appreciating her she despises, and only to the apt, the pure, and the true does she resign herself and reveal her secrets.
>
> —Johann Wolfgang von Goethe

Chapter 1

Change Your Thinking

There is a law in psychology that if you form a picture in your mind of what you would like to be, and you keep and hold that picture there long enough, you will soon become exactly as you have been thinking.

—William James

Once upon a time there was a woman, about 30 years old, married with two children. Like many people, she had grown up in a home where she was constantly criticized and often treated unfairly by her parents. As a result, she developed deep feelings of inferiority and low self-esteem. She was negative and fearful, and had no confidence at all. She was shy and self-effacing, and did not consider herself to be particularly valuable or worthwhile. She felt that she was not really talented at anything.

One day, as she was driving to the store, another car went through a red light and smashed into her. When she awoke, she was in the hospital with a mild concussion and complete memory loss. She could still speak, but she had no recollection of any part of her past life. She was a total amnesiac.

At first, the doctors thought it would be temporary. But weeks passed and no trace of her memory returned. Her husband and children visited her daily, but she did not know them. This was such an unusual case that other doctors and specialists came to visit her as well, to test her and ask her questions about her condition.

2 ◄   CHANGE YOUR THINKING, CHANGE YOUR LIFE

■ STARTING OVER

Eventually, she went home, her memory a complete blank. Determined to understand what had happened to her, she began reading medical textbooks and studying in the specialized area of amnesia and memory loss. She met and spoke with specialists in this field. Eventually she wrote a paper on her condition. Not long afterward, she was invited to address a medical convention to deliver her paper, answer questions about her amnesia, and share her experiences and ideas on neurological functioning.

During this period, something amazing happened. *She became a new person completely.* All the attention in the hospital and afterward made her feel valuable, important, and truly loved by her family. The attention and acclaim she received from members of the medical profession built her self-esteem and self-respect even higher. She became a genuinely positive, confident, outgoing woman, highly articulate, well informed, and very much in demand as a speaker and authority in the medical profession.

All memory of her negative childhood had been wiped out. Her feelings of inferiority were wiped out as well. She became a new person. She changed her thinking and changed her life.

■ THE BLANK SLATE

The Scottish philosopher David Hume was the first to propose the idea of the tabula rasa or blank slate. This theory says that each person comes into the world with no thoughts or ideas at all, and everything that a person thinks and feels is learned from infancy onward. It is as though the child's mind is a blank slate that every passing person and experience leaves a mark on. The adult becomes the sum total of everything he or she learns, feels, and experiences growing up. What the adult does and becomes later is the result of this early conditioning. As Aristotle wrote, "Whatever is impressed is expressed."

Perhaps the greatest breakthrough in the field of human potential in the twentieth century was the discovery of the *self-concept.* This is the idea that each person develops a bundle of beliefs regarding oneself, starting at birth. Your self-concept then becomes the master program of your subconscious computer, determining everything you think, say, feel, and do. For this reason, all change in your outer life begins with a change in your self-concept, with a change in the way you think and feel about yourself and your world.

The child is born with no self-concept at all. Every idea, opinion, feeling, attitude, or value you have as an adult you learned from childhood. Everything you are today is the result of an idea or impression you took in and accepted as true. When you believe something to be true, it becomes true for you, whatever the fact may be. "You are not what you think you are, but what you think, you are."

■ FIRST IMPRESSIONS ARE LASTING

If you were raised by parents who continually told you what a good person you were, who loved you, encouraged you, supported you, and believed in you, no matter what you did or didn't do, you would grow up with the belief that you were a good and valuable person. By the age of three, this belief would *lock in* and become a fundamental part of the way you view yourself in relation to your world. Thereafter, no matter what happens to you, you would hold to this belief. It would become your reality.

If you were raised by parents who did not know how powerful their words and behaviors could be in shaping your personality, they could very easily have used destructive criticism, disapproval, and physical or emotional punishment to discipline or control you. When a child is continually criticized at an early age, he soon concludes that there is something wrong with him. He doesn't understand why it is that he is being criticized or punished, but he assumes that his parents know the truth about him, and that he deserves it. He begins to feel that he is not valuable or lovable. He is not worth very much. He must therefore be worthless.

Almost all personality problems in adolescence and adulthood are rooted in what psychologists refer to as *love withheld*. The child needs love like roses need rain. When children feel unloved, they feel unsafe and insecure. They think, "I'm not good enough." They begin to engage in compensatory behaviors to make up for this inner anxiety. This sense of love deprivation is manifested in misbehavior, personality problems, bursts of anger, depression, hopelessness, lack of ambition, and problems with people and relationships.

■ YOU ARE BORN UNAFRAID

The child is born with no fears, except those of falling and loud noises. All other fears have to be taught to the child as he or she grows up.

The two major fears we all develop are the fear of *failure* or *loss* and the fear of *criticism* or *rejection*. We begin to learn the fear of failure if we are continually criticized and punished when we try something new or different. We are shouted at and told, "No! Get away from there! Stop that! Put that down!" Physical punishment and the withholding of love, possibilities that scare us and make us feel insecure, often accompany these shouts and criticisms.

We soon begin to believe that we are too small, too weak, incompetent, inadequate, and incapable of doing anything new or different. We express this feeling with the words, "I can't, I can't, I can't." Whenever we think about doing something new or challenging, we automatically respond with feelings of fear, trembling, and a churning stomach. We react exactly as if we are afraid of getting a spanking. We say, "I can't" over and over.

The fear of failure is the primary reason for failure in adult life. As the result of destructive criticism in childhood, we hold ourselves back as adults. We sell ourselves short. We quit before we even try the first time. Instead of using our amazing minds to figure out how to get what we want, we use our reasoning ability to create reasons why we can't, and why the things we want are not possible for us.

■ THE NEED TO BE LOVED

The second major fear that holds us back, undermines our confidence, and destroys our desire for a happy life is the fear of *rejection*, and its expression, *criticism*. This emotion is learned in early childhood as the result of our parents expressing disapproval of us whenever we do something they don't like, or don't do something that they expect. As a result of our displeasing them, they become angry and withdraw the love and approval we need so much as children.

The fear of being unloved and alone is so traumatic for a child that she soon conforms her behavior to do whatever she thinks her parents will approve of. She loses her spontaneity and uniqueness. She begins to think, "I have to! I have to! I have to!" She concludes, "I have to do whatever Mommy and Daddy want me to, or they won't love me, and I'll be all alone!"

■ CONDITIONAL LOVE

As an adult, a child raised with what is called "conditional love" (as opposed to unconditional love, the greatest gift one person can give to another) becomes hypersensitive to the opinions of others. In its extreme form, he cannot do anything if there is the slightest chance that someone else may not approve. He projects his childhood relationship with his parents onto the important people in his adult life—spouse, boss, relatives, friends, authority figures—and tries desperately to earn their approval, or at least not lose it.

The fears of failure and rejection, caused by destructive criticism in early childhood, are the root causes of most of our unhappiness and anxiety as adults. We feel, "I can't!" or "I have to!" continually. The worst feeling is when we feel, "I can't, but I have to!" or "I have to, but I can't!"

We want to do something, but we are afraid of failure or loss, or if we are not afraid of loss, we are afraid of disapproval. We want to do something to improve our lives, at work or at home, but we are afraid that we may fail, or that someone else may criticize us, or both.

For most people, their fears govern their lives. Everything they do is organized around avoiding failure or criticism. They think continually about playing it safe, rather than striving for their goals. They seek security rather than opportunity.

■ DOUBLE YOUR RATE OF FAILURE

The author Arthur Gordon once approached Thomas J. Watson Sr., the founder of IBM, and asked him how he could succeed faster as a writer. Thomas J. Watson, one of the giants of American business, replied with these profound words: "If you want to be successful faster, you must double your rate of failure. Success lies on the far side of failure."

The fact is that the more you have already failed, the more likely it is you are on the verge of great success. Your failures have prepared you to succeed. This is why a streak of good luck seems to follow a streak of bad luck. When in doubt, "double your rate of failure." The more things you *try*, the more likely you are to *triumph*. You overcome your fears only by doing the thing you fear until the fear has no more control over you.

■ YOUR MENTAL HARD DRIVE

Everything you know about yourself, all your beliefs, are recorded on the hard drive of your personality, in your self-concept. Your self-concept precedes and predicts your levels of performance and effectiveness in everything you do. Because of the law of correspondence, you always behave on the outside in a manner consistent with your self-concept on the inside. All improvement in your life therefore begins with an improvement in your self-concept.

You have an *overall* self-concept that is made up of all your beliefs about yourself and your abilities. This bundle of beliefs includes all the experiences, decisions, successes, failures, ideas, information, emotions, and opinions of your life up to now. This general self-concept determines how and what you think and feel about yourself, and measures how well you are doing in general.

■ YOUR MINI-SELF-CONCEPTS

You have a series of "mini-self-concepts" as well. These mini-self-concepts combine to make up your overall self-concept. You have a self-concept for every area of your life that you consider important. This mini-self-concept determines how you think, feel, and perform in that area.

For example, you have a self-concept for how healthy and fit you are, and how much you eat or exercise. You have a self-concept for how likable and popular you are with others, especially with members of the opposite sex. You have a self-concept for what kind of a spouse or parent you are, for how good a friend you are to your friends, how smart you are, and how well you learn. You have a self-concept for every sport you play, and for every activity you engage in, including how well you drive your car.

You have a self-concept for how well you do your work, and for how well you do each part of your work. You have a self-concept for how much money you make and how well you save and invest it. This is a critical area. The fact is that you can never earn much more or less than your self-concept level of income. If you want to make more money, you have to change your beliefs about yourself relative to income and money. This is an important part of this book.

■ CHANGE YOUR BELIEFS

In every case, if you want to change your performance and your results in any area of your life, you have to change your self-concept—or your beliefs about yourself—for that area. Fortunately, your beliefs are largely subjective. They are not always based on facts. Instead, they are based largely on information you have taken in and accepted as true, sometimes with very little evidence or proof.

The very worst beliefs you can have are *self-limiting beliefs* of any kind. These are beliefs about yourself that cause you to feel somehow limited or deficient in a particular area. These beliefs are seldom true, but if you accept them as valid estimates of your ability, they become true for you, exactly as if they were correct.

The starting point of unlocking your potential, and accomplishing more than you ever have before, is for you to *challenge* your self-limiting beliefs. You begin this process of freeing yourself from self-limiting beliefs by imagining that, whatever they are, they are completely untrue. Imagine for the moment that you have no limitations on your abilities at all. Imagine that you could be, do, or have anything you really wanted in life. Imagine that your potential is unlimited in any way.

For example, imagine that you could be earning twice as much as you are earning today. Imagine that you could be living in a bigger house, driving a better car, and enjoying a more expensive lifestyle.

Imagine that you have the ability to be one of the top people in your field. Imagine that you are one of the most popular, powerful, and persuasive personalities in your social and business world. Imagine that you are calm, confident, and unafraid of anything. Imagine that you could set and achieve any goal you put your mind to. This is how you begin changing your thinking and changing your life.

The starting point of eliminating your fears, and releasing your potential, is to reprogram your mental hard drive with new, positive, constructive, and courageous beliefs about yourself and your future. Throughout this book, you will learn how to do this.

■ THREE PARTS OF YOUR SELF-CONCEPT

Your self-concept has three parts, like a pie divided into three wedges. Each is linked with each of the others. All three elements together make up your personality. They largely determine what you think, feel, and do, and everything that happens to you.

Your *self-ideal* is the first part of your personality and your self-concept. Your self-ideal is made up of all of your hopes, dreams, visions, and ideals. Your self-ideal is composed of the virtues, values, and qualities that you most admire in yourself and others. Your self-ideal is the person you would most like to become, if you could be a perfect person in every way. These ideals guide and shape your behavior.

Great men and women, leaders, and people of character are very clear about their values, visions, and ideals. They know who they are and what they believe in. They set high standards for themselves, and they don't compromise those standards. They are men and women that others can look up to and depend on. They are definite and distinct in their interactions with others. In everything they do, they strive to live up to their ideals.

■ THE WAY YOU SEE YOURSELF

The second part of your self-concept is your *self-image*. This is the way you see yourself and think about yourself. It is often called your "inner mirror." It is where you look internally to see how you should behave in a particular situation. Because of the power of your self-image, you always perform on the *outside* consistent with the picture you have of yourself on the *inside*.

The discovery of the self-image, pioneered by Maxwell Maltz, is a major breakthrough in understanding human performance and effectiveness. By visualizing and imagining yourself performing at your best in an upcoming situation, you send a message to your subconscious mind. Your subconscious mind accepts this message as a command, and then coordinates your thoughts, words, and actions so that they fit a pattern consistent with the picture you created.

All improvement in your life begins with an improvement in your mental pictures. Your internal images influence your emotions, your behaviors, your attitudes, and even the way other people respond to you. The development of a positive self-image is a vital part of changing your thinking and changing your life.

■ HOW YOU FEEL ABOUT YOURSELF

The third part of your self-concept is your *self-esteem*. This is the emotional component of your personality, and is the most important factor in determining how you think, feel, and behave. Your level of self-esteem largely determines much of what happens to you in life.

Your self-esteem is best defined as *how much you like yourself*. The more you like yourself, the better you perform at anything you attempt. And by the law of reversibility, the better you perform, the more you like yourself.

Your self-esteem is the "reactor core" of your personality. It is the energy source that determines your levels of confidence and enthusiasm. The more you like yourself, the higher will be the standards you will set for yourself. The more you like yourself, the bigger the goals you will set for yourself and the longer you will persist in achieving them. People with high self-esteem are virtually unstoppable.

Your level of self-esteem determines the quality of your relationships with others. The more you like and respect yourself, the more you like and respect others and the better they feel toward you. In your business life and career, your personal level of self-esteem will be the critical factor that determines whether or not people will buy from you, hire you, enter into business dealings with you, and even lend you money.

The better your self-esteem, the better you will be as a spouse and parent. High self-esteem parents raise high self-esteem children. These children develop high levels of self-confidence and associate with other high self-esteem children. High self-esteem homes are characterized by love, laughter, and happiness for everyone who lives there.

■ THE DETERMINANT OF SELF-ESTEEM

Your level of self-esteem is largely determined by how closely your self-image—your current performance and behavior—matches your self-ideal—your picture of how you would perform if you were at your very best. You are always comparing your actual performance with your ideal performance at an unconscious level. Whenever you feel that you are living up to your very best, you feel terrific about yourself. Your self-esteem soars. You feel happy and fulfilled.

Whenever you do or say something that is *not* in keeping with your ideals or the best of which you feel you are capable, your self-esteem goes down. Whenever there is a wide separation between the person you are in the moment and the ideal person you want very much to be in the future, you feel badly about yourself. This is why you get angry with yourself whenever you fail at something, or behave badly in a situation with other people. Your self-ideal continually reminds you of how much better a person you can be.

■ THE CORE OF PERSONALITY

Psychologists agree today that your self-esteem lies at the core of your self-concept and your personality. Every improvement in any part of your personality or performance boosts your self-esteem, and causes you to like and respect yourself even more. The more you like yourself, the better will be your self-image and subsequent performance, and the faster you will move toward becoming more like your self-ideal.

The best news of all is that there is an *inverse relationship* between your level of self-esteem and your fears of failure and rejection. The more you like yourself, the less you fear failure. The more you like yourself, the less concerned you are with the opinions of others, and the less you fear criticism. The more you like yourself, the more you make your decisions based on your own goals and standards, and the less you care what others think or say.

■ CONTROL YOUR INNER DIALOGUE

Just as you become what you think about, *you also become what you say to yourself.* The most powerful words you can repeat to yourself, especially if you are feeling tense or uneasy about an upcoming event, are the words, "I like myself! I like myself! I like myself!"

Whenever you say, "I like myself!" your fears diminish and your courage increases. The words, "I like myself!" are so powerful and positive that they are immediately accepted by your subconscious mind as a command. They instantly affect your thoughts, feelings, and attitudes. Your body language immediately improves, and you stand straighter. Your face becomes more positive and cheerful. Your tone of voice becomes stronger and more confident. You feel better about yourself, and as a result, you treat everyone around you in a warmer, friendlier way.

You begin the process of changing your thinking and changing your life by going to work on your self-concept. You start by developing a clear, positive, exciting, and inspiring self-ideal, consistent with the very best person you can imagine yourself becoming. You develop a positive self-image by imagining yourself performing at your very best in everything you do. Finally, you develop high and unshakable levels of self-esteem by loving and accepting yourself unconditionally as a valuable and worthwhile person.

■ EXAMINE YOUR BASIC PREMISES

Most of your thoughts and your responses to the events and people of your life are determined by your *basic premises*. These are the ideas, beliefs, opinions, and conclusions you have come to as the result of inputs and experiences starting in childhood. They constitute not only your self-concept, but also your *philosophy of life*. The more adamant and convinced you are of your basic premises, the more they predict and control everything you do, say, and feel.

If you believe yourself to be an excellent person, loaded with talent and ability, friendly and popular, healthy and energetic, curious and creative, and destined to have a wonderful life, these basic premises will lead you to set goals, work hard, develop yourself, treat others well, bounce back from adversity, and ultimately succeed. Nothing will be able to stop you in the long run.

It is not what happens to you in life that is important. It is only *how you react* to what happens. It doesn't matter where you're coming from, either. All that really matters is where you are going. And where you are going is limited only by your own imagination. And since your imagination is unlimited, your future is unlimited as well. *These* are the basic premises and beliefs you need to fulfill your potential.

■ DISSOLVING THE MYTHS

Unfortunately, there are several myths that we accept as we grow up that can sabotage our hopes for success, joy, and fulfillment later in life. Let's look at these self-limiting beliefs one at a time.

The first and worst is summarized in the feeling, "I'm not good enough." This is the basic premise that causes feelings of inferiority and inadequacy. We assume that other people are better than we are just because, at the moment, they are *doing* better than we are. We feel that they must be worth more than us. Therefore, we must be worth less than them. This feeling of *worthlessness* sits deep in the psyche and causes us to sell ourselves short. We settle for less than we are truly capable of. Rather than to fail at a new goal, we don't set it in the first place.

The correct basic premise for you to develop, or belief for you to have, is that not only are you good enough, but you have the ability to be excellent in any area that is important to you. You have unlimited potential to be, do, and have more than you have ever achieved up to now. As William Shakespeare said in *The Tempest*, "What's past is prologue." Whatever you have accomplished in the past is only a hint of what you can do in the future.

■ TALK TO YOURSELF POSITIVELY

The most powerful words in your vocabulary are the words that you say to yourself and believe. Your self-talk, your inner dialogue, determines 95 percent of your emotions. When you talk to yourself, your subconscious mind accepts these words as commands. It then adjusts your behavior, your self-image, and your body language to fit a pattern consistent with those words.

From now on, talk to yourself only in terms of what you want to be and do. *Refuse to say anything about yourself that you do not sincerely desire to be true.* Repeat the powerful, positive words, "I can do it!" over and over. Prior to any event of importance, repeat the words, "I like myself!" Say, "I'm the best! I'm the best! I'm the best!" again and again like you really mean it. Then, stand up straight and strong, put a confident smile on your face, and do the very best of which you are capable. Soon it will become a habit.

■ YOU DESERVE THE BEST

As the result of previous destructive criticism, people accept another myth, or self-limiting belief. It is that they don't really believe that they *deserve* to be successful. This deep inner feeling of undeservingness is quite common among those of us who started off with very little in life, or who came from families that had little money when we were growing up. It can also be caused by people who told us at a young age that to be poor is virtuous but to be rich is sinful.

If you have grown up feeling undeserving of good things, for any reason, and you do achieve success in your field, you may experience what is called the "imposter syndrome." You will feel that you are an imposter in your success, and that you are going to be found out. No matter how successful you become as the result of your hard work, you will have a nagging fear that it will all be taken away from you.

If you feel like an imposter, you will often feel guilty for achieving greater success than others. To escape these feelings of guilt, many people engage in *self-sabotage*. They eat too much, drink too much, take dope, ignore their families, engage in unpredictable behaviors, and often throw their money away in extravagant living and unwise investments. They feel deep down inside that they don't deserve their success. As a result, they often drive it away.

■ DEDICATE YOURSELF TO SERVING OTHERS

The truth is that you deserve everything you can rightfully earn by doing an excellent job, and producing or distributing products or services that improve people's lives and work. In a market society such as ours, all transactions are *voluntary*. People buy something only if they feel that they are going to be better off as a result. You can therefore be successful in the long run only by providing people with the things they want to improve their lives and work. The more and better you serve other people, the more you both deserve and earn.

The word "deserve" comes from the two Latin words, "dē" which means "from" and "servire" which means "to serve." Therefore, the word "deserve" means "from service." The people who do the best in our society, with few exceptions, are those who are serving other people better than someone else. Your whole focus in your career should be on serving other people better. Then you will deserve every dollar you earn.

Abraham Lincoln once said, "The very best way to help the poor is not to become one of them." In our society, the more financially successful you are, the more taxes you are likely to pay. These taxes help pay for the schools, hospitals, roads, welfare, Medicare, military expenditures, and all the important things that our society offers. You can be proud to be financially successful. By making a lot of money, you make a significant contribution to lots of people. You do well for yourself by doing well for others.

Repeat the words, "I deserve every penny I earn as the result of serving others with the products and services they need to improve their lives. I am proud of my success."

■ YOU ARE AN EXCELLENT PERSON

You are a thoroughly good person. You are honest, decent, truthful, and hardworking. You treat other people with courtesy, respect, and warmth. You are dedicated to your family, friends, and your company. You are strong, confident, and responsible. You are knowledgeable, intelligent, and experienced. You are important not only to the people closest to you, but also to your community. You were born for a special reason, and you have a great destiny to fulfill. You are an excellent person in every way.

The preceding paragraph is a statement of your real personality and character. It may not be true for you 100 percent of the time, but it is a good general description of who you really are inside, and where you are going with your life. When you unconditionally accept that you are a truly valuable and worthwhile person, you will express it in everything you say and do. Over time, it will become true for you. Your ideal will become your reality.

Repeat to yourself, "I like myself and I love my life. I am a thoroughly good person in every way, and I always do my very best at anything I attempt."

■ THE MENTAL SOFTWARE STORE

Imagine that there was a store that sold mental programming. You could purchase any self-concept, belief, or attitude that you wanted and install it in your brain, and that is the person you would be from then on. If such a store existed, and you could buy any set of beliefs, what would you choose?

Here is a suggestion. Look around you and find out what the happiest and most successful people in your world have developed as their core beliefs, and then get the same set of beliefs for yourself. Load them onto your mental hard drive and start running the same programs they are running.

Fortunately, based on hundreds of interviews with successful people, we know exactly how they are programmed and what beliefs they have developed from an early age. The most important core belief you can adopt for yourself is this: "I am a thoroughly good person and I am going to be a big success in life. Everything that happens to me, good or bad, is simply a part of the process of achieving the great success and happiness that is inevitable for me."

If you absolutely believed that you were guaranteed to be happy and successful, and that every setback or obstacle was sent to you to teach you important lessons that you needed to know to achieve your goals, you would be completely unstoppable. You would be positive and optimistic most of the time. You would set big goals for yourself and bounce back quickly from any temporary defeat. Your belief would eventually become your reality. By changing your thinking, you would change your life.

■■■■■

Throughout the pages that follow, I will share with you a series of time-tested and proven methods and techniques that you can use to take complete control over every area of your thinking. I will show you how to think so positively and effectively that you will feel yourself capable of accomplishing anything. You will learn how to program and reprogram your self-concept so that your inner world is consistent with the person you want to be and the life you want to experience on the outside. You will learn how to become *unstoppable*.

ACTION EXERCISES

1. Define your ideals clearly. If you could be an excellent person in every way, what qualities would you have? How would you behave?

2. You become what you think about most of the time. Identify one or more areas of your life where your thinking is having a major influence on your emotions, attitudes, or actions.

3. In what area of activity do you perform at your best? How do you visualize yourself in that area? How could you extend this act of visualization to other areas?

4. What kind of people do you most admire and respect? Why? How could you change your behavior so that it is more consistent with that of the best people you know?

5. In what areas of your life do you like yourself the most? What sorts of activities give the highest levels of self-esteem and personal value? How could you do even more of these things?

6. You are a thoroughly good person. From this day forth, see yourself as the very best you can be, and refuse to accept any limitations on your possibilities.

7. Change your self-concept by continually thinking, talking, and acting as if you were already the person you would like to be, enjoying the life that you want and deserve.

Chapter 2

Change Your Life

If you paint in your mind a picture of bright and happy expectations, you put yourself into a condition conducive to your goals.

—Norman Vincent Peale

The way you think and feel about yourself, including your beliefs and expectations about what is possible for you, determines everything you do and everything that happens to you. When you change the quality of your thinking, you change the quality of your life, sometimes instantly.

You have complete control over only one thing in the universe— your thinking! You can decide what you are going to think in any given situation. Your thoughts and the way you interpret any event trigger your feelings—positive or negative. Your thoughts and feelings lead to your actions and determine the results you get. It all starts with your thoughts.

■ POSITIVE THINKING

Positive thoughts are life enhancing. They *empower* you and make you feel stronger and more confident. Positive thinking is not just a motivational idea. It has measurable, constructive effects on your personality, your health, your levels of energy, and your creativity. The more positive and optimistic you are, the happier you will be in every area of your life.

Negative thoughts bring about the opposite. They *disempower* you and make you feel weaker and less confident. Whenever you think or say something negative, you give your power away. You feel angry and defensive. You feel frustrated and unhappy. Over time, negative thinking can make you physically ill, and even poison your relationships.

Positive thinking leads to mental health and peak performance. Negative thinking leads to mental illness and decreased effectiveness. Your goal, therefore, if you want to live a wonderful life, is to cultivate positive emotions and get rid of negative emotions.

The elimination of negative emotions is the most important single step you can take toward health, happiness, and personal well-being. Each time you take complete control over your thoughts and feelings, and discipline yourself to keep them positive, the quality of both your inner and outer lives improves. In the absence of negative emotions, your mind automatically fills with the positive emotions that generate feelings of happiness and fulfillment.

■ YOU CAN CHOOSE YOUR THOUGHTS

The Law of Substitution says, *"Your mind can hold only one thought at a time, positive or negative. You can substitute a positive thought for a negative thought whenever you choose."* You can apply this law by deliberately thinking about something positive whenever you want to cancel out a thought or feeling that makes you angry or unhappy.

The Law of Habit says, *"Any thought or action that you repeat over and over will eventually become a new habit."* When you repeatedly react and respond in a positive way, you take full control over your conscious mind. Soon it becomes automatic and easy to think and act in that manner. By using willpower and repetition, you develop new habits of thinking and acting. By applying this law, you can become a completely positive person and change your life.

■ STARVE YOUR NEGATIVE EMOTIONS

Your negative emotions have all been learned, beginning in childhood. And what has been learned can be *unlearned*, sometimes quite quickly. You can learn any habit or skill that you consider to be either desirable or necessary. Especially, you can learn positive, constructive ways of thinking about people, money, health, and other factors to cancel out negative ideas that limit your potential and interfere with your success.

Many negative ideas or attitudes are based on false premises. Sometimes a negative idea about a subject, or a negative attitude toward a person, can be completely reversed with a single piece of new information. You could suddenly learn that an idea you had about yourself or another person was not true. As a result, you could change your thinking in an instant. Be open to this possibility.

Negative emotions exist only because we give them life and then keep them alive. We feed them by continually thinking and talking about things that make us angry or unhappy. Fortunately, you can change this situation by applying the Law of Emotion. This law states, *"A stronger emotion will dominate and override a weaker emotion, and whichever emotion you concentrate on grows and becomes stronger."*

What this means is that whatever emotion you *dwell upon* grows and eventually dominates your thinking in that area. If you withdraw your mental energy from a person or situation that makes you sad or angry by refusing to think about it, the emotion connected with that situation eventually dies away. Like a fire with no fuel, it goes out.

You have experienced this many times already. For example, as we grow up, we have relationships with the opposite sex. Most of them do not work out over time. When they end, we are often emotionally distressed and hurt. We are often sad, angry, depressed, preoccupied, and unhappy. These feelings last for a certain period. Then we recover. We meet someone else. Gradually we forget about the unhappy ending of the earlier relationship. Months or years later, we look back or even meet the other person, and we cannot imagine how emotionally involved we were with him or her. Because we did not feed them, the feelings have died away completely. This is an example of the laws of substitution and emotion in action in your own life.

■ THE SOURCES OF NEGATIVE EMOTIONS

There are four basic causes of negative emotions. According to the Russian philosopher Peter Ouspensky, in his book *In Search of the Miraculous*, these are: (1) justification; (2) identification, (3) inward considering, and (4) blame. The greatest leap forward in changing your thinking and changing your life will take place when you systematically eliminate all four of these causes of negative emotions from your life.

■ STOP JUSTIFYING

Justification is what you do when you rationalize or create a reason for your anger and unhappiness. You tell yourself, and whoever else will listen, how badly you were treated and how dreadfully the other person behaved. You continually rehash the situation in your mind. You repeat all the reasons you have for being upset. Each time you think of the person or situation, you become angry. You feel entitled to your anger, as if you have paid a high price for it, especially since, in your estimation, you were such a good and virtuous person.

The way you *short-circuit* the natural tendency toward justification and rationalization is by refusing to engage in it. Instead, you stop justifying. You use your marvelous mind to think of reasons not to justify your negative emotions. Remember, your negative emotions do you no good. They are totally destructive. They do not affect the other person or change the situation. They simply undermine your happiness and self-confidence, making you weaker and less effective in other areas of your life.

Instead of justifying your anger and unhappiness, you should use your intelligence and imagination to *excuse* the other person, or to let go of the unhappy situation. For example, if someone cuts you off in traffic, instead of becoming angry, you say, "Well, I'd better be more careful next time," "I guess he is having a bad day," or "He must be late for an important appointment."

■ MAKE EXCUSES FOR OTHERS

Since your mind can hold only one thought at a time, the instant you start *excusing* the other person you withdraw the energy or fuel that the negative emotions of anger and resentment require to get going and stay burning. You reassert your mental control. You keep yourself calm and positive. In a little while, the situation passes and you forget all about it. By substituting a positive thought for a negative thought, you get rid of the negative emotion, whatever it is.

If you have a major life problem, such as a divorce, a lost job, or a failed investment, the same rule holds true. Stop telling yourself (and anyone who will listen) why you are entitled to be angry or unhappy. Instead, make excuses for the other person each time you think about the situation until the negativity dies away. When the fire of negative emotion goes out, you can then turn your attention to something positive.

One of the most important rules for success and happiness is, "Don't be upset or worry about something that you can't do anything about." Don't criticize anyone for something that the person cannot change. A famous law says, "If there is no solution, there is no problem."

■ TWO TIME PERIODS

There are two time periods in life, the past and the future. The present is only a brief, fleeting moment. You can choose to focus your attention on what has happened, which cannot be changed, or on the future, on what is possible, over which you have some control.

Many people spend most of their emotional energies being upset and angry about events that occurred in the past. Unfortunately, this energy is completely wasted. Nothing good can come of constantly complaining about the past. Even worse, the negative emotions kept alive by reliving past events rob you of the joy and excitement that you could experience by thinking about future possibilities.

■ LET IT GO

A psychiatrist with more than 25 years' experience working with unhappy people wrote that the two most common words he heard in his practice were the words "if only." It seemed that most unhappy people are held back by some event that occurred in the past that they cannot let go of. They are still resentful, angry, or depressed over something that someone did or did not do or say. They are angry with one or both parents, a sibling, a previous relationship or marriage, a boss or business relationship, a failed investment or financial mistake.

The fact is that your life will be a continuous series of problems, difficulties, setbacks, and temporary failures. These unexpected and unwanted reversals and disappointments are a normal, natural, and unavoidable fact of growing up. To change your thinking and change your life, you must make a decision to get over them and to get on with your life, no matter what happened. Until you do, you remain a slave to the past, which cannot be changed in any case. Make a decision today that, from now on, you are going to eliminate all the "if only's" from your life.

■ REINTERPRET EVENTS DIFFERENTLY

The author and speaker Wayne Dyer says, "It's never too late to have a happy childhood." He means that at any time you can reinterpret the unhappy events of your early life in a positive way. You can practice the Law of Substitution and look into those negative experiences for something good, and think about that instead. You can focus on how your unhappy experiences have made you a better, wiser person. You can actually be grateful to people who have hurt you in the past because they have made you so much stronger in the present. And in any case, it could not have happened otherwise.

Your parents had no experience with raising children. In addition, they were a product of the way they were raised. Like all humans, they came to parenting with their problems and weaknesses, just as you have today. Nonetheless, they did the best they could with what they had. They were the people they were, and they could not have raised you any differently than they did. It is silly to continue to be unhappy about things they did or didn't do that they were incapable of doing otherwise. Let it go and get on with your life.

■ DON'T TAKE IT PERSONALLY

The second major cause of negative emotions according to Ouspensky, is *identification*, or attachment. This occurs when you take something personally or you become attached to a person or thing. You see the unhappy outcome of an event or circumstance as a personal affront or attack on you or on something you believe in or hold dearly. You become emotionally involved in a situation and identify so strongly with it that it affects your emotions and your reason in a negative way.

The great spiritual teachers, such as Buddha and Jesus, have emphasized the importance of separating yourself emotionally from the situation (*disidentification*), in order to regain your calmness and composure. Psychologist and philosopher William James of Harvard wrote, "The first step in dealing with any difficulty is to be willing to have it so." He encouraged people to say, "What cannot be cured must be endured." In other words, practice detachment from any person or situation that makes you feel angry or upset. Withdraw the emotional energy from it so that you can regain your calmness and composure.

This approach does not suggest that you passively accept anything that happens to you. Instead, it encourages you to use your willpower to keep your mind and emotions under control. You discipline yourself to stand back mentally and deal with the problem intelligently. You use your mind to see the situation objectively and make better decisions to resolve it.

Nothing and no one can have any control over you unless there is something you still want from them. They must have something that they can still give you or withhold from you. As soon as you detach emotionally from a person or object and no longer want anything from them, you are free. This ability to practice detachment is a power you can develop through practice. It can make you the master of a situation that might otherwise cause you to become upset and angry.

One of the kindest things you can do to help others is to encourage them to stand back from a problem situation and be objective about it. Encourage them to view the difficulty as if it was happening to someone else. Ask them what advice they would give to another person who was facing this same problem. By detaching from the emotionally charged situation, you and others will become much more capable of dealing with it effectively.

■ THE OPINIONS OF OTHERS

The third major cause of negative emotions, according to Ouspensky, is *inward considering*. This occurs when you become overly concerned with the way people are treating you. If you perceive that someone is not giving you the respect that you feel you deserve, you can feel insulted and angry, and want to strike back. If people are rude or indifferent to you, you can experience their behavior as an attack on your personality or character. This interpretation of their attitude or behavior can make you angry or depressed.

Psychologists say that everything we do is to increase our self-esteem and sense of personal value, or to protect it from being diminished by other people or circumstances. If your self-esteem is not as high as it could be, you will be sensitive to the actions and reactions of other people toward you. You will take everything *personally*, exactly as if what they said or did was consciously and deliberately directed at you. However, this is seldom the case.

The fact is that most people are preoccupied with themselves and their own problems. As much as 99 percent of the time, people are wrapped up in their own thoughts about themselves. They devote the other 1 percent of emotional energy they have available to everyone else in the world, including you. The person who cuts you off in traffic is so involved with his own thoughts, he is not even aware of your existence. It would be silly to become angry or upset over his thoughtless action.

■ SET YOUR OWN SAILS

There is a rule that I have learned from experience: *Never do or refrain from doing something because you are concerned about what people might think about you. The fact is that nobody is even thinking about you at all.*

Of course, I am not talking about criminal or antisocial behaviors. But it is amazing how many people make decisions to get into or to *not* get into relationships, businesses, new endeavors, adventures, and other things for fear that someone else might not approve. They stay in marriages they hate, they work at jobs they dislike, or they turn down business opportunities for fear that someone, anyone, might criticize them. The truth is that no one cares more about your key life decisions than you do. Plan accordingly.

In Abraham Maslow's studies of self-actualizing people, those 1 or 2 percent of men and women who are fully mature, fully functioning adults, he found a particular quality that they all had in common: *They were completely honest with themselves.* They were objective and clear about their own strengths and weaknesses. They did not hope or pretend that they were other than they were. This self-acceptance was a foundation stone of their self-esteem and self-respect.

Because they knew who they were, and who they were not, they did not feel that they had to continually earn the approval of others. They took the opinions of others into consideration, but then they made their own decisions. They were not overly influenced by the possible approval or disapproval of other people. You should do the same. You are the one who cares the most and who is most affected, in any case.

■ THE RESPECT OF OTHERS

When Somerset Maugham, the famous English author, was asked by a reporter for his chief motivation for writing, he replied, "I write to earn the respect of the people I respect."

The fact is that much of what you do, or fail to do, is influenced by the same concern. You do many things in your social life to earn the respect of the people you respect, or at least not to lose it. In fact, the people whose respect is most important to you largely determine how good you feel about yourself, both at home and at work. The respect of others has an inordinate influence on your self-esteem because it is so closely linked to your self-ideal and your self-image.

Exceptional men and women look up to and seek the respect of men and women of character and accomplishment. They strive, at an unconscious level, to behave and to live up to their ideals of how an excellent person would behave.

One of the most important decisions you make as you go through life is to decide for yourself the specific people whose respect is of the greatest value to you. Once you are clear about who you respect and why you respect them, you can then organize your life in such a way that you continually earn that respect, whether they know of your actions or not.

■ SET HIGH STANDARDS

In the famous book *In His Steps*, by Charles M. Sheldon (Christian Library, 1984), an entire town agrees, prior to every act or decision, to ask the question, "What would Jesus do?" and then to behave accordingly. The eventual outcome for the townspeople was that the problems that had divided them were soon solved and the town became happy and prosperous. They created an *ideal* for themselves and then built their lives around living up to it.

In a study of successful men and women, most of whom had started from humble beginnings, researchers found that these people had almost all been avid readers of biographies and autobiographies when they were young. As they read the life stories of famous men and women, they imagined themselves having the same qualities and characters of the people they were studying. When they became adults themselves, those qualities and virtues had become part of their thinking and guided their choices and decisions in later life.

Modeling has been used as a powerful way to develop personality and character throughout history. Young people have been encouraged to study school heroes and heroines, and emulate them as much as possible. In the military, the heroic acts of soldiers and sailors from the past are taught as part of the curriculum, encouraging young soldiers and sailors to think and act like them when the situation demands it.

The people you most admire and look up to have an inordinate influence on how you think and feel about yourself, and the kind of decisions you make. Who are *your* role models?

■ CHOOSE YOUR ROLE MODELS WITH CARE

There is nothing wrong with being thoughtful and concerned about the feelings and reactions of others toward you and your choices. When you select admirable people to look up to, you develop an inner guide that leads you to conduct yourself in an excellent way yourself.

What is silly and self-defeating however, is for you to allow yourself to be inordinately influenced by the fleeting opinions of people whose regard and respect is of no concern or value to you. If you have been raised with destructive criticism, you can easily slip into the trap of organizing your life around trying to gain the approval, or escape the disapproval, or people you don't even know or care about.

Here is the way to avoid this form of negative emotion: Decide for yourself the men and women you most admire, and the qualities they have that you would most like to emulate. From now on, when you have to make a decision, think about someone you admire and ask, "What would he or she do in this situation?"

When you ask this question, you actually connect at an unconscious level with a higher power that will then give you guidance and insight. You will experience a deep inner knowing of exactly the right thing to do or say. You will make the right decision and achieve the desired result. This is a technique used by many successful men and women. Give it a try and see what happens.

■ THE WORST NEGATIVE INFLUENCE OF ALL

The fourth major cause of negative emotions, according to Ouspensky, and the trigger of anger, resentment, envy, jealousy, and frustration of any kind is *blame*. It is blame especially that generates *anger*, the worst of all the negative emotions. Anger is more destructive than any force in the human world. Uncontrolled anger destroys health, relationships, families, businesses, and societies, and is the chief generator of wars, revolutions, and social conflict.

The primary cause of anger can be traced back to destructive criticism in early childhood. Whenever a person is criticized, he reacts exactly as if he is being attacked, with defensiveness and resentment. Since any behavior that you repeat over and over becomes a habit, many people develop the habit of responding with anger to every problem, disappointment, or frustration they experience. Eventually, they reach the point where they are always angry about something.

To become angry, a person must be able to blame someone for something that has happened or not happened that they don't like or approve of. Many people are so preoccupied with blaming others for their problems that they lose contact with reality. They see the entire world through a lens of blame and its sister emotion, guilt.

Whenever there is a problem, personal or public, the angry person automatically concludes that someone must be to blame. The individual then spends his time and emotion apportioning blame among various parties. This obsession with blame and anger, leading to resentment and envy, can often consume the person who experiences it.

■ NO ONE IS GUILTY

Here is a common example. Two people in love get married. Both of them have the best of intentions and the highest of expectations for the future, or they wouldn't get married in the first place. Unfortunately, people and situations change over time. The couple finds that they are no longer happy together and decide to divorce. But then the problems really begin.

Instead of agreeing, like adults, that they have reached a point where they are incompatible and they no longer want to live together, blame must be apportioned. Someone must be guilty. The guilty party must be punished. Lawyers and judges now have to get involved. Detectives and accountants are hired to dig up dirt on each party. The situation gets worse and worse, until it finally ends in anger, bitterness, accusations, and even hatred.

The best of solutions, when a marriage or a relationship does not work out, is to accept that fact as an unfortunate reality, make reasonable provisions for each party, and then for each person to get on with his or her life. Many couples are doing this today through mediation rather than going through the bitterness of a traditional divorce. The results turn out to be better for everyone involved.

It is a psychological fact that most people feel that they are right in whatever they do. But as soon as one person starts to blame the other, and even worse, demand that the other person admit to being guilty, the emotional and legal battles begin. The saddest part of these legal battles is that they usually end where they started, with no one having gained very much.

■ ACCEPT RESPONSIBILITY

The best way to eliminate anger of all kinds is to *accept responsibility*. The acceptance of responsibility immediately short-circuits the emotion of anger. All the energy that anger requires for its existence is cut off. As soon as you say, *"I am responsible!"* your anger stops. Because of the Law of Substitution and the fact that your mind can hold only one thought at a time, you cannot accept responsibility for your situation and be angry at the same time. The idea of blame, on which the emotion of anger is based, is canceled out by the decision to accept responsibility.

■ POSITIVE VERSUS NEGATIVE WORLDVIEWS

There are two basic ways of looking at your world. You can have a positive and *benevolent* worldview or a negative and *malevolent* worldview. By taking responsibility for yourself and what happens to you, you become positive. You see the world in benevolent terms. You become more optimistic toward yourself and your possibilities. You become a happier and more effective person.

In contrast, when you take a negative or malevolent worldview, you see problems and injustice everywhere. You see oppression and evil. You see guilty people all around you. You see limitations and unfairness rather than opportunity and hope. Worst of all, you spend your time apportioning blame to various people and institutions for all the problems you see.

■ DIFFERENCES IN RESULTS

For example, in this country, some people are better off than others. This has been true of all societies throughout human history. This can be for various reasons. It may be the result of different people having different talents, ambitions, and desires. It may be the result of some people working harder, having a better start at life, being born with greater intelligence, or simply being at the right place at the right time to catch a favorable trend in the economy.

In any case, people who are well off are not to blame for the fat that other people are not well off. People who are healthy are not to blame for the fact that other people are sick. People who are successful and happy are not to blame for those who are unsuccessful and unhappy. People who are building a good life for themselves and their families are not at fault because other people are not.

Success does not cause failure. *Correlation is not causation.* Because both situations occur simultaneously, this does not mean that one caused the other. An honest acceptance of this simple fact would solve many arguments and disagreements at the philosophical and political levels.

■ THE POWER OF FORGIVENESS

The root cause of negative emotions, the main factor that predisposes a person to blaming and to anger and resentment, fear and doubt, envy and jealousy, is the *inability to forgive* someone we feel has hurt us in some way.

As we develop as children, we go through a phase where "justice" is very important to us. We fixate on the concept of "fairness." We are upset by any situation in our lives that does not seem to be fair and equitable to anyone, especially if it concerns ourselves. Whenever we feel that we or anyone else has been unfairly treated, for any reason, we take it as a personal attack. Our fragile self-esteem is threatened. We react with anger and resentment. This is a normal developmental phase of growth that we go through as we move toward adulthood.

However, some people fixate at this stage and never grow beyond it. If we are not taught the importance of letting go of our grievances as children, we will come into adulthood with a gunnysack of unforgiven experiences. If we are not careful, we will then build our lives around our anger toward people who we feel are to blame for something they did or that we disapprove of. Many psychotherapists and psychiatrists spend their entire careers helping people confront and deal with these unhappy past and current experiences.

The most powerful and liberating decision you can make is to forgive everyone who has ever hurt you in any way. Only by freeing the other person, in your mind, by forgiving him or her can you be free *yourself*. This is why most religions stress the importance of forgiveness as the first step toward peace of mind and earthly bliss.

Just imagine how you would feel if you had no anger toward anyone at all in the whole world. Imagine being a completely positive, optimistic, cheerful person, with high levels of self-esteem and enthusiasm and unlimited self-confidence. Imagine being a warm, friendly, loving person filled with feelings of calmness and inner peace. All this is possible for you when you practice forgiveness.

In contrast, the refusal or failure to forgive lies at the base of negativity, anger, stress, anxiety, mental and physical illness, and most unhappiness. The refusal to forgive keeps you trapped. Forgiveness sets you free. And it is always a choice you make. It has nothing to do with the other person or situation.

■ IT TAKES TWO

Some people hold themselves back from forgiving with a false basic premise. They think that by forgiving they are condoning the behavior of the person they are mad at. They think that, if they forgive the other person, they are doing that person a favor. They even think that they are letting the other person go free, which they are determined not to do.

The fact is that it takes two to make a prison, the prisoner and the jailer. Both are in the jail. When you let the other person go free, you liberate yourself. You don't have to condone the behavior or *like* the person who hurt you. You just have to forgive him or her so that you can get on with the rest of your life. Forgiveness is therefore a totally *selfish* act. It really has nothing to do with the other person at all. It has only to do with your own mental integrity and peace of mind.

The comedian Buddy Hackett once said, "I never hold grudges; while you're holding grudges, they're out dancing!"

When you remain angry with another person, you give away your emotional control to that person each time you think of him or her. You allow him or her to control your emotions at long distance. By not forgiving, you allow that person to run your emotional life, exactly as if he or she were right there with you and the situation was occurring all over again.

■ THE PATH TO FORGIVENESS

The way you forgive is simple. Each time you think of the other person, you use the Law of Substitution and say, *"God bless him/her; I forgive him/her for everything, and I wish him/her well."* It is not possible to bless and forgive another person and simultaneously be angry or upset. The positive thought cancels out the negative thought.

You can speed up the process of personal liberation by *accepting responsibility* for your share of what happened. Very few negative events that lead to anger and resentment occur in a vacuum. Almost invariably, you did *something* to contribute to the situation. You therefore need to have the maturity to take your share of the responsibility.

You can then say, *"I am responsible. I shouldn't have gotten into the situation in the first place, or stayed in so long. I should not have done what I did. I forgive him/her completely and let it go."*

It may be difficult for you to forgive at first. These words will be hard for you. Many people have built their entire adult lives around their grievances. They are afraid that they will have nothing else to talk about if they stop complaining about their parents or their bad marriages. But don't worry.

When you forgive others and let them go, you soon begin to feel lighter and happier. As the thoughts of anger and resentment fade away, your mind will fill with positive thoughts. You will have more energy and enthusiasm. You will feel stronger and more confident. Your whole future will open up before you, like a summer sunrise.

Don't worry about what your friends think or say when you decide to forgive people who have hurt you. They are probably tired of hearing your complaints about the unfortunate events of your past. In fact, when you start forgiving, you will often find that the only common bond between you and certain people is your gripe sessions. When you decide to forgive others, you may no longer find them very interesting to talk to.

■ THE PEOPLE YOU MUST FORGIVE

There are four groups people you need to forgive if you are serious about changing your thinking and changing your life.

The first is your *parents*, living or dead. You must absolutely forgive them for every mistake they ever made in bringing you up. At the very least, you should be grateful to them for giving you life. They got you here. If you are happy to be alive, you can forgive them for everything else. Never complain about them again.

Many of my seminar participants have phoned or visited their parents and told them that they forgive them for everything. Often this simple act of courage and character has had a profound effect on their relationship with their mother or father. From that day onward, they have become good friends, which lasted the rest of their lives together.

In contrast, by not forgiving your parents, you remain forever a child. You block your own chance to grow up and become a fully functioning adult. You continue to see yourself as a victim. Even worse, you keep your negative feelings of inferiority and anger alive.

If your parents die without your having forgiven them, it can bother you for the rest of your life.

■ CLOSE PERSONAL RELATIONSHIPS

The second group you must forgive is the people from your *close relationships* that didn't work out. Marriage and other intimate relationships can be so intense, and so threatening to your feelings of self-esteem and self-worth, that you can be angry and unforgiving toward those people for years.

But you were at least *partially* responsible. Have the personal strength and integrity to say, "I am responsible," and then forgive the other person and let him or her go. Say the words, "I forgive him/her for everything and I wish him/her well." Each time you repeat this, the negative emotion attached to the memory will diminish. Soon it will be gone forever.

■ THE LETTER

Many of my graduates have found that "the letter" is the key to putting a bad relationship behind them forever. This is a powerful technique that can free you from feelings of anger and resentment almost instantly.

Here is how it works: You to sit down and write the other person a letter of forgiveness. It consists of three parts.

First you say, "I forgive you for everything you ever did that hurt me."

Second, you write out a description or list of every single thing that you are still angry about. Some people write several pages in this part.

Third, you end the letter with the words, "I wish you well."

You then take the letter to the mailbox and drop it in. At that moment, you will feel a huge sense of relief, and you will be free at last.

By the way, don't worry about how the other person might react. That is not your concern. Your goal is to free yourself, to regain your peace of mind, and to get on with the wonderful life that lies ahead of you.

■ CLEAR YOUR SLATE

The third group you must forgive is *everyone else* in your life who has ever hurt you in any way. Let them go. Forgive every boss, business partner, friend, crook, or betrayer who has ever caused you grief of any kind. Clean the slate. Wipe each of their names and images off by saying, "I forgive him/her for everything, and I wish him/her well." Repeat this statement each time you think of the person or situation until the negative feelings are gone.

■ SET YOURSELF FREE

The fourth and final person you have to forgive is *yourself*. You must absolutely forgive yourself for every silly, senseless, wicked, brainless, thoughtless, or cruel thing you have ever done or said. Stop carrying these past mistakes around with you. That was then and this is now.

Think of it this way: When you did those things in the past that you still feel badly about, you were not the person you are today. At that time, you were a different person, younger and less experienced. You were not your true self. You were an immature version of the person you have become with experience. Stop beating yourself up for something that occurred in the past that you cannot change.

In psychotherapy, when a person feels burdened with a deep sense of guilt or shame as the result of a childhood trauma, the cathartic moment comes when he or she suddenly realizes, "It's not my fault." Sometimes you did things, or things were done to you, when you were too young or inexperienced to know what was going on or to change the situation. It was not your fault. You did the best you could. You are okay. Forgive yourself and let yourself off the hook.

Just say, *"I forgive myself for every mistake I ever made. I am a thoroughly good person and I am going to have a wonderful future."* Whenever you think of that event or situation, just repeat, "I forgive myself completely." And then get on with your life. Focus on the future rather than the past. Look at where you are going rather than where you have been.

Finally, if you did something that hurt someone, and you still feel badly about it, you can go to that person, or write, and apologize. Tell the person you are sorry for what you did or said. Whatever his or her reaction, positive or negative, it doesn't matter. The very act of *repentance*, of expressing regret, will set you free.

■ A FINAL WARNING

Most people are open to the idea of forgiveness. It is among the core beliefs of most religions, and is taught in psychology and metaphysics. You are probably comfortable with the idea of forgiving most of the people in your life who have hurt you in some way. But there is a great danger.

The danger is that *your refusal to forgive just one major grievance can be enough to sabotage your entire life.* Your insistence on holding onto just one person or situation by not forgiving can put the brakes on all your forward progress. There are countless men and women who ruin their lives because of their anger and resentment toward a single person. They can't let go of it, and so they never get free.

Don't let this happen to you. You must have the courage and character to forgive *everyone*, without exception. There should be no one in your life with whom you are still angry. Your mind should be calm and clear. You should be able to say, *"I do not have a negative or unforgiving thought toward anyone in the world; I freely forgive them all."*

■ TAKE CONTROL OVER YOUR EMOTIONS

The starting point of eliminating negative emotions is for you to take full control over your thoughts and actions, and to discipline yourself not to *express* negative emotions when they arise, as they surely will. You may not be able to stop the initial negative reaction to a disappointment or a frustrated expectation, but you can refuse to express it, either to yourself or to another. You can cancel it instantly by saying, *"I am responsible!"*

There are some who say that it is healthy to express the negative emotions of anger, hurt, fear, and doubt. But the fact is that *whatever you dwell upon and talk about grows in your reality.* A small negative experience is like a spark that can be fanned into a blaze by thinking and talking about it. Instead, snuff it out the instant it arises by saying, "I am responsible!" Then look for reasons why you might be responsible. You will always find them.

■ THE TRUE GODS ARRIVE

An English poet once wrote, "When the false gods go, the true gods arrive." When you stop thinking about, talking about, and rehearsing negative events and the emotions they trigger, the "true gods" of positive emotions will fill your mind and heart. When you let go of the thoughts, opinions, prejudices, and attitudes that make you unhappy, you will begin to experience the thoughts and emotions that make you feel good about yourself and your life.

Nature is on your side. Nature wants you to be happy, healthy, prosperous, and fulfilled. Your destiny is to experience joy, harmony, love, and the greatest of all human blessings, *peace of mind*. And just as a gyroscope knocked off balance returns to an upright position, your life and emotions return to peace and joy just as soon as you stop doing and saying the things that move you away from a sense of inner peace.

Decide this very day to give up your negative emotions. Resolve from this moment forward to become a positive, optimistic, happy, enthusiastic person in every part of your life. Change your thinking about yourself and your possibilities, and you change your life.

ACTION EXERCISES

1. Resolve today that you are going to be a completely happy person. Now ask, "What is it in my life that makes me unhappy or causes me stress?" Whatever your answer, decide to deal with it and eliminate it.

2. Recall an experience from your childhood that you are still angry about. Now reinterpret that experience positively and view it as a valuable learning experience.

3. In what areas of your life are you angry or resentful because you are still blaming someone for something he did or didn't do? Whatever it is, accept responsibility and get on with your life.

4. Who is there in your past that you have not forgiven? What previous experience causes you the most anger still today? Whoever or whatever it is, resolve to forgive and let it go.

5. Don't take things personally anymore. From now on, when people do not respect you or treat you as you wish to be treated, rise above it and go about your business.

6. Make a decision today to forgive everyone in your past toward whom you still feel any negative emotion. Let them go and let yourself go at the same time.

7. Forgive yourself for every mistake you have ever made. If it is appropriate, go and ask forgiveness of the other person. Set yourself free.

Chapter 3

Dream Big Dreams

Dream lofty dreams, and as you dream, so shall you
become. Your vision is the promise of you shall at
last unveil.

— John Ruskin

Your mind can be your best friend or your worst enemy. Your
thoughts alone have the power to make you healthy or sick, rich or
poor, popular or unpopular. Your mind is like a powerful force that
can be turned in any direction to bring about wonderful results, or
wreak havoc and destruction. Your main goal in life must be to har-
ness your amazing powers and direct them intelligently and systematically toward achieving everything you really want.

■ A JOURNEY THROUGH ITALY

Let me tell you a story. Some years ago, I took my family to Italy on
vacation. We toured several of the great art museums of Rome and
Florence. In Florence, there is a special museum that was built to
house the statue of David created by Michelangelo several hundred
years ago. This is perhaps the most beautiful piece of sculpture in
the world. The actual physical experience of being in the same room
with it is something that none of us has ever forgotten.

The story of the creation of the *David* is very interesting and
contains a lesson for all of us. Michelangelo was commissioned
by the Medicis to create a statue for the main square in Florence.

The Medicis were the wealthiest and most powerful family of Italy at the time. A commission for a statue from the Medicis was not only a great honor; it was also a task that could not be refused. For two years, Michelangelo searched for a block of stone out of which he could create the kind of masterpiece the Medicis were looking for.

Finally, on a side street of Florence, partially overgrown with weeds and covered with dirt, he found a huge slab of marble lying on wooden trestles. It had been hauled down from the mountains years before and had never been used.

Michelangelo had walked past this street many times, but this time he stopped and looked more closely. As he walked back and forth studying the block of marble, he actually envisioned the statue of David and saw it in its entirety.

■ GREAT SUCCESS REQUIRES LONG, HARD WORK

The sculptor quickly arranged to have workmen haul the block of marble to his studio some distance away. He then began the long, hard job of hammering and chiseling. It took him two solid years of work to create the rough outline of the statue. He then put his hammers and chisels aside and spent two more years polishing and sanding before the statue was complete.

Michelangelo was already famous as a sculptor, and the news that he was working on a major commission for the Medicis spread all over Italy. When the day came for its first public viewing, thousands of people came from all over Italy and gathered in the main square. When it was unveiled, the crowd stood gaping in awe. It was breathtakingly beautiful. People cheered. Women fainted. The audience was amazed at the incredible beauty of the enormous statue. Michelangelo was immediately recognized as the greatest sculptor of his age.

Afterward, when Michelangelo was asked how he was able to create such a masterpiece, he replied by saying that he saw the *David* complete and perfect in the marble. All he did was to remove everything that was *not* the *David*.

■ YOU ARE A MASTERPIECE

There are many parallels between yourself and the *David*. You are very much like a great masterpiece enclosed in marble as well. But the marble that envelops you, and most other people, is the marble of small, limited thinking and excessive worry about the possibilities of loss or failure, rather than an excited anticipation of the rewards of success and achievement.

To realize your full potential, your greatest need is to break out of your limited thinking by dreaming big dreams and imagining unlimited possibilities. You need to remove all the negative beliefs that hold you back from becoming all you are capable of becoming.

But remember, even after the *David* had been released from the marble, it took Michelangelo two solid years of sanding and polishing to turn it into a masterpiece. In the same way, you also have to work on yourself, sanding and polishing, learning and practicing, for days, weeks, months, and even years, to develop and bring out all the talents and abilities that lie deep inside of you.

■ YOU CAN BECOME UNSTOPPABLE

The central purpose of this book is to help you change your thinking in such a way that you become absolutely *unstoppable* in achieving any goal you can set for yourself. Your goal is to develop yourself to the point *psychologically* where you become like an irresistible force of nature. You will be like the tide coming in, or like a powerful storm that sweeps across the land.

Your aim is to become so confident, courageous, strong, and resolute that you can set any goal for yourself with the firm knowledge that you can learn what you need to learn, and do what you need to do, to eventually achieve it. You will become so persistent and determined that nothing and no one can slow you down or alter your course. You will become truly unstoppable!

■ DREAM BIG DREAMS

You begin the process of becoming unstoppable by dreaming big dreams. Since everything you create in your world begins with a thought, the bigger the dreams you dream, the bigger the goals you will achieve. All successful men and women are dreamers. All peak performers are what are called "blue-sky thinkers." They continually allow their minds to float freely when they think about what is possible for them. They look at the unlimited blue sky above them as the only limit to everything and anything that they could possibly be, or have or do.

Successful people continually practice "back from the future" thinking. They project into the future several years and imagine what their lives would look like if they had achieved all of their goals. They look back to the present, from the mental vantage point of the future, like looking from the top of a high mountain down to where they are actually standing in the valley, in the present. They then look at the path that they would have to take to get to where they want to be in the future.

By the law of correspondence, whatever you can clearly see on the inside, you will eventually experience on the outside. You should therefore visualize your goals with as much clarity and *vividness* as possible. Visualize your goals *intensely* and create within yourself the same feeling that you would have if you had already achieved your goals. Visualize your goals *frequently*. Replay a picture of your goal, as if you had already realized it, on the screen of your mind as many times a day as you possibly can. Visualize your goals for *as long* as you possibly can, preferably just before falling asleep each night.

Repeat these exercises of visualization—vividness, intensity, frequency, and duration—until your goals become absolutely clear, living, breathing, exciting, clear pictures in your mind. The more skilled you become at moving from the dream through the goal to the visualization, the more motivated and determined you will be. The more clarity you develop, the more courage and confidence you will have, and the more unstoppable you will become.

■ CREATE YOUR IDEAL FUTURE VISION

The most important part of dreaming big dreams is for you to define your *ideal future vision*. It is for you to think about what you *want* before you begin to think about what is *possible* for you. You dream big dreams by looking into the future and imagining that you have no limitations holding you back from achieving anything you set your mind on.

Detach yourself from your current situation and allow yourself to dream. Pretend for the moment that you have all the time and money you need. Imagine that you have all the connections and contacts, all the resources and opportunities, all the education and knowledge, all the skills and experience that you require to be, have, or do *anything* that you could dream of.

Imagine your ideal lifestyle. Imagine your ideal job or income. Imagine where you would like to live and how you would like to spend each day, each week, each month. Imagine your ideal family life. Imagine your ideal state of health. Design your perfect life in every respect.

■ MAKE YOUR OWN DREAM LIST

Here is an exercise for you. Take out a piece of paper and at the top write the words "Dream List." Underline these words and then write down everything that you can think of that you could ever possibly want if you had no limitations whatsoever.

Most people are held back by their self-limiting beliefs. The way you burst these mental chains is with a dream list. The very fact that you can write down something that you would love to have someday means that you probably have within you, right now, the ability to achieve it. Let your mind float freely as you write. There will be lots of time to organize and evaluate your dreams later.

■ WHAT WOULD YOU DARE TO DREAM?

Here is a great question: "What one great thing would you dare to dream if you knew you could not fail?"

If you were absolutely guaranteed of success in the achievement of any one goal, big or small, long-term or short-term, what would it be? If a billionaire took a liking to you and offered to write you a check to cover any goal that you could clearly define, what one goal would you choose?

If you could have any job, what would it be? If you could work for any kind of company, what kind of a company would you select? Where would it be, and what would it be doing? If your family life and your relationships could be perfect in every respect, what would they look like? Answer these questions clearly. Write them down.

■ START WORK ON YOUR FUTURE

You begin the creation of your ideal future by making up your dream list. You write down everything that you would want to be, do and have, exactly as if you had no limitations at all. You make up your list as if you were absolutely guaranteed of success. Then you can begin refining your list, step by step to develop a detailed blueprint for your life.

Henry David Thoreau once wrote, *"Have you built your castles in the air? Good, that's where they should be built. Now, go to work and build foundations under them."* Once you have broken free from your limited thinking, like a balloon casting loose its moorings and rising high into the sky, you can begin to turn your dreams and fantasies into concrete practical goals with specific plans of action.

Your ability to set goals and to make plans for their accomplishment is the "master skill" of success. With this master skill, there are no limits on what you can accomplish. Putting your goals on paper is the next step in the process.

■ HOW TO ACHIEVE ANY GOAL

There is a seven-step method for goal setting and achievement that you can use, over and over, in any situation, to accomplish anything you could ever want for yourself. These seven steps constitute a powerful, proven formula that you can use to change your life immediately.

■ STEP ONE: DECIDE EXACTLY WHAT YOU WANT

A real goal is clear, specific, measurable, and time bounded. A non-goal—a wish or a hope—is fuzzy and unclear. It is a fantasy that floats in the air. People with clear, specific goals, who know exactly what they want, are very different from people who are going through life hoping for the best. Your ability to decide *exactly* what it is you want in each area of your life is one of the most important responsibilities of adult life.

People often approach me at my seminars and ask what their goals should be. I reply that only they can decide. It is amazing how many of them tell me how hard it is to set goals, and I agree with them. It is hard, but it is also essential. With clear goals, you can do almost anything. Without them, you can do virtually nothing.

One of the major reasons that people fail in life is because they waste so much of their time doing things of low value or no value at all. And the reason they waste so much time is because they have no real idea of what they really want. Once you have clear goals, your ability to manage your time improves dramatically.

■ USE YOUR TIME WELL

Here is a way to decide whether something is a good use of your time. Just ask, *"Does this move me toward the achievement of one of my goals?"* If the activity helps you to achieve a goal you have set for yourself, it is a good use of time. If it doesn't, it is a poor use of time.

When you get into the habit of only doing those things that move you toward your goals, your life will take off. Your results will improve. You will soon find yourself busy every hour of every day doing things that are helping you in some way. You will have no time left to spend on activities that aren't helping you to achieve one of your goals.

When you set clear goals for yourself, and you know exactly what you want, you will become increasingly impatient with activities that are not helping you in some way. You will watch less television. You will listen to less radio. You will read the newspapers quickly, if at all. You will become far more selective with your friends and your social activities. You will spend time only with people you enjoy, people you can learn and benefit from. But, as the old saying goes, *"If you don't know where you're going, any road will take you there."*

■ STEP TWO: WRITE DOWN YOUR GOALS

Write your goals down on paper. There is something quite incredible that happens between the brain and the hand. When you take a paper and pen and write down your goals, you activate the Laws of Expectation, Attraction, and Correspondence simultaneously. You intensify your belief and deepen your conviction that your goals are possible for you. The very act of writing down your goals gives you a sense of control and personal power. Written goals increase your resolve and determination to do whatever is necessary to achieve them.

The speed at which you will begin to achieve your goals after you have written them down is nothing short of miraculous. The very act of writing out your goals increases the likelihood of your achieving them by as much as 10 times—1,000 percent!

Many thousands of my graduates have written or come back to tell me about the amazing things that have happened in their lives that started immediately after they began putting their goals in writing.

■ STEP THREE: BE WILLING TO PAY THE PRICE

Determine the price you are going to have to pay to achieve your goal. Make a list of everything that you are going to have to do if you want to make your goal a reality.

Are you going to have to start each day's work a little earlier, work a little harder, and stay a little later? Write it down. Are you going to have to upgrade your knowledge and skills, and take additional courses? Again, write it down. Are you going to have to change jobs, change industries, or change careers in order to achieve everything that is possible for you? Write it down.

The Law of Cause and Effect is the iron law of the universe. For everything that you want, there is a price that must be paid. This price must be paid *in full* and *in advance*. The Law of Sowing and Reaping is not the Law of Reaping and Sowing. You have to *put in* before you *get out*. You have to *give* before you *receive*. You have to pay the price before you enjoy the reward.

Your willingness to do whatever you need to do, pay whatever price is required, go whatever distance is necessary, and make whatever sacrifice is demanded is the measure of how badly you really want your goal.

Many people sabotage their own success by deciding that they want a particular goal, and although they are willing to pay a high price for it, they are not quite willing to pay the *full price* that the goal demands. This is like wanting to win in a poker game but not being willing to match the final bet made by the other player. You end up losing the whole hand, just as by failing to make a total commitment people end up losing the entire goal.

■ STEP FOUR: MAKE A DETAILED PLAN

Make a plan, in writing. Remember, the ability to develop written goals and create plans for their achievement is the master skill of success. A plan begins with your making a list of all the things that you can think of that you are going to have to do to achieve your goal. Once you have made your list, you can add new items as they occur to you.

You then organize your list in terms of priority and sequence. What are the *most important* things on the list that you will have to do to achieve your goal? What are the things that you will have to do *before* you do something else? Which items on your list are dependent on your completing other items *first*?

A plan of action gives you a track to run on. It increases your level of belief and intensifies your desire for the goal. You gradually become convinced that your goal is actually possible and achievable for you. You begin to see possibilities that you may not even have been aware of in the absence of a written plan.

■ STEP FIVE: TAKE ACTION ON YOUR PLAN

Take action of some kind in the direction of your goal. Once you have set a goal, written it down, determined the price that you are going to have to pay, and made a plan, you must take some action immediately. Even if you only make one phone call or collect one piece of information, be sure to do *something*. In the Bible it says, "Faith without deeds is dead."

There is something powerful in your willingness to take a specific action, in faith, in the direction of your goal, with no guarantee of success. Your action itself seems to trigger all kinds of other powers and forces in the universe. You activate the Law of Attraction to help you. When you take action, you demonstrate to yourself, and to others for that matter, that you are really serious about your goal.

Until you have taken a specific, irrevocable action of some kind, you have merely engaged in an enjoyable exercise, like daydreaming. You have put your key into the ignition but you haven't turned it on.

■ STEP SIX: DO SOMETHING EVERY DAY

Do something every day that moves you toward your most important goal. This is a vital success principle that generates energy and enthusiasm. For you to maintain your courage, confidence, and self-motivation, you must be doing something every single day that gives you a feeling of forward motion and progress. Your job is to build yourself up to the point where you genuinely feel *unstoppable*, and the only way that you can do this is by refusing to stop, by doing something daily.

■ STEP SEVEN: NEVER GIVE UP

Resolve in advance that you will never quit once you have started toward your goal. No matter how many setbacks or obstacles you experience, make the decision that you will keep on picking yourself up and persisting until you eventually succeed.

By deciding in advance that you will persist, no matter what the difficulty, you give yourself a psychological edge. When the difficulties *do* arise, you will be mentally prepared to plow through them rather than quitting. Your willingness and ability to persist are what will eventually guarantee your success.

■ SECRETS OF SELF-MADE MILLIONAIRES

If money is your goal, remember that most of the people who are wealthy today started out with no money at all, or even deeply in debt. Almost everyone who is on the top today was once at the bottom. Almost everyone who is at the front of the line of life was once at the back of the line. Almost everyone who is wealthy today was once poor.

Most of the five million millionaires in the United States are self-made. That is, they started out with nothing and worked their way up. Our world today has more than 300 self-made *billionaires* and multibillionaires as well. Many of these are people who started with little or nothing, and by changing their thinking, they unleashed their own inner potentials to achieve extraordinary financial results. And almost anything that anyone else has done, within reason, you can do as well. What are *your* goals?

■ THE POWER OF COMMITMENT

One of my favorite quotations is from the mountain climber Charles Murray.

> *Until one is committed, there is hesitancy, the chance to draw back, always ineffectiveness. Concerning all acts of initiative and creation, there is an elementary truth, the ignorance of which kills countless ideas and splendid plans; that the moment that one definitely commits oneself, then providence moves too.*
>
> *All sorts of things occur to help one that would never otherwise have occurred. A whole stream of events issues from the decision, raising in one's favor all manner of unforeseen incidences and meetings and material assistance that no man could have dreamed would have come his way.*

He finishes off his statement with these words from Goethe:

Are you in earnest? Seek this very minute,
Whatever you can do, or dream you can, begin it.
Boldness has genius, power, and magic in it.
Only engage and the mind grows heated.
Begin and then the task will be completed.

ACTION EXERCISES

1. What one great goal would you set for yourself if you were absolutely guaranteed success?

2. Make out a "dream list"; write down everything you would like to have in your life someday, exactly as if you had no limitations.

3. Imagine your perfect lifestyle; if you were financially independent and you could live any way and anywhere you wanted, what would you change?

4. Make a list of 10 goals you would like to accomplish in the next year. From that list, select the one goal that would have the greatest positive impact on your life if you could achieve it right now.

5. Write your most important goal on a separate piece of paper. Make it measurable and set a deadline for its accomplishment.

6. Make a written plan to achieve this one goal. Write out a list of everything you can think of that you will have to do to accomplish it.

7. Take action on your plan immediately. Once you have started, discipline yourself to do something every day that moves you toward that goal. Never miss a day until you have achieved it.

Chapter 4

Decide to Become Rich

Thought is the original source of all wealth, all success,
all material gain, all great discoveries and inventions, and
of all achievement.

—Claude M. Bristol

We have passed from a world based on material limitations into a
world that is determined by *mental* concepts. We have moved from
the age of *things* into the "Psychozoic Age," the age of the *mind*.
Wealth and opportunities are contained more in the person you *are*
and the way you *think* than in the assets you have acquired in life so
far. Your future lies more in your ability to apply your mind and intelligence to your work and your life than it does in your current job
or situation.

Because health, wealth, and happiness are essentially mental,
there are very few limits on how much of them you can acquire for
yourself. In this chapter, and in subsequent chapters, you will learn
many of the simple, practical, proven methods, techniques, and
strategies used by high-achieving men and women in every field to
accomplish far more than they, or the people around them, ever
dreamed possible. You will learn how to break the bonds of limited,
conventional thinking, expanding your desires and ambitions so
dramatically that you will be able accomplish any goal that you
could ever set for yourself.

■ THREE MAJOR FORCES

There are three major forces reverberating through our world today, transforming everything they touch and creating unlimited opportunities for the creative minority. These three forces are the incredible growth in *information*, *technology*, and *competition*.

➤ Information and Knowledge Explosion

The *information* revolution, combined with the speed of computerized information processing, the Internet, and wireless communications, is enabling knowledge in every field to double every two or three years. Fully 90 percent of all the thinkers, inventors, engineers, scientists, writers, entrepreneurs, and creators of all kinds who ever existed are living and working today. The results of their efforts are becoming almost instantaneously available to each other, thereby doubling and tripling their outputs.

➤ Technological Advances

The explosion in *technology* and high-speed computers is literally breathtaking. Today, you can e-mail a message around the world to dozens, hundreds, or even thousands of people simultaneously, in a matter of seconds, at a cost of pennies. The World Wide Web gives you access to tens of millions of other Internet users, as well as to the accumulated knowledge stored in more than 50,000 libraries and research institutes. Instantaneous transmission of data enables the money markets to move a trillion dollars per day, sometimes in seconds, making it impossible for countries to control their currencies, much less their economies.

In the twenty-first century, you will own a laptop computer with a microchip that can process one billion commands per second. It will have a long-life battery and a built-in cellular telephone, connected to cells and satellites that will enable you to communicate instantaneously with almost anyone, almost anywhere in the world. You will have your own personal telephone number that will enable anyone in the world, anywhere, to telephone you, wherever you are, whether or not they even know what country you are in. And this telephone technology will probably fit on your wrist like a large digital watch does today.

➤ Thriving Competition

The third major factor driving our lives is *competition*. Every business organization wants to generate sales and make profits, locally, nationally, and internationally, if possible. To survive and thrive, each person and business must be continually seeking faster, better, newer, cheaper, easier ways to deliver value to their customers.

Every advance in knowledge and technology creates opportunities that fleet-footed competitors can grab and run with to create new products and services to leapfrog each other in their markets. All three forces—information, technology, and competition—are multiplying times each other to create the greatest rate of change in human history. And if anything, the rate of change is going to increase in the years ahead.

■ CHANGE CREATES OPPORTUNITIES

Fully 80 percent of the products and services that you will be using five years from now will be brand-new or completely transformed from today. Probably 80 percent of the jobs being done in five years will be new jobs or jobs that have been completely transformed by the onrush of information, technology, and competition. And the good news is that every single change that takes place opens up more opportunities and possibilities for you to achieve your goals and make greater progress, faster than ever before.

The forces of change impact everything you do. The rate of change is accelerating week by week and month by month. The speed and variety of change is something over which you have no control, and about which you have no choice. The only decision you have to make is whether you are going to be a "master of change" or a "victim of change." Are you going to be a *creator* of circumstances or a *creature* of circumstances? Are you going to ride the wave and stay ahead of the curve of change, or are you going to be bowled over by it and left in its wake? It will be one or the other, but the impact of change will be forced upon you, whatever you do.

■ LEARN FROM THE EXPERTS

If you want to learn how to cook, you study cooking. If you want to be a lawyer, you study law. If you want to be an engineer or an architect, you study engineering or architecture. And if you want to be financially successful, you study others who have become financially successful before you. You find out what they did, and you do the same things, over and over, until you get the same results.

Making money is a *skill*, like riding a bicycle or operating a computer. Because it is a skill, it is therefore learnable by anyone who wants to acquire wealth. If in the past you have accepted the false idea that you cannot make or keep all the money you want, it is now time for you to get rid of that idea. It is a false belief. It is time for you to decide to become financially independent.

■ THE GREAT LAW

The Greek philosopher Aristotle first articulated the foundation principle of Western philosophy in about 350 B.C. It became known as the Aristotelian Principle of Causality. Today, we call it the Law of Cause and Effect. This law says that for every effect in your life, there are specific causes. It says that everything happens for a *reason*. Success is not an accident. Failure is not an accident, either. What happens to you is not determined by luck or by coincidence. It is the result of unchanging law.

My journey from unemployment and poverty to success and financial independence started when I began to study the most successful people in our society. My idea was simple: I would find out what they had done to accomplish so much, and then I would do the same things. Why reinvent the wheel? What I discovered changed my life. It will change yours as well.

■ MILLIONS OF MILLIONAIRES

When I began my reading and research in the 1960s, there were seven hundred thousand millionaires in the United States, mostly self-made, having started with nothing. By 1980, according to the IRS, there were 1,800,000 families or individuals with a net worth of more than one million dollars. Today, there are more than five million millionaires, an increase of 277 percent in 22 years. And most of them are self-made as well. These are men and women who started with little or nothing, often broke or deeply in debt, and who gradually accumulated enough money to become financially independent.

Self-made millionaires come from every walk of life, with every level of education and skill, and with every difficulty, obstacle, handicap, and challenge to overcome that you could ever dream of.

Some are young and some are old. Some are new immigrants who arrived in America unable to speak English, and some are from families that have been in America for generations. Some have excellent educations from the finest universities, and some are high school dropouts. Some have superb physical health and others are in wheelchairs, hard of hearing, blind, or have other physical limitations.

The most important thing to remember is that no matter what difficulties you have, no matter what problems you feel are holding you back, someone else, and probably thousands of other people, have had far greater obstacles to overcome than you could possibly dream of, and they have gone on to become successful nonetheless. And what others have done, you can do as well.

■ EXHAUSTIVE RESEARCH

Dr. Thomas Stanley of the University of Georgia spent more than 30 years studying self-made millionaires. He interviewed thousands of them and compiled his findings into a variety of books, research studies, and reports, including two best-selling books, *The Millionaire Next Door* and *The Millionaire Mind*. His research shows that every single kind of person, from every walk of life, has been able to start from nothing and pass the magic million-dollar mark by doing certain things in certain ways, over and over again.

■ START WHERE YOU ARE

When I began studying self-made millionaires, I was living in a rented apartment with rented furniture. I had a used car that was not paid for and I was deeply in debt. I was between jobs and living off credit cards.

The first thing I found was that self-made millionaires did things *differently* from average people, and I was tired of being *average*. I therefore decided to stop doing what I was doing, which wasn't working, and to start doing what they were doing. My life has never been the same since this decision.

It wasn't easy to change my thinking about money and my financial future, but eventually these efforts began to pay off. Like a large ocean liner changing direction, one degree at a time, my habits began to change. Within five years, I was out of debt and making good money. In another five years, I passed the million-dollar mark. When I look back, I see that it was no miracle. All I really did was to learn what other successful people had done before me and then do the same things until I got the same results.

■ GET RID OF THE MYTHS

There are a great many myths about self-made millionaires. If you want to become a self-made millionaire yourself, you must dispel these myths from your own mind. Remember, as the humorist Josh Billings once said, "It's not what a man knows that hurts him; it's what he knows that isn't true."

Many people have fixed ideas or beliefs about themselves and money that are holding them back. These ideas may be completely untrue, but they will cut off your chances of success nonetheless. You must get over them. *To achieve something you've never achieved before, you will have to think in ways that you have never thought before.*

One myth is that you have to have a great education to become rich. Another myth is that you have to start off with a lot of money. Some people are convinced that financial success depends on getting a lucky break of some kind, like picking a hot stock in the stock market.

None of these myths are true. In fact, a survey of members of the Forbes 400, the 400 richest men and women in the United States, found that high school dropouts in the group who made it to the list were worth, on average, $300 million more than university graduates on the list.

■ THE LAND OF OPPORTUNITY

The most successful immigrant group per capita in the United States, in terms of starting and building successful businesses, are Russians. Why is this so? It is because the Russians have come from a system where it has been so extraordinarily difficult to succeed that when they arrive in America, believing that America is the land of opportunity, they find that it is much easier to succeed than they have ever experienced.

As a result, Russians start business after business and achieve successes that the average American continually claims are no longer possible. Because they absolutely believe that it is possible for them, they make their dreams come true. Their beliefs become their realities.

■ THE REALITY PRINCIPLE

The past president of General Electric Company, Jack Welch, was considered to be one of the best business executives in the world. He said that the most important single quality of leadership is what he calls the "reality principle." The reality principle says that *you must deal with the world as it is, not as you wish it would be.* You must strive to be completely honest with yourself and your situation. You must refuse to engage in self-delusion and the hope that things will work out whether or not you do anything about them.

Especially when it comes to building wealth, you must be totally honest with yourself. You cannot afford to play games with your own mind if you truly want to be wealthy. You cannot wish and hope and pray that somehow you are going to win the lottery or strike it rich as a result of luck or some remarkable external circumstance.

■ YOU CREATE YOUR OWN LUCK

Often people ask me about the role of *luck* in success. They are convinced that luck is a critical factor in achieving anything worthwhile. They feel that some people are just lucky and some are not. They talk about luck as if it were a matter of fate or destiny, largely inexplicable. They insist that a person gets to the top of his field largely as the result of getting lucky breaks, which they, of course, did not get.

I have studied the concept of luck for many years. My conclusion is that luck is a word that people use to explain away things that turn out much better than could have been expected. If a person achieves great financial success at a young age, people say he was "just lucky."

Some people use luck to describe something remarkably good that happens that is out of the ordinary. But it is not luck at all. The fact is that all so-called lucky outcomes are really the result of *probabilities*. There is no such thing as luck.

The Law of Probabilities says that there is a probability for everything that happens. These probabilities can often be determined with considerable accuracy. The entire insurance and underwriting industry is based on probabilities, which are expressed in actuarial tables.

■ BECOMING A MILLIONAIRE

There is a probability that you will become a millionaire in the course of your working lifetime. Today in America, one family in 20 has a net worth of more than one million dollars. This means that your likelihood of acquiring a million dollars is one in 20, or 5 percent.

However, this also means that your likelihood of *not* acquiring one million dollars, should that be your goal, is 95 percent. These are not good odds. Your job must be to improve the odds in your favor. Your aim should be to dramatically increase the probabilities of achieving financial independence by doing more and more of those things that will help you to achieve your goal. This principle applies to anything you want to accomplish.

The more different things you do that are likely to help you to achieve your goal, the more likely it is you will do the right thing at the right time. If you set clear, written goals, make detailed plans, and continually upgrade your skills to increase your income, you increase the probabilities that you will earn a good living.

If you study money and investments, save and put aside 10 percent to 20 percent of your income every month, keep tight control over your expenses, and think long-term about your financial life, you will eventually become a millionaire. It is not a matter of luck. It is just a matter of probabilities.

■ PROBABILITIES ARE EVERYTHING

Imagine you are an inexperienced dart thrower, slightly inebriated, in a darkened room, standing some distance from the dartboard. Even under these conditions, if you throw enough darts in the direction of the dartboard, you would eventually hit it. And if you continued to throw darts, almost in spite of yourself you would become more accurate. As a result, by the law of probabilities, you would eventually hit a bull's-eye.

This metaphor explains why people who start off with high levels of desire and determination ultimately succeed. They just keep trying. And by the law of probabilities, they finally win. It is not luck. They create their own luck by what they do, or what they fail to do.

Now, imagine the conditions are different. Imagine that you are a skilled dart thrower, and that you practice every day to get better. In addition, you are fully rested, clear-headed, and completely prepared. The lights in the room are bright and you stand at a reasonable distance from the dartboard. Under these conditions, all of which are under your control, the time it would take you to hit a bull's-eye would be greatly reduced. And of course, when you do hit a bull's-eye, everyone would tell you how "lucky" you were. But you made your own luck.

Throughout your life, you must be constantly thinking about all the things you can do, in every area, to increase the probabilities that you will be successful in achieving your goals. You should leave nothing to chance. You should refuse to wish or hope, or trust to luck. You must take control of your situation. You are responsible.

■ YOU ARE RESPONSIBLE

You will achieve financial success only after you accept that everything that you ever become is completely up to you. You are responsible. No one is going to do it for you. Keep repeating, *"If it's to be, it's up to me!"*

Fortunately, in America there are more opportunities for wealth creation and personal success than have ever existed previously in all of human history. The United States is the only country on earth that is commonly referred to overseas as "the land of dreams." In 2003, it was rated as *the most entrepreneurial country* in the world. This means that it is easier to start and build a successful business in the United States than it is anywhere else on earth.

As information and technology continue to expand and multiply times each other, and competition continues to intensify, more and more opportunities are opening up every day for the creative minority who are willing to take advantage of them. Your job is to find these opportunities, and if you don't find them, *create them* for yourself.

■ THE COMMON DENOMINATOR

One of the discoveries in the research on self-made millionaires is the finding that most of them start off with little or no money. Most of them start off by saving their money carefully for a long time until they have enough to start a small enterprise or business. Some of the biggest companies in America were started on a kitchen table or in a garage, like the Hewlett-Packard Company or Apple Computer. Some of the newest millionaires in America come from the field of multilevel marketing. Working from home, they paid $50 for a sample kit and went out to work. They sold something, made a profit, reinvested their profits, grew larger, and eventually achieved financial independence.

In Dr. Thomas Stanley's interviews with self-made millionaires, he discovered their common denominator of success. The most important quality that self-made millionaires used to explain their success was the habit of *hard, hard work.*

Self-made millionaires work much harder than the average person. They start earlier, work harder, and stay later. According to many studies and interviews, self-made millionaires work an average of 59 hours per week. Some work considerably more, especially at the beginning.

■ WASTING TIME AT WORK

The average employed person puts in about 40 hours per week on the job, but only about 32 hours of that is officially working time. Fully 50 percent of time spent at work is wasted in idle socializing with co-workers, personal telephone calls, and personal business. Average employees start a little later, take long coffee breaks and lunch hours, and leave a little earlier. Even managers privately report that they spend fully half of the time they are at work doing things that have absolutely nothing whatever to do with the job.

Only about 5 percent of people working today work full-time on their jobs from the time they begin each day until the time they finish. These people are the ones on the fast track in their careers. They are moving upward and onward, getting paid more and being promoted faster. They are the movers and shakers in every business, and everyone knows who they are.

■ LOW-VALUE ACTIVITIES

The saddest part of the research into employee work habits is not just that people waste a lot of time at work. It is that in the *other* 50 percent of the time, when people are actually *working* on company tasks and responsibilities, they tend to work on low-value, low-priority tasks. As a result, they contribute little of value to their companies. Low productivity leads to lower wages and fewer opportunities.

Every year, hundreds of thousands of people are laid off from large and small corporations, often from white-collar, midmanagement jobs. Why is this? The answer is simple. The companies have finally learned that they are paying high salaries to people who are producing very little of value. No company can survive very long under these conditions, and these companies are determined to survive. So the redundant staff has to go.

■ YOU CAN DO IT

If you are serious about becoming financially independent, or even better, becoming a *self-made millionaire* over the course of your career, here are two facts: First, it is definitely possible. Hundreds of thousands of men and women become financially independent each year after having started from nothing. Whatever others have done, within reason, you can do as well. The very fact that someone else has achieved a particular financial goal is proof it is possible for you. The only question is, how badly do you want it?

Second, the reality principle says that if you want to be successful in any area, you have to find out what other successful people have done to succeed in that area, and then do the same things over and over until you get the same results. As long as you don't try to fool yourself and look for shortcuts, you are virtually assured of eventually achieving, and even exceeding, your goals.

■ THE 40 PLUS FORMULA

Begin today to apply the "40 Plus Formula" to your work and your career. This formula says that you work 40 hours per week in the United States for *survival*. If you work only 40 hours per week—if you work only the number of hours that are required of you—then all you will ever do is survive. You will tread water financially. You will make enough to pay your bills and perhaps a little more besides, but you will never get ahead and you will never be successful.

According to the 40 Plus Formula, every hour that you put in over 40 hours on your job, or on yourself, is an investment in your future success. You can tell where you are going to be five years from now by simply looking at how many hours per week you put in on your job. Every hour over 40 that you invest in getting more results for your employer and your customers adds up and contributes to your long-term success.

■ GIVE YOURSELF AN EDGE

If you work 45 to 50 hours per week, you give yourself an edge over your co-workers. If you work 55 to 60 hours per week, your long-term success is virtually guaranteed. You put yourself on the side of the angels. Many self-made millionaires work 70 to 80 hours per week to get established in their careers. There are no shortcuts to lasting success.

I have studied successful men and women in America for more than 25 years. I have never found a single successful person who got there working only 40 hours, or five days per week. The idea of the five-day week, which was promoted by the labor unions as a great advance in the life of the working person, has been the cause of more financial underachievement and failure than perhaps any other single myth.

The fact is that, especially at the beginning of their careers, all really successful people work much harder than the average person. They work 10 to 12 hours per day, six days per week. They work at this rate for many months and years, before they reach the point where they can slow down. The average self-made millionaire has taken 22 years to get from being broke to having a net worth of more than one million dollars. It is not easy and it is not quick. But it is definitely possible if you want it badly enough.

■ WORK ALL THE TIME YOU WORK

A key part of success at work is to *use your time well*, to focus on results, and avoid the time-wasting social activities of the poor performers. In correlation with this is the need for you to "work all the time you work."

This is a remarkable idea for many people. Often employees think about work as if it was an extension of school. When they were growing up, they came to think of school as a place where you go to socialize. You take the required courses, but the most important part is spending time with your friends between classes. School becomes a form of play.

Many people think, when they take their first job, that work is also a place where you go to spend time with your friends. This is why fully half of the working day is spent socializing, and in idle conversation on the telephone with friends and family. Work is seen as a giant sandbox where you continue to play as you did in school. You do a little work when the boss is watching, get a paycheck, and then go home.

But this is not for you. If you are determined to succeed greatly and be paid the very most, you must *work all the time you work*. When you go to work, you must put your head down and work wholeheartedly.

■ SOCIALIZING WITH CO-WORKERS

Many people believe the myth that you have to spend a lot of time getting along with your co-workers. They say, "Work is supposed to be fun!" And this is true up to a point.

Of course, it is important for you to be positive and agreeable person to work with. But you can accomplish this in a few minutes of pleasant interaction each day. You don't have to spend endless hours chatting about sports, television shows, and family activities. Your job is to work all the time you work.

When you work, you work. You do not pick up your dry cleaning or drop off your laundry during working hours. You do not socialize with your friends or chat on the phone with your family. You do not take long coffee breaks and extended lunch hours. You work all the time you work. You commit yourself to getting the very most done that you possibly can in the time that you have available to you.

■ GET BACK TO WORK

Your goal is to earn the reputation around your company as being the hardest-working person in the organization. If someone wants to shoot the breeze with you, explain to him or her that you would be pleased to chat after work, but right now you have to get back to work. Keep repeating to yourself, "Back to work, back to work, back to work!"

People who achieve great financial success, either in their own businesses or working for other organizations, are people who very early develop a reputation for hard, hard work. There is a saying in business: *"Everyone knows everything."* There are no secrets. Everyone knows who works the hardest in every organization, and who doesn't.

There is no quality that will bring you to the attention of people who can help you *faster* than your developing a reputation for being one of the hardest-working people in your company.

■ START EARLIER, STAY LATER

Napoleon Hill, the author of *Think and Grow Rich*, once told the story of a young man who started at the bottom of a large organization and eventually moved up into the top ranks of executives, passing all the people who had started with him at the same level. His strategy was simple. He noticed that his boss came in a little earlier than the rest of the staff, stayed to finish up his work, and left a little later than the others. This young man therefore resolved to arrive 15 minutes before his boss and to leave 15 minutes after his boss left.

He put his resolution into action the next day. This is another hallmark of high achievers: They don't procrastinate when they have a good idea; they take action immediately. The young man began coming in 15 minutes before his boss and going straight to work, continuing all day. When his boss left he would still be at his desk, working away.

■ BE PATIENT AND PERSISTENT

The boss said nothing for several weeks. Finally, after work one evening, his boss came over to his desk and asked him why he always seemed to be there, even though all his co-workers had left. The young man said it was because he was really determined to be successful in this company, and he knew he couldn't be successful unless he was willing to work harder than anyone else.

The boss smiled and nodded and went on his way. Soon after that, the boss asked him to do something that was not part of his job description. He did it quickly and well, delivered it to his boss, and went back to his desk. Soon after, he was given another assignment, which he also completed quickly. Within a year, the young man had been given several additional responsibilities, each one of which he accepted and fulfilled immediately.

In his second year, he was promoted to a higher position. He studied, upgraded his skills, and continued to work hard. Within a couple of years he had surpassed all of his rivals. He had earned the respect and esteem of the other managers. They soon promoted him so that he was one of them, rather than one of the staff. His career took off. Eventually he became a vice president of the company.

This is a simple strategy that works for anyone who is willing to do more than is expected of him or her. It works for almost anyone, anywhere, over and over again, year after year.

■ LOOK FOR WAYS TO ADD VALUE

If your goal is to become wealthy, you have to know how wealth is created. The answer is contained in two words: "add value." All wealth comes from adding value in some way. All wealth comes from serving and satisfying your customers better than they could be served and satisfied by someone else. Wealth is the result of adding value to them in a way that no one else can match.

In your job, you should be looking for ways every day and every week to add value and to become more valuable than you were before. Throughout your career, your main focus must be to constantly seek out ways that you can add value to your boss, to your co-workers, to your customers, to your suppliers, and to everyone else and anyone upon whom you rely for your success. This should become your motto: *"Add value, add value, add value!"*

■ THE NEW PARADIGM OF WORK

One of the major revolutions in thought that has taken place in the world of work in the past few years is the idea that you must justify your position anew every day.

It used to be that a person would work hard for a few years until he had achieved a certain level in his job. He could then coast along at that level for many years, if not for the rest of his career. His attitude was, "Well, I've paid my dues. I earned my position. I did a great job. Now I am entitled to this job indefinitely."

But this is no longer good enough. Today, everybody wants to know, *"What have you accomplished lately?"* In the fast-moving, highly competitive business world of today, your boss wants to know what you have done to add value recently. You have already been paid for what you did last year, last month, and even last week. Now you must earn and justify your paycheck anew. There is a race on and you are in it, whether you know it or not.

■ TWO SOURCES OF VALUE

There are two major sources of value in the world of work today. The first is *time* and the second is *knowledge*. Today, time is the currency of modern business. Everyone must be focused on reducing the amount of time that it takes to get the same results. Customers will pay dearly for anyone who can reduce the time needed to get them the products and services they want. People will pay more for someone who can satisfy their needs faster than someone else. This is why most of the major improvements in modern management are those that reduce the amount of time that it takes to get the job done.

The most important measure of time is *speed*. The most important quality that you can develop with regard to time is a "sense of urgency." This is the habit of moving fast when opportunity presents itself to you. Develop a bias for action. Fast tempo is essential to success. All successful people not only work hard, hard, hard, but they work fast, fast, fast!

■ DO IT NOW!

Procrastination is not only the thief of time; it is the thief of life. To outperform your competition, both inside and outside your organization, you must develop the habit of moving *quickly* when something needs to be done. You must develop a reputation for speed and dependability. Study after study shows that those individuals with the best reputations for speed and dependability are the most valued in any organization. They are very quickly promoted onto the fast track in their careers.

The wonderful advantage of developing the habit of moving fast is that the faster you move, the *better* you get. This is because the faster you move, the more experience you get. The faster you move, the more you learn and the more competent you become. The faster you move, the more energy and enthusiasm you have. People who move fast as a way of life soon develop a totally different temperament and personality than people who move slowly or who take a casual attitude toward their work.

■ WORK IN REAL TIME

Whenever possible, do your work in "real time," as soon as it comes up. Do it now. It is amazing how much time you can waste by picking up a task, looking at it or starting it, and then putting it down and coming back to it again and again. As a general rule, small tasks should be done immediately, as soon as they appear. This habit of taking action quickly will enable you to get through an enormous amount of work in a day. It will earn you a reputation for being the kind of person to give jobs to when someone needs them done quickly.

■ SUCCESS COMES FROM GOOD HABITS

Fully 95 percent of everything you do throughout your day is based on habit. Successful people are those who have developed the habits of success. Successful people form good habits and ensure that those habits govern their behaviors. Unsuccessful people allow bad habits to form, and these bad habits then lead to frustration and failure.

My friend Ed Foreman says, *"Good habits are hard to form but easy to live with. Bad habits, on the other hand, are easy to form but hard to live with."*

A habit is defined as "a conditioned response to stimuli." It is an automatic way of responding or reacting in a particular situation. You develop a habit by repeating a specific act or way of thinking and reacting. Once it becomes a habit, it becomes easier to do it that way than to do it some other way. What kind of habits do you have?

Successful people are simply those who developed successful habits. They have trained themselves, like athletes, to do certain things in a certain way, over and over again, until they do them automatically, without even thinking about them. You may have heard the old saying:

Sow a thought and you reap an action;
Sow an action and you reap a habit;
Sow a habit and you reap a character;
Sow a character and you reap a destiny.

■ A KEY SUCCESS HABIT

One of the habits of success is that of *early rising*. Successful people get up a little bit earlier, read and prepare, plan and organize their day on paper in advance, and get going before the average person has even started. Thomas Jefferson said, "The sun has never caught me in my bed."

A woman in one of my seminars some years ago told me that she discovered the magic of early rising. She had found that by going to bed early she could get up at four o'clock in the morning. She could then do the equivalent of a full day's work by seven or eight o'clock, before the average person even got started. In no time at all, she was producing and earning double the amount of her co-workers. She was continually promoted and paid more money because she was getting far more done than anyone else.

Successful people make a habit of getting up early, usually by 6:00 or 6:30 in the morning, sometimes earlier, and then getting going immediately. This gives them a great jump on the day.

The average person, on the other hand, takes a full hour to get up and get going in the morning. Then they drag themselves off to work, thinking about lunchtime, and what they are going to do in the evening.

When *your* alarm clock goes off, get up immediately and get going right away. Start moving. Develop the habit of rising early and starting right to work on your most important task. This habit can do as much to assure your success as any other habit you develop.

■ PRACTICE LOMBARDI TIME

When Vince Lombardi took over the Green Bay Packers, the players had developed the habit of not showing up until the last moment for games or buses. Often they were late, and everyone had to wait. So Lombardi introduced "Lombardi time." This was defined as 15 minutes earlier than the scheduled time. Eventually everyone began arriving early, and the problem was solved.

You should go onto Lombardi time as well. Make a habit of punctuality by resolving to be on time, and then practicing it over and over until is natural and easy. Less than 2 percent of people are punctual, and everybody notices it, one way or the other. Make it a game to be on time—or better yet, *early*—for every appointment.

■ MAKE EVERY MINUTE COUNT

Get into work before anyone else gets there, and when you do arrive, begin working immediately. Don't waste time reading the newspaper, drinking coffee, or socializing with co-workers. Develop a reputation for being the kind of person who is always working, and always working on high-priority tasks.

Work all the time you work. Discipline yourself to keep yourself focused on the most valuable use of your time. Don't allow other people to put you "off your game." When you have coffee breaks or lunches, have them when they best suit you, not when they best suit the clock.

■ DOUBLE YOUR PRODUCTIVITY

Here is a powerful three-step formula you can use to double your productivity and perhaps even double your income over the next 12 months. It is simple and powerful, and it works for anyone who uses it.

First, make a decision to come into work an hour earlier. This does not take very much effort, and it allows you to beat the traffic. Have your work planned out for the day so that when you get into work you can then put your head down and go full blast. You will be amazed at how much you can get done before anyone else comes in. Research proves that you can do three hours of office work in one hour of uninterrupted time.

Second, work through lunch, using the hour when your co-workers are all off together eating to get ahead of your work. Resist the tendency to take an hour off at "lunchtime" or to go for lunch with whoever is standing there.

Third, work one hour later, after everyone has left. This third uninterrupted hour will enable you to wrap up your work from the day and plan the next day in detail. Also, by working later, you will miss the rush hour traffic.

By starting one hour early, working through the usual lunch hour, and staying one hour later, you will double your productive working time each day. When you combine this with working all the time you work and focusing on high-value tasks, you will more than double the amount of work you get done. You will quickly become one of the most valuable people in your organization.

■ SCHEDULE YOUR FIRST APPOINTMENT EARLY

If you are in sales, schedule your first appointment as early as possible. Many of the most important people you could want to see get into the office at 7:00 and 7:30 in the morning. Arrange to meet them at that time.

A salesman friend of mine, who is at the top of his field, found that the key to getting appointments with the key decision makers was to call their offices at 7:00 or 7:30 in the morning or 6:30 or 7:00 in the evening. He discovered that at these times all the staff either weren't in yet or had gone home. The only people working were the key people. They would answer the phone personally and he would get an opportunity to talk to them and arrange to see them later.

■ CREATE YOUR OWN OPPORTUNITIES

Develop the habit of moving fast. Successful people in every field have a sense of urgency. Only a small percentage of the population moves quickly when opportunity or responsibility presents itself. You must be a member of this small percentage.

When I was younger, I used to think that when my opportunity came along I would take advantage of it at that time. I soon learned that your opportunity never does just come along.

Russell Conwell made this point in his famous story, *Acres of*

Diamonds (Berkley, 1986). In summary, it says that in most cases your greatest opportunities lie under your own feet. They are right where you are. They lie within your current talents, skills, ability, and experience. They lie within your own business or industry. They lie within your own background or career. Your acres of diamonds are very close at hand, and that is where you should begin your search.

■ TAKE ACTION RIGHT WHERE YOU ARE

Theodore Roosevelt once said, *"Do what you can, with what you have, right where you are."* This is the key to success. *"Do what you can, with what you have, right where you are."*

Focus on the present moment and on your current situation. Don't wait for things to be "just right." It is you who will make things just right. By throwing your whole heart into what you are doing every minute, you will open up doors of opportunity that are not now visible to you.

Look around you at this very moment and ask yourself, "What could I do to add value to the most important people in my work life?" What could you do to make things faster, easier, or better for the people who are depending on you? Be proactive rather than reactive. Be the kind of person who reaches out and grabs opportunities, and if you don't have any opportunities, create them personally through your own efforts.

■ MAKE YOURSELF INDISPENSABLE

A secretary in Boca Raton, Florida, told me an interesting story at one of my seminars. She had listened to one of my audio programs on personal achievement. As a result, she had set a goal to increase her income by 50 percent over the coming year from her current income of $1,500 per month. She told me that she didn't really think it was possible to earn that much more because she was part of a large secretarial pool where salaries were fixed. Everyone made almost exactly the same.

Nonetheless, she decided to look for ways to add value to her boss. She noticed that he spent a lot of time replying to routine correspondence. One day, she took all of his regular mail and wrote replies to them. She then took the finished letters to him to edit and sign. He was delighted with her work and encouraged her to do more of it. Soon, she was handling 90 percent of his routine correspondence.

She then began to take additional courses to upgrade her skills in word processing, page making, and report preparation. Bit by bit, she began to take his smaller tasks and handle them herself. Each time she took over a smaller task, she freed her boss to work on more important tasks. And he noticed.

■ SOWING AND REAPING

After about three months her boss called her in and closed the door. He said that he really appreciated the work that she was doing for him, and he wanted to increase her pay. He asked her not to tell anyone else so that it didn't create any waves around the office. He then raised her salary from $1,500 to $1,750 per month.

She thanked him, and continued looking for ways to help him in his job. Three months later, he increased her pay again, and three months later, he increased her salary once more. By the end of the year, she was earning $2,250 per month, a 50 percent increase, while the other secretaries around her were still earning an average of $1,500.

She said it was absolutely amazing what happened when she began to focus all of her energies on adding value to her boss and to her company. And this same strategy can work for you.

■ SERVE PEOPLE BETTER

Every job is an opportunity for you to solve problems and to satisfy the needs of other people. Since the problems and needs that people have are unlimited, your opportunities to create value are unlimited as well.

Every fortune begins with an idea to serve people better in some way. Almost all entrepreneurs who start and build successful companies have worked for other organizations where they continually looked for ways to increase their value to the company.

The primary sources of value, the keys to wealth building, are *time* and *knowledge*. Your job is to continually increase your knowledge so that the value of what you do becomes greater and greater. Over 400 years ago Francis Bacon said that *knowledge is power*. But this is only partially true. Only when knowledge is applied to some good purpose is it power. Your job is to gather the knowledge that you need so that you can do your job fast and well.

There is a saying in Texas that goes, *"It's not the size of the dog in the fight; it's the size of the fight in the dog."*

What is most important is not the hours you put in, but the value of the work you put into those hours. Your success is determined by your ability to contribute value to your current job, either as an employee or as an employer, as a company worker or a company owner, that determines your income and your financial future.

■ PRODUCE MORE VALUE

In its simplest terms, successful people are *more productive* than unsuccessful people. Successful people have better habits. They dream bigger dreams. They work from written goals. They do what they love to do, and they concentrate on getting better and better at it. They use their natural abilities to the fullest. They are continually generating ideas to solve problems and to achieve company goals. They focus on using every minute of their time to get maximum results.

Above all, they are constantly looking around them for opportunities to add value to everything they do. They have a sense of urgency and a bias for action. They work all the time they work. They develop and maintain a sense of forward momentum. As a result, they soon become *unstoppable*.

ACTION EXERCISES

1. Identify the most valuable things you do at work. How could you organize your time so that you do more of them?

2. Resolve today to develop the habit of punctuality. Go on Lombardi time, and start arriving 15 minutes early for appointments.

3. Organize your day so that you come in and get started one hour earlier than your co-workers. Work through lunchtime, and stay one hour later.

4. Work all the time you work. Don't waste a minute. If someone tries to distract you, say you have to get back to work, and then do it.

5. Look under your own feet for your personal acres of diamonds, opportunities to add more value right where you are. What could they be?

6. Resolve today to become financially independent. Become a student of money, wealth accumulation, and wealth creation. Becoming rich is a skill that you can learn.

7. Begin today to implement the 40 Plus Formula in your daily work life. Work on your job, or work on yourself to get better at what you do, 50 to 60 hours each week. Put yourself on the side of the angels.

Chapter 5

Take Charge
of Your Life

The only limit to our realization of tomorrow will be our
doubts of today. Let us move forward with strong and
active faith.

—Franklin Delano Roosevelt

■ THE GREAT TRUTH

*"You can learn anything you need to learn, to accomplish any goal you
can set for yourself."* This principle offers a way for you to take complete control over your future. When I was young and struggling,
failing and frustrated, this principle came along to change my life.

Generally speaking, *no one is smarter than you, and no one is better
than you.* Just because someone is *doing* better than you doesn't
mean that he *is* better than you. It usually means that he has just
learned how to succeed in his particular field before you have. And
whatever someone else has done, you can probably do as well.
There are few limits.

This is not an easy rule, but it is definitely *simple.* You, too, can
learn anything you need to learn to accomplish any goal you can set
for yourself.

Once I learned this idea, I was unafraid to change jobs, and even
industries. I learned how to sell advertising, investments, automo-
biles, and office supplies. I worked in real estate sales and leasing,

and then real estate development. Then I engaged in importation and distribution, then banking, printing, consulting, and eventually speaking, writing, recording, and corporate training.

■ LEARN WHAT YOU NEED

Every time I entered into a new field, I went out and learned everything I possibly could about that field, and then applied it as fast as I could. At first, I checked out the books from the local library. Then, I bought my own books and built my own library. I listened to every audiocassette I could buy on the subject, and attended every seminar.

When I was 31, I studied and prepared myself, and then took the entrance exams to get into a major university. I invested several thousand hours of study to get a business degree. I learned the intricacies of micro- and macroeconomic theory, statistics, probability theory, management science, and accounting. I studied marketing, management, administration, and strategic planning. I became devoted to the concept of learning.

■ THE GREAT MYSTERY

I thought I had come late to the party, that everyone knew that learning was the key to the future. I was amazed and perplexed to find, when I looked around me, that very few other people were doing what I was doing. Most people, by their own admission, were "living lives of quiet desperation," in Thoreau's words. They were working at jobs they didn't like, earning salaries far below their potentials, staying in relationships they didn't enjoy, and living lives that gave them no satisfaction.

I tried to tell them that the way out was *up*. I told anyone who would listen that they could learn anything they needed to learn to achieve any goal they could set for themselves. There were no limits. But few people seemed to be listening.

■ REASONS FOR EVERYTHING

We live in an orderly universe. Everything happens for a reason. When I found that the people around me didn't seem to be interested in changing their situations, I began looking for the reasons underlying their behaviors. And I found them.

Psychologists and scholars have spent many years researching the psychology of success and the psychology of failure. And most of the studies conclude that there are two major mental blocks that hold people back. The first is what Dr. Martin Seligman of the University of Pennsylvania, in his book, *Learned Optimism* (Knopf, 1990), calls "learned helplessness." According to his research, this attitude afflicts fully 80 percent of the population to some degree, and for many people it is their major obstacle to success and fulfillment.

■ FEELING TRAPPED

As the result of childhood experiences, especially destructive criticism and early failure experiences, people eventually reach the point where they feel helpless to change or to take action in different areas of their lives. The majority of men and women feel overwhelmed by things that seem to happen to them, and the many things going on around them. They feel that there is nothing they can do to influence events or to improve their lives. The most obvious proof that an individual is experiencing learned helplessness is the repeated use of the words "I can't."

People feel that they can't lose weight, can't get a better job, can't improve or change their relationships, can't increase their incomes, can't upgrade their knowledge and skills, and can't do many other things that they really want to do. They have tried unsuccessfully so many times in the past that they have come to conclude automatically that there is very little they can do to change the future. They become passive and accepting of their situations. Their lives consist of getting up in the morning, going to work, socializing a bit, coming home, eating dinner, watching television for four or five hours, and then going off to bed.

■ THE TRAP OF COMPLACENCY

The second mental condition that holds people back is called the "comfort zone." Human beings are creatures of habit. They begin an activity of any kind and they soon become comfortable with it. They then become extremely reluctant to change what they are doing, or change the situation they are in, even if they are not particularly happy or satisfied with it. They become somewhat content and complacent. Eventually, they become afraid to change, for any reason. They get into a rut, and the longer they stay in their rut, the deeper it grows, until they finally give up all hope of ever changing or improving their lives.

Learned helplessness, in combination with the *comfort zone*, creates a person who feels trapped and helpless, weak and powerless, and unable to take control or to make any real difference in his life. The individual in this mental state then strives for security rather than opportunity, and often feels like a victim of circumstances over which he has no control.

■ NO REAL LIMITS

But the reality is that there are no real limits on what you can accomplish with your life. Within reason, whatever someone else has done, you can do as well. The very fact that you can set a clear goal for yourself means that you probably have the ability to achieve it. Nature does not give you a burning desire for something without also equipping you with the talents and abilities you need to acquire it.

If you think back over your life, you will recall that almost everything that you ever really wanted long enough and hard enough you finally achieved. You are not helpless, and you are not stuck in a rut. Your true potential is limited only by your own imagination and determination.

■ OUR BIGGEST ENEMIES

The two factors that contribute most to the feeling of helplessness and the comfort zone are *fear* and *ignorance*. Fear is and always has been your greatest enemy. Fear and self-doubt do more to hold you back from dreaming big dreams, and accomplishing great things, than any other factors.

It seems that the *less you know* about a subject, the *more fearful* you are of trying something new or different in that area. Your ignorance makes you reluctant to reach out for something better than what you are doing today. Fear and ignorance reinforce each other, growing until they induce in you a form of mental paralysis that leads inevitably to underachievement and failure.

Here is a wonderful discovery. Aggressively *learning* about any subject builds your confidence and diminishes your fear in that area. As your knowledge or skill increases, you soon reach the point where you are ready to take action and make changes. But if you are completely ignorant in a particular area, if you have not read or learned anything about a subject, it will seem too difficult and may even appear overwhelming to you. Your lack of knowledge will make you afraid to take the actions necessary to improve your life in that area.

■ NEUTRALIZING YOUR FEARS

The antidotes to fear and ignorance are *desire* and *knowledge*. The only real limitation on what you can accomplish is the level of intensity of your desire. If you really want something badly enough, there are almost no limits on what you can achieve. And the more you learn about any subject, the greater will be your desire to accomplish something in that area. As your knowledge grows, you become more confident in taking the necessary steps to make your goals a reality.

As you *increase* your levels of desire and knowledge, you *decrease* the self-limiting effects of fear and ignorance, and their companions, learned helplessness and the comfort zone.

With desire and knowledge, you eventually replace fear and ignorance with *courage* and *confidence*. The more you learn about anything that is important to you, the more courage you will have to attempt to achieve it, and the more confident you will be that you can eventually succeed. As Henry Ford once said, "If you believe you can do a thing, or you believe you cannot, in either case, you are probably right."

■ YOU ARE RESPONSIBLE

My first big breakthrough in life came when I discovered that I could learn anything I needed to learn to achieve any goal I could set for myself. My second breakthrough was when I realized that I was completely responsible for myself and everything that happened to me. *No one was going to do anything for me.* If I wanted something, it was completely up to me to do whatever was necessary to get it. If I had a problem or limitation, it was up to me to solve it or overcome it. I was on my own.

The acceptance of *personal responsibility* for your life is the giant step from childhood to maturity. Prior to that decision, people criticize, complain, and blame others for their problems. After that decision, they see themselves as the primary creative forces in their own lives. Before you take total responsibility for your life, you see yourself as a *victim*. Afterward, you see yourself as a *victor*.

■ ALL CAUSATION IS MENTAL

My third breakthrough came when I learned that *all causation is mental*. Everything you create in your material world begins with a thought of some kind. If you want to change something on the outside, you have to begin by changing it first on the inside. You have to change your thinking if you want to change your life. This is the greatest discovery of all.

You create your world with the continuous stream of thoughts, feelings, and images passing through your own mind. You control and determine your future by the thoughts you think in the present. Nothing around you has any meaning except for the meaning you give it by the thoughts and emotions you attach to it. As Shakespeare wrote in *Hamlet*, "There is nothing either good or bad, but thinking makes it so."

■ THE LAW OF BELIEF

Remember, *whatever you believe, with feeling, becomes your reality.* The greater the intensity of your belief, the more emotion you combine with it, the greater the impact it has on your behavior and on everything that happens to you.

If you absolutely believe that you are destined to be a great success, and you hold to this belief no matter what happens, then there is nothing in the world that can stop you from becoming that great success.

If you absolutely believe that you are a good person with tremendous abilities and that you are going to do remarkable things with your life, that belief will express itself through all of your actions and will eventually become your reality. The biggest responsibility you have to yourself is to change your beliefs on the inside so that they are consistent with the realities you wish to enjoy on the outside.

You can always tell what your beliefs really are by looking at what you do. You always express your true values in your actions. You always act on the outside consistent with who you really are, and what you really believe, on the inside.

One of the best ways to determine your true beliefs is to think about how you behave when you are angry, upset, or under pressure of any kind. This is when they come out. As Terrance wrote, *"Circumstances do not make the man; they only reveal him to himself."* (And to others!)

By using the Law of Reversibility, you can develop within yourself the values, beliefs, and qualities you most admire by *acting as if* you already had them, whenever they are called for by the circumstances of your life. To develop courage, force yourself to act courageously, even when you are afraid. To develop integrity, speak and act with complete honesty, even if you feel like shading the truth or cutting corners. Soon your beliefs will mirror your acts, and your acts will mirror your beliefs.

■ THE LAW OF EXPECTATIONS

The Law of Expectations says that *whatever you expect, with confidence, becomes your own self-fulfilling prophecy.* You are continually telling your own fortune when you talk about how you think things are going to turn out in a particular area. Your expectations then determine your attitude, and your attitude causes people to behave toward you in a way that reflects what you are thinking inside.

If you expect to be successful, you will eventually be successful. If you expect to be happy and popular, you will be happy and popular. If you expect to be healthy and prosperous, admired and respected by the people around you, that is what will happen.

You can tell your true expectations by listening to the words you use to describe an upcoming event. Always think and talk positively about the future. Start every morning by saying; *"I believe something wonderful is going to happen to me today."* Then, throughout the day, expect the best. Be open and alert to the possibility that each thing that happens, positive or negative, contains something good. You will be amazed at the effect this approach to life has on your attitude, and on the way you are treated by the people around you.

■ POSITIVE SELF-EXPECTANCY

Successful, happy people continually maintain an attitude of positive self-expectancy. They expect to be successful in advance, and they are seldom disappointed. They expect to make more sales than they lose. They expect to learn something valuable from every experience. They expect to eventually achieve their goals, and they remain open to the possibility that those goals may be achieved in a way that they didn't expect.

The very best way to predict the future is to *create* it, and you create your future by the way you approach everything that happens to you today, either positively or negatively. If you approach each situation confidently expecting to learn from it or gain from it, you will continue to grow and progress and move toward your goals. You will also be a happier, more optimistic person that other people will want to be around and to help.

■ THE LAW OF ATTRACTION

The Law of Attraction is considered by many people to be the most important law of all in explaining both success and failure. This law says that you are a "living magnet" and that you inevitably attract the people and circumstances into your life that *harmonize* with your dominant thoughts, especially those thoughts that you emotionalize strongly.

By this law, or natural force, the more you think about something you want, the more excited you will become about achieving it. The more excited or convinced you become, the more you will attract that goal into your life, like a magnet attracts iron filings. Your thoughts will create a force field of energy that will attract the people, circumstances, ideas, opportunities, and resources that you need to achieve your goals. When you change your thinking about yourself and your possibilities, you will attract into your life the forces necessary to turn those big thoughts and ideas into real-life experiences.

■ THE LAW OF CORRESPONDENCE

This law says that *your outer world corresponds to your inner world,* that what you experience on the outside is a reflection of your inner world. Whatever you see when you look around you, you see something in yourself. *"Wherever you go, there you are."* Your outer world of wealth, work, relationships, and health will mirror back to you the pictures and images that are going on inside you. Nothing can permanently stay in your life unless it corresponds with something within you.

To have happier relationships, you must become a more loving person, not in thought alone, but genuinely, in your heart. As you become a more loving person on the inside, your outer world of relationships will change, and sometimes immediately. To become more financially prosperous on the outside, you must become more prosperous on the inside. To be healthier and fitter in your body, you must think like a healthy and fit person in your mind.

In 1905, Dr. William James of Harvard said, "The greatest revolution of my generation is the discovery that individuals, by changing their inner attitudes of mind, can change the outer aspects of their lives."

■ TAKE CHARGE OF YOUR LIFE

There is only one thing over which you have complete control, and that is the content of your own mind. Only you can decide what you are going to think, and how you are going to think about it. This power, this control, is all you need to create a wonderful life for yourself. Your ability to steer your thoughts toward a destination of your own choosing is sufficient to enable you to overcome all obstacles, and make up for all limitations, on your road to success.

The Laws of Belief, Expectations, Attraction, and Correspondence, used consciously and deliberately, are the keys to your accomplishing wonderful things with your life. When you begin to change your thinking about your goals and possibilities, your beliefs and actions will change. You will find yourself doing more and more of the things you need to do to make your dreams come true.

You will continually expect good things to happen to you, and you will seldom be disappointed. You will begin attracting all kinds of wonderful people and opportunities into your life. Your whole world will begin to correspond, on the outside, with the wonderful goals and pictures that you are creating on the inside.

Successful and happy people have a generally positive mental attitude. Prosperous and wealthy people have a prosperous and wealthy mind-set. Kind, patient, gentle, loving people, who enjoy happy and fulfilling relationships with their families and friends, have kind, patient, loving ways of thinking. When you develop the same mind-set that other successful people have, you will soon enjoy the same results and experiences that they do.

■ START WHERE YOU ARE

You may think that you lack the education, opportunities, or resources that other successful people seem to have. Don't worry. The fact is that most people start off with few advantages. The story of most successful people is the story of people who started with nothing and did something worthwhile with their lives.

I used to feel sorry for myself because I entered my twenties with no money and a limited education. Then I learned that most people start off with little or no money. If they do get a good education, most of it turns out to be largely useless in the real world once they get out of school.

Then I felt sorry for myself because I had no natural talents to help me, and I couldn't find a good job. I soon learned that most people start off in the same boat. Most people try and fail at a lot of things before they find the right situation for their talents and abilities.

The fact is that everything you ever achieve you are going to have to do *yourself*. No one is going to do it for you. But if you keep learning and growing, trying lots of things, you will eventually get the breaks. Everyone does. Just remember that opportunities are like a fumble in a football game. If you don't personally pick up the ball and run with it, it just lies there and has no effect on the score. When you get your chance, take action on it immediately.

■ IT'S A WONDERFUL WORLD

We are living in a wonderful world today, probably the best period in all of human history. You are surrounded by more opportunities and possibilities to achieve your dreams than have ever existed before. There are no limits to what you can accomplish except for the limits that you put on yourself with your own thinking.

The feeling of learned helplessness and the lure of the comfort zone are the two major mental obstacles to changing your thinking, dreaming big dreams, and setting big goals for yourself.

The way to overcome fear and ignorance is with desire and knowledge. The two qualities that flow out of intense desire and increased knowledge are the courage and the confidence you need to do whatever is necessary to achieve anything you really want.

You translate your dreams into concrete realities by turning them into goals. You decide exactly what you want, write it down, set a deadline, and determine the efforts you are going to have to make to achieve it. Make written plans of action to achieve your goal and then do something every day to move toward it. Resolve in advance that you will never, ever give up.

■ MAKE PROGRESS, NOT EXCUSES

Mark Twain once wrote, *"There are a thousand excuses for failure, but never a good reason."*

When I stopped making excuses, I started making progress. When I stopped blaming other people and feeling sorry for myself, I began thinking about specific actions I could take to improve my situation. When I began to set goals and make plans for their accomplishment, I felt in control of my life and my future. When I began learning what I needed to know to achieve my goals, I felt more confident and competent in other parts of my life as well. And as I began achieving my goals, one by one, just as you will achieve yours, my thinking changed completely.

■ CHANGING YOUR LIFE

Success is an inside job. It is a state of mind. It begins within you and is soon reflected in the world around you. When you change your thinking for the better, you become a better person. By dreaming big dreams and envisioning an exciting future, you become a leader. By writing down your goals and making plans to accomplish them, you take full control of your life. And by practicing the ideas taught in this book, you can and will become *unstoppable*.

ACTION EXERCISES

1. Resolve today to accept 100 percent responsibility for everything you are or will ever be. Instead of making excuses, decide to make progress.

2. Identify one area where you use the words "I can't" when you think of the need to change or do something different. Now imagine that your limitations in that area are all in your mind.

3. In what parts of your life have you become comfortable, so much so that you resist change, even if it would be an improvement? What could you do to get out of this comfort zone?

4. Identify one area where fear and doubt are holding you back from doing something that you want to do. Imagine that you were absolutely guaranteed success in that area. What would you do differently?

5. What are your favorite excuses for not making the decisions or taking the actions you need to if you want to achieve all your goals? What if your excuses were not true?

6. Desire and knowledge are the antidotes to fear and doubt. What could you do immediately to increase your knowledge in an area where you want to take action?

7. Identify one key area of your life that you have created with your own thinking. How could you change your thinking in that area to be more successful?

Chapter 6

Commit to Excellence

> The quality of a person's life will be determined by the depth of their commitment to excellence, no matter what their chosen field.
>
> —Vince Lombardi

The starting point of great accomplishment is for you to break loose from the mental bonds that hold you back. Dreaming big dreams and setting big goals provide the starting point of thinking, seeing, and feeling yourself to be capable of achieving far more than you ever have before.

How you think and feel about yourself is largely determined by how *effective* you feel you are in the important things you do, especially in your work or career. It is not possible for you to feel happy and confident as a person if you are not competent and capable in the areas of your life that are central to your personal identity.

One of the most powerful ways for you to change your thinking about yourself is for you to *commit to excellence*. It is to make the decision, right now, to be the best, to join the top 10 percent in your field, no matter how long it takes. The very act of thinking of yourself as *potentially* excellent at what you do actually changes your mind-set and improves your personality. It makes you happier and raises your self-esteem. You like and respect yourself more, just by deciding to be the best.

The market pays superior rewards only for superior performance.

It pays average rewards for average performance, and below-average rewards, unemployment, and bankruptcy for below-average performance. Today, the race is on in every area. Your competitors are more capable and determined than they have ever been before, and will grow even more so next year, and the year after, and for the rest of your career. You have to run faster just to stay in the same place.

■ THE GOOD OLD DAYS

At one time, you had to be excellent to rise to the top of your field or market. Today, however, excellence is taken for granted. Today, you have to be excellent just to get into the market in the first place. Then you have to constantly improve, getting better and better, week by week and month by month, if you want to keep up with the competition.

In every field, the top 20 percent of companies make 80 percent of the profits in that business or industry. The top 20 percent of salespeople make 80 percent of the sales and 80 percent of the income. The top 20 percent in every field enjoy most of the great rewards of money, pride, satisfaction, and reputation that go along with being the best at what they do. Your job is to join them, as quickly as possible.

■ THE CONTROL VALVE ON PERFORMANCE

Perhaps the most important quality of high-achieving men and women is that of *ambition*. They see themselves, think about themselves, and conduct themselves every day as though they were among the elite in their fields. They set high goals for themselves and continually work to exceed those goals. For them quotas are minimums, not maximums. They look upon the accomplishments of everyone else as challenges to themselves to be even better. And so must you.

The core of your personality is your level of *self-esteem*. Your self-esteem is a measure of how much you value yourself, and how much you think of yourself as an important and worthwhile person. Your self-esteem is the power source of your personality. It determines your levels of energy, enthusiasm, motivation, inspiration, and drive. The more you like and respect yourself, the better you do at everything you attempt. And the better you do, the more you like and respect yourself. Self-esteem and personal excellence reinforce each other.

■ THE BETTER YOU DO

Self-esteem and *self-efficacy* are flip sides of the same coin of personality. You can genuinely like and respect yourself only when you know, deep in your heart, that you are really good at what you do. A sense of *personal mastery* is absolutely essential to the healthy human personality. Every single thing that you do in an excellent fashion boosts your self-esteem and makes you feel better about yourself. It makes you feel even more confident of performing at even higher levels.

Achieving your full potential requires high levels of courage and confidence. Great success requires a continual willingness to move out of your comfort zone, and to break the bonds of learned helplessness that hold most people back.

The higher your self-esteem, the more powerful, positive, and determined you will become. The more you like yourself, the more willing you will be to take chances, to step out in faith, and to persist longer than anyone else. The better you become in your chosen field, the stronger and more confident you will become in every other part of your life as well.

■ THE ABSOLUTE PREREQUISITE

The fact is that it is impossible for you to be truly happy or successful until you know in your heart that you are very, very good at what you do. For this reason alone, you must resolve to overcome any obstacle, pay any price, and go any distance to achieve this level of excellence. You must set a goal to be among the top 10 percent of performers in your field, and then do whatever it takes to get there.

Fortunately, getting to the top is easier than you think. The great majority of people seldom think about personal excellence. And if the thought crosses their minds, they quickly dismiss it and go back to average performance. Most of the people around you are content to do their jobs, for better or for worse, and then go out with their friends, or go home and watch television. However, when you begin to make those extra efforts that enable you to excel, you will find that, like a runner going into a sprint, you soon move ahead of the pack of the average performers.

■ DEVELOP THE WINNING EDGE

One of the most important of all success principles is the "winning edge" concept. This concept explains success and failure, and has been demonstrated over and over. This principle says: *Small differences in ability can lead to enormous differences in results.* It seems that the top people in every field are usually just a little bit better than the average in the critical things that they do. But consistency in being a little bit better in your key skill areas eventually adds up to an enormous difference in results.

In fact, all you need is to be about 3 percent better in each of the key result areas of your job to develop the winning edge. This edge enables you to move to the front in the race of life. Once you get a little ahead, you can then maintain and increase this gap by continuous self-improvement. You can continue to get better and better with learning and practice. With this strategy, you will soon emerge in the top 10 percent, or even the top 5 percent, of people in your field.

■ KEY RESULT AREAS

Success in any job requires a minimum level of performance in one or more tasks or functions. These are the key result areas (KRAs) of the position. Key results areas are the tasks that you absolutely, positively have to do well to be successful in your overall job, whatever it is. As it happens, there are seldom more than five to seven key result areas in any job, position, company, or area of responsibility. Your job is to identify the KRAs of your job and then make a plan to improve in each one.

The reason they are called "key result areas" is because they are the essential skills necessary for you to do your job completely and well. A weakness in any one of them can hold you back from excellent performance in your overall job. You are successful because of your strength in certain key result areas, but your *weakest* key result area determines the degree of effectiveness with which you will be able to use all the others. Your weakest key skill area largely determines your income.

■ IDENTIFY YOUR KEY SKILLS

Each job or desired result can be defined in terms of the key skills necessary to achieve it. For example, there are seven key result areas in selling. A weakness in any one of them can hold you back from selling as much as you can. They are: (1) prospecting; (2) establishing trust and rapport; (3) identifying the customer's problem or need; (4) presenting your product or service as the ideal solution to the problem; (5) answering objections and concerns; (6) getting agreement to proceed; and (7) obtaining resales and referrals. If you perform well in all seven of these areas, you will soon be at the top of your field. If you are poor in any area, your performance in that area will determine your income.

In management, there are also seven key result areas. They are: (1) planning; (2) organizing; (3) selecting the right people; (4) delegating; (5) supervising; (6) measuring; and (7) reporting, both upward and downward. If you are excellent at every key skill except for one, that one weakness alone will hold you back in your career as a manager.

There are critical success factors in almost every area of life. For example, there are four critical success factors that determine your physical health. They are: (1) proper diet; (2) proper weight; (3) proper exercise; and (4) proper rest. Almost all of your health problems can be traced back to a problem or deficiency in one of these four areas.

The starting point of personal excellence is for you to identify the key result areas of your job. Define them clearly and write them down. Make a list of the tasks, in order, that you must perform to get the results expected of you in your job. Evaluate your current performance in each of these key result areas. Where are you strong? Where are you weak? Be honest.

■ SET STANDARDS OF PERFORMANCE

If you want to lose weight, the first thing you do is weigh yourself. If you want to improve in any area, you first measure how well you are doing in that area today, and then use that as a *baseline* for improvement.

Once you have determined the results that you absolutely, positively have to get to perform at your best in a particular aspect area of your life or work, you then give yourself a score of 1 to 10 in each key result area, with 1 being the lowest and 10 being the highest. You must be at a 7 level or above in each area to do your overall job in an excellent fashion. Wherever you are scoring 7 or below, you must set a goal to improve in that area.

Always start your program of personal improvement where you can get the greatest result the *fastest*. This will invariably be in the key result area where you are the weakest. Identify your lowest-scoring KRA and then make a plan to improve in this skill area as quickly as possible. Simultaneously, you develop a plan to gradually improve in each other area where you are weak.

Every step you take toward improving yourself in one of your key result areas will improve your results in your job. The better you get at your job, the more you will like and respect yourself. The more you like and respect yourself, the better you will feel, and the more energy and enthusiasm you will have. You will soon become unstoppable.

■ PERSONAL STRATEGIC PLANNING

In the business world of the twentieth century, it was generally agreed that corporations should conduct strategic planning on a regular basis. Individuals, though, were encouraged to set personal goals. In the twenty-first century, however, the situation is different. Today, each individual, just like a company, must engage in a regular process of *personal* strategic planning.

In personal strategic planning, you view yourself as a business organization. With this perspective, you make more detailed, long-range plans for your goals and activities in every part of your life.

Today, you must spend far more time thinking about your future than ever before. You must invest more energy and effort analyzing and planning the steps you need to take to translate your future dreams into present realities. You must *manage* yourself better than ever before. You have to take complete control over everything that happens to you.

■ AUDIENCE PARTICIPATION

Sometimes I ask my audiences, "How many people here are self-employed?" Usually, about 10 to 15 percent of the audience will raise their hands. I then stop the seminar and ask them again, "How many people here are *really* self-employed?" And then I wait.

It doesn't take them very long. People look at each other and then back at me and then at each other again. Soon, one hand after another begins to go up. Eventually, everyone has his or her hands raised. Everyone realizes that they are *all* self-employed.

The biggest mistake that you can make is to think that you ever work for anyone else but yourself. The fact is that you are always self-employed, from the time you take your first job until the time you retire. No matter who signs your paycheck, you are working for *yourself.* You are the president of an entrepreneurial personal services company with one employee—*yourself.* In the long run, as a result of the things that you do or fail to do, you determine how much you earn. If you want an increase in pay, you can go to the nearest mirror and negotiate with your "boss."

■ YOU DETERMINE YOUR OWN INCOME

People sometimes argue with me about this. They say that the pay structures in their business or industry are determined by factors over which they have no control. But then I point out to them that it was *they* who decided to go to work in that business or industry. And it is they who decide to stay there. They are in charge. They are on their own payroll.

If you are not happy with any part of your work, it is up to you to change it. Benjamin Disraeli said, "Never complain and never explain." If there is a part of your work or personal life that you don't like, don't waste your time complaining about it. Instead, take action. As Shakespeare's Hamlet expresses it, "take arms against a sea of troubles, and by opposing end them."

Seeing yourself as the president of your own personal services corporation requires that you accept total responsibility for everything you are, and everything you ever will be. This is an enormous thought for many people. It is both scary and exhilarating.

Just imagine! You are where you are and what you are because *you* have decided to be there. Everything you accomplish, for the rest of your life, will be largely determined by the actions that you take, or fail to take. You are responsible. You are in charge. You are in control. You are your own boss. And there are no limits except the limits that you allow the outside world to place on yourself and on your thinking.

■ THE AIM OF STRATEGY

When you begin thinking of yourself as a *personal services corporation*, you separate yourself from all those people who think they work for someone else. When you take charge of your career, you begin thinking in terms of personal strategic planning, just like a large business. You begin making plans for the long term.

The parallels between corporate planning and personal planning are very similar. The purpose of strategic planning in a business is to achieve the highest *return on equity* (ROE) invested in the business. All strategic plans and tactics are aimed at reorganizing the resources and activities of the company in such a way that it achieves a higher rate of financial return on its resources than it was achieving before.

In its simplest terms, strategic planning is aimed at increasing the ratio of outputs to inputs. All of the management practices popular today, such as *restructuring, reorganizing, reengineering,* and *reinventing,* are aimed at improving the functioning of the organization so that it earns more money. They are aimed at increasing outputs and rates of return on equity.

■ INCREASING YOUR RETURN ON ENERGY

If return on financial capital is called return on equity, your personal ROE is your *return on energy*. Personal strategic planning is focused on organizing and reorganizing your life, restructuring and reengineering your activities, to increase the quality and quantity of rewards you get from the investment of the hours and days of your life in what you do.

Let us say, for example, that you have decided that you want to double your income in the next three to five years. This is a reasonable goal that many people around you are already achieving. It is not that difficult to achieve. Simply put, to double your income, you merely have to double the value of your output relative to your input. You have to double the value of your contribution.

Financial results come as the result of performing a function or producing valuable goods and services that someone is willing to pay for. If you want to increase the amount you get out, you have to make a plan to increase the amount you put in.

■ YOUR AREA OF EXCELLENCE

What is the critical factor that determines the success or failure of any company? It is its *competitive advantage*, or "area of excellence." Every company comes into being and survives because it has a unique capacity to offer the market something that is better in some way than anything being offered by its competitors. It stays in business as long as it continues to satisfy its customers in a particular area better than anyone else.

The competitive advantage or *unique selling proposition* of a company determines its rate of growth, its level of sales, its profitability, and its very survival. Companies without a competitive advantage soon disappear from the marketplace, to be replaced by other companies with clear, unmistakable, competitive advantages that customers can and will pay for.

You are no different. As the president of a company of *one*, you, too, must develop and maintain meaningful competitive advantage. You must develop an area of uniqueness. You must be absolutely excellent in the work that you do so that you can rise to the top of your field. Your choices and decisions about what your competitive advantage is, and will be, are the critical determinants of your financial success in your life and career.

■ SUCCEEDING THE HARD WAY

Some years ago, a friend of mine went to work for a stock brokerage firm. The recruiting and training program was highly technical and the sales training was virtually nonexistent. When he finally got his brokerage license, he was given the yellow pages and told to begin "dialing for dollars," phoning anybody he could get on the other end of the line and pitching them on his products. He soon learned that this was one of the hardest ways in the world to crack the professional sales field and make a living.

One day he had a sudden insight that changed his career, and eventually made him one of the top financial advisers in the country. He realized that his entire career, and everything that happened to him—his family lifestyle, his bank account, and his future—would be determined by how good he was on the telephone. So he made a decision to become absolutely outstanding at using the telephone as a prospecting and selling tool.

He read every book he could find on effective telephone techniques. He took every course and studied every piece of information on the subject. He became so good at using the telephone that he could recognize 19 different kinds of hesitancy in the voice of the person he was calling. He developed appropriate responses to each one so that he could reassure his prospects and clients that what he was recommending was the right thing for them.

Today, he earns more than five million dollars per year buying and selling investments for his clients over the phone on straight commission. Fully 99 percent of his business is done by telephone and now by computer, e-mail, and fax. He seldom meets his clients personally. But on the phone, he is a master communicator. He definitely and specifically identified and developed a competitive advantage that he used to move to the top of his field. What could it be for you?

■ BECOME A DO-IT-TO-YOURSELF PROJECT

Here is an exercise: Complete this sentence: "If I could _____ really well, I could make all the money I wanted." Your job is to fill in the blank.

What one skill, if you developed and did it consistently in an excellent fashion, would have the greatest positive impact on your income? If you could wave a magic wand and be absolutely outstanding in any one part of your work, which part of your work would you choose? Whatever your answer, this is the key result area that you need to begin work on right away.

All lasting success in your business or career will come as a result of your doing something extremely well, something that others value and are willing to pay for. And anything that anyone else can do in an excellent fashion, you can learn to do as well. Remember, everyone in the top 10 percent started in the bottom 10 percent.

Everyone who is doing well today was once doing poorly. All of the people at the top of your field were at one time in some other field altogether. The way to get to the front of the buffet line of life, where all the good things are to be found, is simple. First, *get in line.* Make a decision to join the top 10 percent, no matter how long it takes. Second, *stay in line.* Once you start moving toward personal excellence, keep learning and practicing until you get there.

Here's the good news. The buffet line of life is moving! It never closes. It is open 24 hours per day. Everyone who gets in line and *stays* in line eventually gets to the front. Nothing can stop you from getting into the top 10 percent except yourself. You are responsible.

■ CLARIFY YOUR COMPETITIVE ADVANTAGE

One of the first questions you ask of yourself is, *"What is my competitive advantage?"* What are you absolutely excellent at doing? What is it that you do better than almost anyone else in your business? What unique set of skills do you have that accounts for most of your success to date? Where are you *really* good?

Your second question is, "Looking at the trends in my industry, what will my competitive advantage be in three to five years?" If things continue on the way they are and you could project yourself three to five years into the future and look around, what will you need to be doing in an excellent fashion at that time?

Many people have trouble answering both of these questions. They are not sure what their competitive advantage is today, and as a result they have no idea what their competitive advantage will be in the future. If you are in this situation, you are in great danger of underachieving and even failing in your career.

■ YOUR POTENTIAL COMPETITIVE ADVANTAGE

Here is the next question: "What *should* your competitive advantage be?" If you could be absolutely outstanding in any one area, what should it be? If you're not sure, go and ask your boss or your co-workers. Ask them, *"If I was really, really good in any one skill, what one skill would have the greatest positive impact on my results?"*

You usually know the answer to this question as soon as you ask it. If you are in doubt about the one skill that could help you the most, ask for advice and input from others. The people around you, especially your boss, can usually tell you quite quickly the answer to this question.

Once you have the answer, you set the development of that skill as your new goal or target to aim at. You change your thinking in a very positive way in that area, and you begin to imagine that you have the ability to be absolutely outstanding in that one area. You write it down, set a deadline, make a plan, and go to work on improving yourself in that area. In no time at all, you will begin to develop the winning edge in your job that will enable you to move ahead of the crowd.

■ FIRE THE STAFF

Some companies today are taking their people through an exercise that can be quite traumatic to their employees. They call everyone together, and then they *fire* the entire staff. They announce that they are going to be rehiring someone for each job, and that each person can *reapply* for their job as though they were outside contractors presenting a proposal.

This proposal for their jobs would include a description of *what* they intend to do, *how* they intend to do it, *how much* they would charge for their work, and *how much* the company would gain or save by paying them the salaries they are requesting for what they are proposing to do.

As you can imagine, many employees are completely baffled when they are confronted with this exercise. The very idea of thinking through their current jobs and describing them in the form of a business proposal, along with a justification for why they should be paid the amount that they are asking, is an over-whelming task. Most people have never thought about their jobs in this way before.

Finally, the boss adds one more detail. He tells them that they will each be competing against other people who will also be sub-mitting proposals for the same jobs. Whoever offers the company the best deal or price will get the position.

■ DETERMINE EXACTLY WHAT YOU DO

If you were put into this position and you had to write out a pro-posal for your job, starting with the most important and valuable things that you do for your company, how would you explain your-self? How would you sell yourself to your current employer? How would make a case for the kind of money you want to earn?

What are your *core competencies*? What special talents and abili-ties do you have that make you valuable and set you apart from oth-ers? What *should* your core competencies be, or what *could* they be in the future? What is it that you do in such an excellent fashion that you are worth the kind of money that you want to earn? Your an-swers to these questions are essential to your success in your career.

■ HOW GOOD ARE YOU?

There is a simple way to determine how good you are at what you do: *Are you in great demand?* If you are very good, people are continually trying to hire you away from your current employment. You receive regular job offers. If you are self-employed, you have more business than you can handle. You get a steady flow of recommendations and referrals from satisfied customers.

When you are in demand, you have complete job security. You know that if something happened to your current job, you could walk across the street and get another job tomorrow. You never worry about the ups or downs in the economy because you always have far more opportunities than you can handle in a 24-hour day.

When you reach this point, you will know that you are one of the very best in your field. You will feel terrific about yourself. You will have complete control over your future.

■ DO WHAT YOU LOVE TO DO

You may be wondering how you go about determining your area of excellence, if you don't already have one. If you are already very good at what you do, you should know that with change taking place so rapidly in your field, within a few years you will probably find yourself in another job, doing something different, with a different area of excellence. Whatever got you to where you are today is not enough to keep you there.

Here is one of the most important parts of changing your thinking. *Successful people do what they love to do.* They do their jobs for the art and joy of it. They would do what they are doing even if they weren't being paid for it. Ask yourself this question: *"What would I choose to work at if I was financially independent and could do anything I wanted?"*

How would you change your life if you won a million dollars? The great majority of people, if they won a million dollars, would immediately quit their current jobs. If you would quit your current job if you won a million dollars, this is a danger signal. It means that you are in great danger of wasting your career and wasting your life.

■ DETERMINE WHAT YOU ENJOY DOING

Self-made millionaires almost invariably say that their secret of success was that they found out what they enjoyed doing, and they did it with their whole heart. Most successful people feel that they don't really work at all. Some of them say, "I haven't worked a day in my life." Their work and their play are intermingled. They don't know where one begins and the other ends. When they are not at work, they think about it and talk about it. And when they are at work, they lose themselves in it.

There are more than 22,000 official job categories in the United States alone. Among these 22,000 categories, there are subcategories that bring the number to easily 100,000 different jobs that you could be doing. And most of the jobs that people will be doing in the twenty-first century have not even been invented yet.

Of the many thousands of jobs that exist, there are numerous jobs at which you could work and earn an excellent living. Your goal must be to select the ideal job for you, the one that gives you the greatest joy, satisfaction, and rewards, and then channel all of your energies into becoming absolutely excellent in that one area.

■ SUCCESS LEAVES TRACKS

The starting point of identifying your special talents and unique abilities is for you to think back into your past. What sorts of activities have given you your greatest results and rewards?

When you were in school, what subjects interested you the most? What subjects did you get the best grades in? You will always be best at doing something that *fascinates* you, that holds your *attention*, that captures your *interest*, and that you are naturally *attracted* toward.

One of the tests for whether something is right for you is your desire to learn more about it. You will enjoy *reading* about it, *talking* about it, and *learning* about it. Not only that, but you will naturally admire the people who are the most successful in the field for which you are ideally suited.

■ GO BACK TO YOUR CHILDHOOD

One way to determine your future is to examine your past. Look back to what you *most enjoyed* doing when you were between the ages of 7 and 14 years old. At that time, you were completely free to pursue any subject that attracted you. What did you most enjoy doing? If you don't remember, go and ask one of your parents. They will usually remember how you spent your time when you were younger.

A participant in one of my seminars told me that this principle applied to him exactly. When he was between the ages of 7 and 14, he loved to build model airplanes. He spent many hours, long into the night, building more and more complex models. Soon, he was building model planes with small engines and entering them in contests. As he grew older, he built larger planes, remote-controlled, and flew them in competitions around the country.

When he finished high school, he attended university and earned a degree in aeronautical engineering. He now owns three companies. In one company, he designs small aircraft. In a second company he leases and charters aircraft, and he owns a third company that does aircraft maintenance. He told me that he was worth several million dollars and he felt that he had never done a day's work in his life. He was still doing what he most enjoyed doing when he was a young man. And he was only 35 years old.

■ YOUR FEELING OF IMPORTANCE

Dale Carnegie once wrote, "Tell me what gives a person his greatest feeling of importance and I will tell you his entire philosophy of life." What gives you your greatest feeling of importance? What gives you a heightened sense of self-esteem when you do it successfully? What do you most enjoy doing, so much so that you are drawn back to it continuously?

Napoleon Hill once said that one of the great secrets of success is to *decide what it is that you most enjoy doing, and then find a way to earn a good living at it.* Most people get it backward. They do what they feel they *have to do* so that they can finally acquire the time and money necessary to do what they really *want to do.* Your goal should be to reverse this order. You should do what you really enjoy doing from the very beginning. In this way, you will get better and better doing more and more of the things that give you your greatest feeling of importance.

■ FACE THE FACTS

One of the most important parts of changing your thinking is the development of the quality of *courage*. I will discuss this subject in greater detail later, in Chapter 12. For the moment, in terms of doing what you love to do, you need courage to face the fact that, right now, you might not be in the right job, place, or relationship for you. You may be on the wrong path.

Most people back into their jobs and their careers, and even their relationships, like backing up their car and hitting something, and then getting out to see what it was. They do not have clear goals, so they accept whatever happens to them. They take the job that is offered to them at the time they are starting work or making the transition from one job to another. They do the work that is assigned to them. They allow their boss to determine their career path.

Their entire work lives soon become organized around the expectations of the people who sign their paychecks. If they are not careful, years will go by and they will completely lose sight of the child in them who started off in life with hopes and dreams, entering a world of untapped possibilities and potentialities.

■ BE TRUE TO YOURSELF

Joseph Campbell, the late professor of mythology, told a story on the *Bill Moyers Special* television show some years ago. It took place in a small local restaurant that he patronized with his wife. One day another couple, along with their young son, came in and sat down for dinner at a nearby table. Halfway through the meal, the boy spoke up and said that he didn't like his dinner, and he wasn't going to eat it. The father became extremely angry and insisted that he eat it whether he liked it or not.

The boy refused and said to his father, "But I don't *want* to eat it!"

At this, the father blew up and shouted, "You don't *want* to? What does that have to do with anything? I never did anything I *wanted* to do in my whole life!"

Campbell went on to point out that many people are in that same situation. Many people feel that they have lived their whole lives doing things that other people wanted them to do because they never had the courage to do just what *they* wanted.

Campbell then said that the key to success and happiness in life was to "follow your bliss." It was to do what you most loved to do. It was to look over the landscape of your life and determine those activities that you enjoyed doing more than anything else, the things that you would do if you had no limitations, and then to build your life around those activities.

■ BE PREPARED TO WALK AWAY

Many of the happiest men and women in our society today are those who, at a certain point, got up and walked away from a situation that they finally realized was not making them happy or fulfilled. They had the courage to decide that they were going to do what they loved to do, rather than what they felt they had to do. They looked deep within themselves and honestly assessed their own natural talents and abilities. This often changed their whole lives.

■ LISTEN TO OTHERS

Some years ago, I began thinking in earnest about what it was that I really wanted to do. My current job was coming to an end, and the prospects for the future, because of the economy, were not very encouraging. Meanwhile, although I had a very good idea of what I wanted to do, I wasn't sure.

At this point, I suddenly asked a friend of mine what he thought I would be good at doing. He replied, without a moment's hesitation, "You'd be excellent at teaching and giving seminars."

That turned out to be exactly what I had been thinking, but I was nervous about directing my whole career into a completely unknown field. My friend's comment made me realize that often the people around you can see clearly what you should be doing, even if you can't see it yourself.

If you are at all unsure about your area of natural talent and ability, ask someone who knows you well what he or she thinks your ideal line of work would be. The people who know you and care about you will often give you ideas and insights that change your whole life. Often these insights will reveal to you your heart's desire.

■ YOUR HEART'S DESIRE

Your heart's desire is that one special thing that you were put on this earth to do. No one else can do it in the same way that you can. It is something that may have been calling to you for many years, like the sound of distant music. It is something that has interested you and attracted you since you were young.

Perhaps you have never told anyone about it. Perhaps, deep in your heart, you were afraid of the enormous changes you would have to make to pursue your heart's desire. But the fact is that you will never be truly happy or satisfied until you let yourself go and throw your whole heart into whatever it is.

Eric Butterworth wrote in his book *Discover the Power within You* (Harper & Row, 1968), "You are not what you *are*; you are what you *can be*."

Imagine! You are not what you are, but rather, *you are what you can be* when you discover and develop your natural talents and abilities to the full.

■ BE HONEST WITH YOURSELF

One of the marks of personal leadership is that you see yourself as you really are. You are completely honest. You recognize and accept that you are completely responsible, the president of your own personal services corporation. You accept that excellent rewards come only from excellent performance in your chosen field. You view yourself strategically, as if you were looking at someone else. You plan every part of your life, knowing that no one is going to do it for you. Especially, you establish your own program for personal and professional improvement to assure that you become one of the very best people in your field.

■ THINK AND PLAN STRATEGICALLY

There are several concepts in personal strategic planning that can improve your results and change your life. As in everything, these are ways of thinking that lead to ways of acting more effectively.

■ DRAW A LINE

The first concept is what I call "zero-based thinking." Call a time-out in your life and work. Draw a line under all your current activities. Now, imagine that you are starting over. Ask yourself, *"Is there anything in my life that, knowing what I now know, I would not get into or start up again today if I had it to do over?"*

This is one of the most important questions you will ever ask and answer. You can apply it on a "go forward" basis to each part of your life. Often the biggest problem in personal strategic planning is your attempting to make something work that you wouldn't even get into in the first place if you had to do it over again.

Often when I consult with companies, they ask me for advice on how to increase sales of a particular product or service. I always ask them, *"Knowing what you now know, would you introduce this product or service again today if you had it to do over?"*

They often tell me that, knowing what they now know, they would never have brought it out in the first place. My advice to them is always the same: "Kill it." One of the smartest things a company can do with a part of the business that is not working, and which has no future, is to discontinue it as quickly as possible. This applies to products, services, processes, methods of sale or advertising, investments, or any other area of activity that consumes time, money, or emotional energy.

■ HOLD YOUR OWN FEET TO THE FIRE

If there is anything in your life or your work that you wouldn't get into today, knowing what you now know, it is an excellent candidate for *creative abandonment*, for being discontinued altogether.

Is there any relationship in your life—personal or business— that, knowing what you now know, you wouldn't get into today if you had it to do over? If there is, your next question is, *"How do I get out of this relationship, and how fast?"*

Think about your business and your career. Is there anything in your work life that you wouldn't get into again today, knowing what you now know? Is there any business process, procedure, activity, or expense that you wouldn't start again today if you had it to do over?

Finally, think about your investments, not only of money, but also of time or emotion. Is there any part of your life that is dragging you down, causing you tension or stress, that you wouldn't get into again today if you were starting over? Sometimes, the fastest way to change your thinking and your life is simply to question everything you are doing today that is making you unhappy. If it is not working, abandon it and do something else.

■ YOUR MOST VALUABLE ASSET

Your most valuable asset is your time. It is also your scarcest resource. You have a limited amount of time, and once it is gone, it is gone forever. Time is essential to accomplishment. Time is perishable. You cannot get more of it, no matter what you do. It can be said that the quality of your life is determined by the way you spend this precious resource.

Results and rewards, however you define them for yourself, are everything. Your ability to achieve the health, happiness, and prosperity you desire is the measure of your effectiveness as a human being. Your job is to use your minutes and hours more effectively to assure that you are achieving the greatest quantity and quality of the things you want in exchange for the time you invest.

■ TRADING YOUR TIME

Everything in life is a trade of some kind. Overall, you trade your time for the results and rewards you want. You can tell what kind of a trader you are by looking around you and evaluating your current situation. Are you satisfied with the results of your trades in life so far?

Some people trade their time for $25,000 per year. Some people trade the same amount of time for $250,000 per year, even though they may be of similar age and intelligence, and have similar educations and backgrounds. But one of them earns 10 times what the other earns! Why is this?

In the simplest of terms, the one earning *more* thinks and acts differently from the one earning *less*. One person is a better "trader" than the other. One person has better information, continually upgrades his skills, starts earlier, works harder, and stays later. A good trader quickly develops the winning edge, and begins to pull ahead of the pack. Soon, he is working and earning at a far higher level than the people he started out with. This must be your goal as well.

■ YOUR TIME IS LIMITED

You cannot save time. You can only spend it differently. Every part of your life today shows the results of how you have spent your time in the past. If you want to have a different future, you have to spend your time differently in the present. You have to change your thinking about yourself and how you use your time to get the things you want in life.

Time, in a way, is like *money*. It can be either spent or invested. If you spend time or money, it is gone forever. You can never get it back. But it you invest your time or money wisely, you will get a greater return in the future. Personal strategic planning and thinking give you the tools to ensure that you achieve the highest return on time invested (ROTI). Put another way, it enables you to get the highest "return on life."

Everything you do that requires your time represents a choice. The choice is to use your time wisely or not. However you choose, the time will be gone forever. If you spend your time on one activity, you will no longer have that same quantity of time available to spend or invest in another activity. Your choices about how you use your time largely determine the quality of your life, both today and in the future.

You must be extremely jealous of your time. You must be adamant about not spending your time on activities of low value. You must downsize, outsource, and eliminate all activities that no longer represent the highest and best use of your time if you want to get the highest return on energy in your life and career. Zero-based thinking will help you to make better choices. It is a key thinking tool that can change your life.

■ THE PARETO PRINCIPLE

Another important strategic planning concept is the 80/20 Rule, the "Pareto Principle," which Italian economist Vilfredo Pareto wrote about in 1895 in Switzerland. This rule says that 80 percent of your results will come from 20 percent of your activities. If you make a list of 10 tasks that you have to do in the coming day, two of those items will be worth more than the other eight items put together.

But the 20 percent of activities that account for most of the value in your work are invariably the most difficult and challenging tasks. The 80 percent of activities that account for only 20 percent of your results are usually fun and easy. Being human, you have a natural tendency to do the *easy* things, even though they are not particularly valuable or important. To get the most done and the greatest results from every minute invested, you must *resist the temptation to clear up small things first.* You must discipline yourself to keep your energies focused on the one or two things that you can do that are more important and valuable than anything else.

■ MARKETING YOURSELF STRATEGICALLY

As the president of your own personal services corporation, you must consider the *four strategic variables* in marketing yourself and your services. Your effectiveness in each of these four areas will determine your income and your future. They are: (1) *specialization*; (2) *differentiation*; (3) *segmentation*; and (4) *concentration*.

These four activities are central to every business and to the success of every product or service offered by any business anywhere. All business growth and profitability are the result of performing well in each of these areas. Problems with sales and profitability are the result of a weakness in one or more of these areas. Each of them applies to you and your career, as well.

■ SPECIALIZE IN YOUR FIELD

Specialization means that you decide exactly what it is that you are going to do, and *do well,* in your field. Successful people in every field specialize rather than generalize. They *focus* their time and talents rather than trying to do too many things. They work to develop a reputation for being very, very good in a specific area. They don't try to be all things to all people or jacks-of-all-trades.

A successful business may specialize in a particular type of customer or in a specific market. It may specialize in a particular product or service for that type of customer. A successful salesperson will specialize in selling a particular product or service to a particular type of customer. A successful person in any field will spend more and more time doing fewer and fewer things that are of higher and higher value in a specific area.

What is your area of specialization today? What will it be in the future? What should it be if you want to move to the top of your field? What could it be if you were to stand back and imagine that you have no limitations, and that you could be excellent at any skill, or in any market, that you desired?

■ SET YOURSELF APART

The second strategic variable in your business or career is *differentiation.* This is the key factor that determines the success of most sales, marketing, and business growth. This is the primary determinant of success in your career.

Differentiation is defined as the way that you separate yourself from everyone else in your field who is offering something similar. Your area of differentiation is, in reality, your *area of excellence,* your area of uniqueness, your unique selling proposition. It is what gives you a competitive advantage over others in your industry.

■ THE KEY QUESTION

Imagine if a very important prospective customer were to ask you, "What is it about your product or service that is different, better, and superior to any other similar product or service offered by any other company in today's market?" How would you answer? If you had to explain how and why your product or service is superior to that of your competitors, what would you say?

Many salespeople, and even business owners, are not sure about the answer to this question. But you must be absolutely clear about your competitive advantage if you want to make more sales in an increasingly competitive market.

As an individual, doing personal strategic planning for your own career, you must ask this question of yourself. What unique skills do you have that make you superior to anyone else offering to do the same job that you are doing? What skills would it be *useful* for you to have? If you are not currently excellent in your field, what steps do you need to take, beginning immediately, to get yourself to the point where you stand out from everyone else?

➤ Identify Your Ideal Customers

The third strategic area in business is that of *segmentation*. This requires that you divide your markets and customers into segments. You do this by identifying those customers who can most benefit from your area of specialization and your competitive advantage within that area.

In segmentation, you identify your *ideal* customers. Who are they? Where are they? What do they have in common? What are their ages, incomes, education levels, backgrounds, positions, experiences, and so on? Today, more and more marketing is focused on *niches* and *micro-niches*. Sales and marketing are increasingly personal and individual, aimed at tightly defined groups of prospective customers with special qualities and characteristics. Who are your ideal customers?

■ CONCENTRATE YOUR ENERGIES

The fourth strategic variable, perhaps the most important of all in sales and marketing, is the principle of *concentration*. This is your ability to focus all of your energies and resources on those specific customers or markets where you have the greatest chance of success in the shortest period of time.

Your ability to concentrate single-mindedly on your highest-value opportunities will do more to increase your return on energy than any other factor. Concentration is a key success principle in every field.

■ SUCCESS VERSUS FAILURE

Dun & Bradstreet has been tracking the results of successful and unsuccessful businesses for more than 50 years. Not long ago, it put all of its research on failed businesses into a computer. The data showed that businesses fail because of "low sales." Businesses succeed because of "high sales." Everything else is commentary.

As the president of your own company, engaged in personal strategic planning for your career, your job is to ensure the highest level of sales of your personal services that you can possibly achieve. This requires that you *specialize, differentiate, segment,* and *concentrate.* As the president of your own life and career, you must become absolutely excellent at doing one or two things that the market will pay the most for. You must then become continually better in those one or two areas.

■ YOU ARE EXTRAORDINARY

The fact is that you are extraordinary. You are born with unique talents and abilities that make you completely different from all other human beings who have ever existed. The odds of there being two people just like you are more than 50 billion to one. In fact, it will never happen.

There is no one who has the unique and remarkable combination of experiences, ideas, thoughts, feelings, education, and imagination that you do. You have within you, right now, the ability to be, have, or do virtually anything you can imagine. You are very much like Michelangelo's block of marble, just lying there. You are like an incredible masterpiece just waiting to emerge.

Great success and happiness come when you identify your natural abilities, and then concentrate on developing along the lines of your inborn talents. It is almost as though you are engineered for success in a specific way, and if you can find the area for which you were specifically designed, you will achieve more in a few years than most people achieve in a lifetime.

■ LEAVE NOTHING TO CHANCE

You leave nothing to chance. You don't hope for miracles or wish for a lucky break. You recognize that if it's to be, it's up to *you*.

Since you know you are going to have to spend the rest of your life working at *something*, you decide in advance that you will do what you love to do. You will become everything you are capable of becoming by developing your unique talents and abilities, wherever they lead. You will work only at something you enjoy, with people you enjoy, doing work that makes a difference in the world.

You set high standards for yourself. You think positively and constructively about your career and your future. You recognize that anything that anyone else has done you can do as well. Once you have decided what it is you want to do, you throw your whole heart into doing it in an excellent fashion. And as a result, you become *unstoppable*.

ACTION EXERCISES

1. What is it that you really love to do? What activity gives you your greatest feeling of importance?

2. If you could be absolutely excellent at any one task or skill, what would it be? Set it as a goal and begin work on that skill immediately.

3. What are the key result areas of your job? On a scale of 1 to 10, how good are you in each area?

4. What one skill, if you developed and utilized it in an excellent fashion, would have the greatest positive impact on your life?

5. What is your area of excellence, your unique selling proposition, and the very best thing you do in your work?

6. If you could do only one thing all day long, what one task or activity would contribute the greatest value to your company and to your work?

7. Identify your heart's desire, the one thing that you were put on this earth to do. If you could accomplish one great thing in your lifetime, what would it be?

Chapter 7

Put People First

Personal relationships are the fertile soil from which all advancement, all success, all achievement in real life begins.

—Ben Stein

The people you know, and who know you in a favorable way, will do more to determine your success, happiness, and level of achievement in life than any other single factor. No one achieves anything of consequence by himself or herself.

In life, relationships are everything. My friend Charlie Jones says, *"You will be in five years what you are today except for the books you read and the people you meet."*

Dr. David McClelland, author of *The Achieving Society* (Van Nostrand, 1961), concluded after 25 years of research at Harvard that your choice of a "reference group" would have more to do with your success than anything else. McClelland interviewed graduates of the university, as well as those who had attended his intensive seminars on achievement in American life. He tracked these people for many years. Many of them took what they had learned and did wonderful things with it. They built profitable businesses and successful careers.

However, many of the graduates failed to turn the information and ideas they had learned into later success. Why not? When he went back and surveyed them, he found that invariably they had returned to the same group of people they had been associating with before they had taken the advanced courses on achievement. As a result, they went back to the same old ways, the same old habits, the same old customs and manners of living. Because they were immersed in their old reference groups, nothing changed for them.

■ YOUR REFERENCE GROUP

Your reference group is defined as the people you consider yourself to be *similar* to. For example, if you belong to a particular church, the members of that church are part of your reference group. You consider yourself to be like them. If you belong to a political party, a bowling league, or a particular profession, people in those groups and organizations are parts of your reference group. You identify strongly with them.

Over time, through a process of *absorption*, you will adopt their attitudes, mannerisms, ways of speaking, levels of aspiration, and even their style of dress. Your reference group will exert an inordinate influence on the kind of person you become. You will adjust your goals, behaviors, and thoughts to be consistent with what you feel they will approve of. You see this with teenagers all the time.

■ MAKE NEW CHOICES

All change in your outer world begins with a change in your inner world. Major changes in your inner world start happening when you change the people with whom you associate and identify. When you select a new reference group, or find yourself in a situation with different people, you unconsciously begin to change, almost in spite of yourself.

This change process works quite quickly. In my speaking and travels, I have worked with countless men and women all over the country and throughout the world who have taken this advice to heart. They have deliberately changed their reference groups. They have begun associating with different people in different organizations. Very soon, they began to think differently about themselves, and their outer worlds begin to change.

■ AS A MAN THINKETH

The Law of Correspondence says that your outer world is a mirror of your inner world. It says in the Bible, "As a man thinketh, so is he." This means that as you see yourself and think about yourself in your conscious mind, your perception of outer world changes and conforms to fit a picture consistent with it. This is the central message of this book.

The most influential factors in your thinking and feeling will almost always be the other people in your life. Successful people are those who form the habit of associating with other positive, success-oriented people. Unsuccessful people, by default, end up associating with people who are not going anywhere with their lives. Both sets of people become more and more like the people with whom they most identify.

■ FORM A NEW REFERENCE GROUP

If you really want to change your thinking and your life, make a decision today to begin associating, in every area of your life, with other men and women whom you admire, respect, and look up to. Resolve to associate with people whom you enjoy and from whom you can learn. Work and socialize only with the kind of people that you want your children to be like when they grow up. When you set these kinds of standards for your interpersonal relationships, your whole life will begin to improve almost immediately.

■ DEVELOP YOUR OWN NETWORK

Your network is composed of the number of people you know, both directly and indirectly. These are people over whom you can exert some influence and who can in turn exert some influence over you.

The most successful people in our society, at every level, are those who know the greatest number of other successful people. They organize their lives to meet these successful people by deliberate design, not by accident. And so can you.

Many men and women, over time, move from one city to another, or from one field or industry to another. They start off with few contacts, yet in no time at all, they become some of the best-known and most respected people in their new field. Why does this happen? It is because they apply the principles of creative networking to their new lives.

They immediately begin to form new, positive reference groups. They put into action a plan to develop as many good, high-quality relationships as possible within the shortest period of time.

■ BUILDING YOUR NETWORK

Here is a great exercise for you. Over the course of the next six months to a year, make a list in a notebook of the 100 most important people in your community. As you gather these names from the newspapers, from conversations, from news broadcasts, and from your work as you move around, begin to think of how you could get to meet and know these people. Remember, the more people you know and who know and think about you in a positive way, the more successful you will be in every area of your life.

Once you have your list of 100 people, you should add to it regularly. Begin to network systematically with these people. Once you have a name, think of how you could communicate with that person. The simplest way of all is to write a letter expressing your opinion on something that the individual is involved in, or simply expressing your congratulations on the person's success for something recently achieved.

Be patient when you start to expand your circle of contacts. Don't expect the person you wrote to call you back or to come in your door to meet with you. You are in the business of sowing seeds. Sometime down the road, you may see that the person has done something else and you can write another letter. Over time, these little efforts will begin to bear fruit.

■ PATIENCE PAYS OFF

I write letters continually to people that I meet throughout the country. I always send a copy of a poem, sometimes a book, sometimes an audio program or something that I feel the other person would enjoy. I have done this over the years for hundreds and perhaps thousands of people. Now, wherever I go, people come up to me and remind me that I wrote to them and sent them something, often years ago.

A couple of years ago, I was in Washington, D.C., at a high-level conference, and a senior person from one of the largest organizations in the nation's capital came up to me and reminded me that I had written to him and sent him something five years before. He still remembered. After this meeting, over time, I got to know him very well. He has now introduced me to a variety of other powerful people. These new relationships have turned out to be very enjoyable and productive for me. They all started with me sitting down and writing a friendly letter.

■ ADVANCING YOUR CAREER

Fully 85 percent of the best jobs in the United States are filled through *contacts*, rather than through want ads or recruitment agencies. Someone has the need for a particular job to be filled and lets it be known within a network. The word goes out from person to person, and an individual who could never be found any other way often surfaces and is directed, as the result of personal connections, to a job for which the person is well suited.

Many people have found that by broadening their contacts whenever they got a chance, they have changed their work lives profoundly. When they did change careers, they just happened to know the right person who was in the right place to make the right introduction to get the right job that saved the individual years of hard work in reaching that same level of responsibility and income.

■ BE A JOINER

The major focus of networking developed by most high-achieving men and women and self-made millionaires is their regular involvement with groups, clubs, and associations that contain members who can be of assistance to them in their particular fields.

In my own experience, moving from one city to another, I found that by joining certain clubs and organizations and getting involved, I was able to develop more friendships and make more progress in a couple of years than many people had made in 10 or 20 years.

Make a decision, right now, to join one or two clubs or associations. The first association you should join should be the one for your profession or occupation. If you are in real estate, join the real estate board. If you are an entrepreneur, join an entrepreneurial association. If you are in sales, join a club like Sales and Marketing Executives International.

When you join a professional association, don't make the mistake of merely attending the meetings and going home. This is what 80 to 90 percent of the members do. They may get some benefit from their membership with the organization, but nowhere near as much benefit as you can get by becoming more involved.

Here is your strategy. When you join a club or organization, get the membership book and look at the various committees. Ask around and find out which of the committees is the most active and important to the organization.

Sometimes it is the membership committee. Sometimes it is the government relations committee. Sometimes it is the education committee or the fund-raising committee. But whatever it is, find out what committee seems to have the greatest impact on the health and growth of the organization, and then *volunteer* to serve on that committee. There will almost always be an opening for someone willing to help.

■ DONATE YOUR TIME

When you attend meetings of that committee, develop the habit of raising your hand. Volunteer for assignments. Volunteer to write things. Volunteer to do work that needs to be done.

The rule is this: In every organization, fewer than 10 percent of the people do most of the work. On any committee, fewer than 20 percent of the people do more than 80 percent of the work on that committee. Your goal is to be among that top 10 to 20 percent.

The most important committees attract the best and most important people in the association. These are the kinds of people that you want as part of your reference group. These are the kinds of people that you want to form relationships with. These are the kinds of people whose names you want for your Rolodex, and who you want to be a part of your professional network.

■ PERFORMING FOR YOUR PEERS

One of the great advantages of serving voluntarily on a committee for your association is that you get an opportunity to perform in front of your peers, but without ever attempting to impress them or to get them to give you anything or do anything for you.

Every time you accept a responsibility and fulfill it completely, they make a silent note of it. They may not say anything aside from an occasional thanks or congratulations, but they are making mental notes, which will serve you in good stead later on.

■ LEARN TO SPEAK ON YOUR FEET

If you have any fears about public speaking, you should make a plan, right now, to get over them. Your ability to make a presentation to a small group or to stand up and give a talk or chair a meeting for a larger group can do more to bring you to the attention of people who can help you than almost any other thing you can do.

Fortunately, public speaking is a skill you can learn with practice. I have urged people over the years to take a Dale Carnegie course or to join Toastmasters International. They are both open to everyone and available everywhere.

When you sign up or join one of these fine organizations, leaders will train you thoroughly in how to speak on your feet. They will teach you how to design a talk—with a beginning, a middle, and an end. They will show you how to speak in a variety of different situations. And the better you get at speaking, by the Law of Attraction, the more you will attract people and opportunities into your life to speak to more and larger groups.

■ LOOK FOR WAYS TO PUT IN

Here's something very important that I learned. The great majority of people, being selfish, are always thinking of how they can personally and immediately gain from any interaction that they have with other people. But this is not for you. Instead, your job is to look for ways to put in. Your goal must be to look for ways to contribute.

This seems to be the strategy used by many of the top people.

Over the years, I have worked with many wealthy men and women. I will never forget a billionaire turning to me at the end of a meeting and privately asking me, "Is there anything that I can do for you?" Later, another man, worth more than $500 million, asked me the same question: "Is there any way that I can help you?"

When I went to work for a man worth over $800 million, in our second or third meeting, he asked me if there was anything that he could do in his position to help me in my personal life. By that simple gesture, even though I could think of nothing, he earned my lifelong loyalty.

Over the years, I have observed that many of the most powerful men and women, at every level of society, got there by continually looking for ways to help other people.

■ LIVING THE LAW

Here is one of the greatest discoveries of the ages: *The more you give of yourself without expectation of return, the more that will come to you from the most unexpected sources.*

Most people think that if they do something good or helpful for a person or group, their rewards should come back directly from that person or group. But this is not the way the universe works. When you do something nice for someone else, you activate the law of attraction. Because it is a *law*, you never have to worry about your reward. As long as you continue to sow goodness, the universe will take care of the reaping. Your good will usually come to you from a completely unexpected source, and at a completely unexpected time. All you have to do is be sure that you are continually putting in. The getting out will take care of itself.

■ THE BEST PEOPLE

As a professional speaker, I work with groups and associations all over the country. Without fail, the best and most talented people in every association are the ones who attend almost every meeting. The top people are the ones who always take the time and make the sacrifice to be there. They are the ones who always sit on the committees and volunteer to help in any way possible.

And I have noticed an interesting phenomenon. Each year, one member of the association will be elected to be the national president. As the president, he or she will have to spend as much as half of his or her time traveling around the country voluntarily, without pay, on association business.

You would think that this would really cut into the person's ability to make a living. But it seems that exactly the opposite happens. All the association presidents I've spoken to found that they made more money, did better in their careers, and made more progress in their field in the year that they took off to work for the association than in any other year of their work lives.

The more you put in, without expectation of reward, the more you get back from the most unexpected sources. And you are in complete control of what you put in. The universe will take care of the rest.

■ KEEP A RECORD

Harvey Mackay, in his audio program, *How to Build a Network of Power Relationships*, says that the most important word *not* in the dictionary (at that time) is the word "Rolodex." He claims that, if your Rolodex is big enough, you are never more than two phone calls away from anyone in the country. Harvey Mackay has a Rolodex with more than four thousand names that he has gathered over the years. He has found that at least one of those people in his Rolodex has direct access to virtually any other person in the country with whom he wants to communicate, including the president of the United States.

■ YOUR MASTERMIND ALLIANCE

Napoleon Hill, after decades of studying the richest men in America, concluded that the formation of a mastermind network was an important step to great wealth. It was the creation or joining of a mastermind group that enabled countless men and women to go from poverty and obscurity to success and affluence.

The core of your personal network of contacts, even before you begin to go outside to join groups and organizations, should therefore be your mastermind network. This is a small group of four or five people with whom you meet and talk on a regular basis.

Getting together regularly, at least once per week or even more often, with other people who think like you do is the key to the success of a mastermind group. Don't worry about being self-serving in these relationships. Include in your mastermind only people you can help (and who can help you).

■ TAKE THE INITIATIVE

You begin the formation of a mastermind group by approaching one or two people you like and admire, and who seem to have the same positive attitude you do. They may be in your field or in another field. They may be younger or older than you, of the same gender or not. It doesn't really matter as long as you have good chemistry.

The most important qualifications are that they have positive mental attitudes and are generally optimistic about themselves and their lives. They should have goals of their own that they are working on each day. They should be open-minded and curious. They should believe in personal development, and already read books, listen to audio programs, and attend courses and seminars.

■ LOOSE OR STRUCTURED

When you get together with members of your mastermind group, you can have an agenda, or no agenda. Your meetings can be structured or unstructured. You can talk about general subjects or specific topics. You may talk about your own business or about theirs. It doesn't matter. The very activity of spending time around other positive people energizes you, makes you more creative, and makes you feel more enthusiastic toward whatever you are doing.

An important element of your mastermind group is the amount of laughter that you experience together. This is the key measure of the quality of any of your relationships. People who laugh a lot together like each other more. They are usually more helpful and supportive of each other. The people you enjoy the most in life will always be the people with whom you laugh and joke the most.

■ TWO PEOPLE TOGETHER

The most important mastermind group that you ever form is with your spouse or partner. A husband and wife together, or a couple, can be the most powerful mastermind of all. When two people are completely attuned to each other, and completely supportive of each other's hopes and dreams, they form a powerful combination that enables each of them to accomplish far more than either could achieve alone.

People who are in an excellent relationship with a person they describe as their *best friend* are some of the happiest, most successful, and most fulfilled people in our society. Two people together can create wonderful things for both of them.

■ MULTIPLE MASTERMINDS

You can have more than one mastermind network. Some people will have a mastermind network in their families. Others will have mastermind alliances with people who participate in the same hobbies or sports. You should definitely have a mastermind network that is specifically focused on your work or career. You can even have interlocking mastermind groups with people who are involved with you in more than one area.

The more you interact with other positive people, the more positive and productive you will be. Constantly talking with and sharing your ideas and experiences with others will give you a steady flow of ideas and insights from their experiences, and help you keep a healthy perspective on what you are doing.

■ GUARD YOUR TIME

Your most valuable asset is your time, and relationships with people are enormously time-consuming. The number of high-quality relationships you can form and maintain is limited. There are simply not enough hours in the day or enough days in the month. You must be selective about the people with whom you associate. You must choose them carefully.

Baron de Rothschild, in his *Maxims for Success*, said, "Make no useless acquaintances."

This may sound a bit cold, but remember, your life is precious, and your life is made up of the minutes and hours of each day. You cannot afford to squander it on relationships with people whom you cannot help, and who cannot help you, to live and enjoy a better life. You must guard your time carefully. As Benjamin Franklin wrote, *"Dost thou love life? Then do not squander time; for that's the stuff life is made of."*

■ BE SELECTIVE IN YOUR CHOICES

Many highly successful people are often described as "loners." However, this does not mean "a-loners." They are not isolated, anti-social individuals. They are loners in that they are highly selective about who they spend time with. They do not drink coffee with whoever is sitting there, or go out for lunch with whoever happens to be walking out the door at the same time. They carefully build and maintain high-quality relationships, and they fastidiously avoid negative people who might hold them back.

If associating with positive people is a key to success, then the flip side is for you to get away and keep away from negative or "toxic" people. Negative people are the primary source of most un-happiness. Problems with such people are most likely your major sources of stress and frustration. Negative people do more to dimin-ish your joy in life than any other single factor.

It's much easier to bounce back from financial loss or reverses in your career than it is to deal with negative people in your work or personal life. One major negative relationship can be enough to cut off all your chances of achieving your full potential in your career. Choose your relationships with care.

■ SEEK OUT A MENTOR

Most successful people have mentors at different stages of their lives. A person whom you know and who knows you and helps you on a regular basis often determines your success in life. The right mentor at the right time can save you from countless mistakes and years of hard work.

At each stage of your life you can benefit from the advice and experience of someone who is further along the path than you. The men who have been there to give me guidance and advice as I have grown up and gone into business at various levels have affected my life dramatically. This type of relationship can have a major impact on your success as well.

Many people are a little bit fuzzy about exactly how mentoring relationships work. A mentor is like an uncle. He or she is an older friend, someone wiser and more experienced than you, who will give you guidance and advice from time to time. A mentor can help you avoid pitfalls that might sidetrack your career or hold you back.

■ DEVELOP A STRATEGY

As it happens, the best potential mentors are successful people who are already very busy. Approaching one of them requires strategy and planning. Here is what you do.

When you decide that you would like a particular person to be your mentor in a particular area, you should contact that person with a specific question or need. Most successful people are open to helping other people who want to be successful as well, but they are busy. They don't have a lot of time. You should not ask for more than 10 minutes.

The best way to approach a prospective mentor for the first time is with a short list of key questions for which you need answers to help you to make current decisions in your life and your career. Do not approach a mentor asking personal questions about his or her life and experiences. Busy people are not interested in sharing their innermost experiences and feelings with someone they have never met before.

■ LOOK FOR COMPATIBILITY

In your first meeting, by asking a few specific questions, you are testing the waters. What you are looking for is a certain form of *chemistry*. You are looking for a person you like and respect and feel comfortable with, and who likes you and will be willing to help you in the future.

For this reason, you must go slowly at first. You must ask for only a few minutes, and then you must get on with your business. You must ask for specific advice about a specific situation. Be respectful, friendly, and businesslike.

Here is the key to developing the mentor/mentee relationship. When you are given advice, follow it. Don't ask for specific advice and do nothing with it, and then attempt to come back for even more advice. This just demonstrates to the prospective mentor that you are wasting his or her time.

Instead, if the person suggests that you take a particular action, do it immediately. If the mentor suggests that you read a book, get it and read it. If he suggests that you listen to an audio program, get it and listen to it. If she suggests that you take a particular course, sign up for it and attend.

■ BE RESPECTFUL OF THEIR TIME

Many people contact me and ask me to be a mentor to them, not only from throughout the United States and Canada but from foreign countries as well. Aside from the fact that I am extremely busy, I respectfully decline all invitations because of the particular approach that they usually take. They call up or write and want me to take complete charge of their lives. They want me to spend many hours of my time guiding, counseling, and directing them, and helping them in their jobs or careers.

The fact is that a prospective mentor is usually very busy and cannot even consider the possibility of spending large blocks of time with a complete stranger.

However, if you go slowly and you follow the advice given to you by a mentor, the individual may conclude that investing time in you is worthwhile. He or she will be willing to spend even more time with you to help you even further. Eventually, a very good relationship can develop.

You may have more than one mentor at the same time, and you may have sequential mentors. This means that as one mentor serves his or her purpose in guiding you, and you evolve and grow in your career, it will often be time to move on to another mentor who is even further along than your first mentor.

■ RESIST RELATIONSHIP ENTROPY

The natural tendency in all relationships is toward *entropy*. Relationship entropy means that relationships run out of energy unless they are continually renewed. People stop doing the things that they had done earlier to establish the relationship in the first place. They work very hard to create the relationship, and then they take it for granted. They forget to communicate with the other person. They just assume that everything is going along fine and that no extra efforts are necessary to maintain the relationship. As it happens, men are more likely than women to let this happen.

But all relationships are a function of the time invested in them. You can only increase the value of a relationship by investing more time in it. This applies to a relationship with your spouse, relationships with your children, relationships with your staff members, and especially relationships with your friends and associates on a personal and professional level.

There is no alternative to personal time invested in building and maintaining a relationship. You must be alert to the danger of relationship entropy and be constantly working to counter it.

■ CUSTOMERS FOR LIFE

It is quite common in business for someone to work very hard to win a customer for the first time and to build the initial relationship. However, once the relationship is established, the businessperson begins to take the customer for granted and go off to work on new relationships that are not yet well established. Then, six months later, the businessperson is astonished to find that the customer has gone to a competitor.

As a businessperson, your customer relationships are some of the most important assets that you develop and maintain over the course of your career. Once you have invested the time and energy required to develop a customer relationship, it is essential that you develop a plan for relationship maintenance. You make sure that you are doing whatever is necessary to keep that relationship alive and growing.

■ THE LAW OF INDIRECT EFFORT

There are several principles that apply to building and maintaining relationships of all kinds. Perhaps the most important is the Law of Indirect Effort. This law says that *you achieve things with people more indirectly than directly.* Here are some examples of this principle.

If you want to *have a friend,* the direct way is by trying to get people to like you. This seldom works. The indirect way is to *be a friend,* to treat other people in a friendly way without expecting anything in return.

If you want to *impress* other people, the direct way is to tell them about your accomplishments and show them how clever you are. The indirect way, which is faster and more effective, is to be *impressed* by them. The more you show that you are impressed by someone, the more they will find you to be an impressive person.

The indirect way of getting people to like you is for you to like them *first.* The way to get people to admire and respect you is for you to admire and respect them in advance.

■ THE LAW OF COMPENSATION

The Law of Compensation seems to apply directly to relationships. This law says that you get out what you put in, and *the more you put in, the more you get out.* The more things that you do for other people, the more things other people will want to do for you. When you offer to help or serve others, they will want to help or serve you. What goes around comes around. Whatever you sow you will eventually reap.

We have entered into the era of the "go-giver" rather than just the go-getter. Each person has a deep desire to reciprocate in his or her relations with others. We want to even things up when anything nice has been done for us. We want to pay people back for any kindnesses or favors. We don't want to feel that we are obligated to another. Nowhere is this principle more important than in relationships.

There are many people who think that the key to success is to get around other successful people and then to exploit this relationship. This strategy seldom works. It is much better for you to become the kind of person that other people want to be around. When you go to work on yourself and become a better person, better people will want to associate with you. This is the indirect way.

■ MARRY RICH

Sometimes people say they want to marry a rich person. If you want to marry a rich person, by the law of indirect effort you had better get busy working on yourself to become the kind of man or woman that a rich person would want to marry. You should become very good at what you do, and develop the manners of an excellent person. Improvement of your life and prospects on the outside begins with your getting better on the inside.

There have been many studies of social climbers, people who have joined clubs and organizations in an attempt to associate with other successful people. Invariably they fail. Why? Because *like attracts like*. People are naturally attracted to people who are at the *same level* that they are. If you have not developed yourself to achieve a certain level of accomplishment in your field, you cannot take a shortcut and begin associating with people at that new higher level. They will not be interested in you, and you will only end up looking and feeling foolish.

■ RELATIONSHIPS ARE EVERYTHING

Keep it foremost in your mind that relationships are everything. Your job is to become a *relationship-creating* individual. You should look for every way possible—in your personal reference groups, in your mastermind networks, in your clubs and associations, and with mentors—to form and maintain high-quality relationships.

Most successful men and women owe their success to the fact that, at an earlier time, they made the effort to establish and maintain a particular relationship that eventually paid off for them. Doors were opened and opportunities created that saved them years of hard work. And this can happen to you as well, if you use creative networking at every stage of your career.

When you know that your Rolodex contains hundreds of valuable names that you can call upon because you have already built a bridge with these people, it gives you a tremendous feeling of personal power and self-confidence. You begin to feel *unstoppable*.

ACTION EXERCISES

1. Make a list of 10 people whom it would be helpful for you to know. Write each of them a letter congratulating them on something they have just done.

2. Select three people with whom you can form a business/career type of mastermind group. Invite them to meet with you weekly for breakfast or lunch.

3. Join at least one association that holds regular meetings in your community and begin attending every one. Volunteer to serve on one of the committees, and get involved.

4. Examine each of the people with whom you regularly associate, in business or socially. Are these the right people for you to have as members of your reference group?

5. Develop a personal development plan to prepare yourself to become the kind of person that you would like to meet and spend time with. Take control of your own future.

6. Take a Dale Carnegie course in public speaking, or join a chapter of Toastmasters International. Learn to speak on your feet.

7. Resist relationship entropy; keep in regular touch with the most important people in your personal and business life. Call or visit someone today.

Chapter 8

Think Like a Genius

Make every thought, every fact, that comes into your
mind pay you a profit. Make it work and produce for you.
Think of things not as they are but as they might be.
Don't merely dream—but create!

—Maxwell Maltz

You are a *potential* genius. Your amazing brain has more than 18 billion cells, each one of which is connected to and interlinked with as many as 20,000 others. This means that the number of possible thoughts you can think is greater than all the molecules in the known universe.

You have the capacity to learn at incredible rates and to retain more information than you can even imagine. It is said that *"when an educated person dies, it is as if a library burned down."* This potential library is contained between your ears.

■ THE ORIGINS OF WEALTH

Throughout human history, value has been contained in land, labor, capital, furniture, fixtures, machinery, and other *hard assets*. Wars and revolutions have been fought over their control. The primary creators of value were those people who could combine these various resources together to produce products and services for the marketplace.

In the twentieth century, however, we have seen change take

place at a speed that is virtually unimaginable. In 1900, 50 percent of the American population lived on farms raising food for the other 50 percent who lived in towns and cities. Today, less than 3 percent of the population lives on farms, and they produce not only enough food for all Americans, but huge surpluses as well that are exported or even given away to the entire world.

We have moved from the agricultural age to the industrial age to the service age to the information age, and we are now entering the *communications* age. The primary source of value today is not land, labor, and other hard assets, but knowledge, information, and ideas.

The greatest wealth you could possibly possess is between your ears. You can create an unlimited future for yourself by tapping into your brainpower and channeling it, like a powerful current, to energize your life and get you anything you really want.

■ TRUE WEALTH TODAY

The richest American today, and perhaps the richest person in the world, is Bill Gates. The net worth of his company, Microsoft, is greater than the net worth of IBM, which has been in business many years longer. Microsoft is based entirely on *brainpower*. It creates wealth by making it easier to process information digitally within computers, and from computer to computer by telephone lines, wireless systems, and satellites.

If you own a company, your chief assets walk out the door every night at quitting time. Your building could burn to the ground, but as long as your people got out safely, you could walk across the street and start your business again. The chief assets of any organization, and of any individual, are contained in the ability to think and to apply that thinking to getting results that other people will pay for. The ability to create wealth is determined by *mental* strength rather than *physical* strength.

■ STARTING CAPITAL

In generations past, it may have taken many years for a person to accumulate enough capital to start and build a successful business in manufacturing or services. Today, such a large investment in physical assets can actually be a liability. A change in technology on the other side of the world can render a $100 million manufacturing plant obsolete in a few months.

But what you have between your ears can be invaluable. It is capable of countless applications and uses. It is completely portable. It is versatile. It is flexible, and can be increased almost without limits, if you learn how.

An immigrant could arrive at a U.S. airport with the ability to create a billion-dollar industry in his head. He could walk up to customs; open his hands and say, "Nothing to declare;" and walk on through. His assets are all in his knowledge and skill. Many of the most successful and respected entrepreneurs and businesspeople in America arrived this way.

■ KNOWLEDGE IS THE GREAT RESOURCE

The primary source of value today is *knowledge*. Since there is no limit to the amount of knowledge you can acquire, there is no limit to the amount of value that you can create. You can start from wherever you are, no matter what your background, and begin to increase your mental assets. You can start work today on improving your ability to perform and get results for which others will pay.

The wonderful thing about knowledge is that it can be reproduced hundreds of thousands, even millions of times without losing its value. It is the one commodity that can actually be infinite in its application. If you or someone else comes up with a new idea to do something faster or better, that idea can be spread around the world in no time at all, and be in the hands of millions of other people who can also use it to improve their lives and work. And you have lost nothing. The idea still has its original value to you. This is absolutely incredible.

■ HARD ASSETS VERSUS BRAINPOWER

Today, our banking and financial industries are struggling to make the shift to knowledge as an asset. Banks, for example, will lend money today only against *hard assets*, things that can be seized as collateral and sold to repay the loan. However, the real assets of a company are not the tangible items at all. They are the thinking ability of the people who work there. They are contained in the combined brainpower of teams of experts working together to solve problems, create innovations, and produce goods and services for the competitive marketplace.

Your ability to utilize your brainpower and unlock your creative abilities is absolutely essential to your success. Today, we know more about how you can become smarter than we ever have before.

■ SMALL DIFFERENCES LEAD TO BIG RESULTS

Often small improvements in the way you think and perform can lead to significant improvements in your performance. It is not necessary for you to attend university and get years of education to bring your knowledge up to the level where it can pay off for you. Sometimes very small changes in what you are doing right now, right where you are, can bring about amazing results.

Here's an example. If a horse runs in a horse race and wins by a nose, it earns 10 times the prize money of a horse that comes in second. Does this mean that the horse that comes in first is 10 times faster? Is it twice as fast? Ten percent faster? No, the horse that wins is only a *nose* faster.

By the same token, your possession of one small piece of information at the right time and in the right place can enable you to make an extraordinary difference in a particular situation. Often a single idea or insight can change your whole life or career.

■ AVOID THE INTELLIGENCE TRAP

The most successful people today are those who are continually investing in learning and expanding their intellectual asset base. They are wide open to new ideas and new approaches. A major mistake made by many people, especially those who have graduated from a university, is that they conclude that everything they know at the moment is all that there is to know about a particular subject.

Sometimes they think that what they know is all they *need* to know about a subject as well.

This is called the "intelligence trap" of the poor performer, the *unconscious incompetent*. This is a person who does not know, and does not know that he does not know. This person cannot be helped, because he is closed to new information. This is why the beginning of all wisdom is often the awareness of how ignorant you really are, of how little you really know.

■ DON'T BE IMPRESSED

I have traveled in many countries and met countless highly intelligent and successful people. I have spoken with many millionaires, multimillionaires, and even billionaires. I have worked at the highest level of government with some of the smartest men and women who have ever lived. And the one thing that these people seem to have in common is that they never become impressed by their own intelligence. In fact, the smarter they get, the humbler they become and the less they look upon themselves as experts in any way.

Over 700 years ago, Roger Bacon of England was considered to be the last *universal* man. He was thought to be current with all the knowledge and science of the day. He, in his day, knew almost everything there was to know about everything that was taught academically.

Of course, at that time, the amount of available knowledge was limited. There were very few books. There were fewer scientists, philosophers, and researchers writing and teaching.

■ KNOWLEDGE GROWS EXPONENTIALLY

Today, however, it is impossible for one person to know everything about even one small subject. Just look at modern medicine. There are great minds who spend their entire lives studying the workings of the inner ear or the trachea or one of the other organs of the body. And even though these highly intelligent and dedicated professionals spend their whole careers specializing in a particular part of the body, they never learn everything there is to know about even that one organ.

Sometimes I ask audiences, "Is there anyone here who is a know-it-all?" Of course, no one raises his or her hand. Then I go on to explain what I mean by a know-it-all.

A know-it-all is a person who feels that he knows everything that he needs to know about a subject. How can you tell if you have become a know-it-all? It is easy. You have stopped learning and growing in your area of specialization. You have stopped reading, listening to audio programs, and taking additional courses.

The very fact that you fail to regularly seek out new knowledge in your field means that you have unconsciously, accidentally, slipped into the intelligence trap of the low performer. You have unwittingly become a know-it-all by the very act of not continuing to learn and grow.

■ THE ANSWERS ARE CHANGING

After giving an advanced test to a graduate class of physics students at Princeton University, Albert Einstein was on the way back to his office when one of his graduate assistants asked the famous professor, "Dr. Einstein, wasn't that the same exam that you gave to this physics class last year?"

Dr. Einstein nodded and said, "Yes, it was the same exam as last year."

The graduate assistant summoned up his courage to ask the great Nobel prizewinning physicist, "But, Dr. Einstein, how could you give the same test two years in a row?"

"Because," Einstein replied, "in the last year, the answers have changed."

In the same way, your answers are changing today at a more rapid rate than ever before. The answers in your field are changing as you sit there. What was true a year ago may not be true today, and what is true today may not be true a year from now. The only way that you can be assured of staying on top of your field is by continually taking in new ideas and knowledge to compare it with what you know today.

■ THE SOURCES OF INNOVATION

Peter Drucker, in his book *Innovation and Entrepreneurship* (Harper-Business, 1985), writes that the greatest business breakthroughs take place as the result of "either the unexpected success or the unexpected failure."

He explains that when something unusual or unexpected happens in any field, the average person dismisses it as a random event or as an accident. The superior person, however, studies each unexpected result as if it were a sign of an underlying trend or an indication of a fundamental change in the nature of things.

When an experiment in growing bacteria failed because a mold had blown across the laboratory and landed on the petri dish, killing the bacteria, the lab assistants were about to throw it out. However, a bacteriologist, Alexander Fleming, became curious about a mold that was so powerful that it could kill such strong bacteria. His research led to the discovery and development of penicillin, which saved millions of lives in World War II and won him both a knighthood and the Nobel prize.

■ KEEP YOUR MIND OPEN

In 1975, IBM commissioned consultants to study the market potential of the personal computer. They came back with the conclusion that the market for personal computers was only a few hundred in the entire world, at best. Based on this information, IBM decided to concentrate its efforts on mainframes, where it was already the world leader, and ignore the personal computer market, leaving it to a little upstart company in Cupertino, California, called Apple Computer.

When the Apple computers hit the market and began to sell by the hundreds, and then thousands, IBM got smart fast. IBM did an about-face and decided to plunge into the small computer business. And the company did. IBM came out with a PC that within four years captured more than 50 percent of the world market for smaller computers.

■ WATCH FOR THE TRENDS

But IBM failed to notice that a major trend to smaller computers had taken place. Ignoring its initial success in PCs, IBM continued to concentrate on the development and sale of mainframes. While IBM's attention was focused on mainframes, more and more competitors rushed into the personal computer field, and eventually IBM was displaced as the world leader.

IBM failed to see that its success in capturing 50 percent of the personal computer market was indicative of a sweeping trend in computers that would change the entire world. Today IBM is scrambling to catch up, competing with companies like Dell Computer, Hewlett-Packard/Compaq, Toshiba, and others. Because IBM missed the trend, it is unlikely that it will ever recover its position in the personal computer market.

■ THINK ABOUT THE FUTURE

Keep your eyes open. There are more changes taking place all around you today than ever before. Any one of these changes may be indicative of a trend that could lead on to fortune and success for you. You must be open, awake, and alert to these changes. Nothing remains the same for very long. All your best opportunities will come from applying your knowledge and brainpower to new products and new services in the future.

All you need to start a fortune is an idea that is 10 percent new. All you need is a product or service innovation that is a little better, faster, or cheaper than something else, and you can quickly move to the front of the line.

Many of the great fortunes being made today in the United States and throughout the world are being created by people who started with nothing. One day, they came up with a breakthrough idea that revolutionized or transformed their industry. What could it be for you?

■ TWO FACTORS THAT HOLD YOU BACK

There are two major factors that stand in the way of you using more of your natural intelligence. They are *psychosclerosis* and *homeostasis*.

Psychosclerosis is another name for "hardening of the attitudes." This is experienced by a particular type of person who is rigid, inflexible, and unchanging. This is the kind of person who develops fixed attitudes on a certain person or subject and then resists any attempt to change his mind. This is often called the *mechanical* way of thinking. You probably know people who suffer from it.

The opposite way of thinking is more open and flexible. This is called the *adaptive* worldview. Adaptive people keep their minds open to new information. They are curious and interested in new ideas and developments. They are more concerned with *what's right* than with *who's right*. They are willing to abandon an old idea if someone can come along and show them that a new idea has more merit. They are more concerned that the new idea works to solve a problem or achieve a goal than they are with being right themselves.

■ THREE QUALITIES OF GENIUS

Geniuses have been studied extensively over the years. One of the most remarkable conclusions the experts have arrived at is that geniuses are not necessarily people with extraordinary high IQs. They are often ordinary people who use their intelligence in a superior way compared to average, or even smarter, people. What this means is that you can function at genius levels if you learn to think the way that geniuses do.

Geniuses seem to have three characteristics in common, each of which you can develop and make into a regular part of your thinking.

First, geniuses seem to have *open minds*. They are curious, questioning, flexible, and willing to consider a wide range of possibilities in dealing with a question or problem. This adaptive mind-set is like an open door that allows ideas to blow through from any direction, or source. This is the mind-set of the genius. And you can learn it by practicing it.

Second, geniuses seem to approach problems and decisions *systematically*. They don't throw themselves at a problem like a dog chasing a passing car. Instead, they approach every difficult situation by asking structured questions in a logical order, like solving a problem in math.

Third, geniuses approach problems with a series of *questions*.

■ QUESTIONING OPENS YOUR MIND

Geniuses first ask, *"What exactly is the problem?"* and *"Why is this a problem in the first place?"* They then ask, *"What would be an ideal solution to this problem?"* and *"What holds us back from achieving such a solution?"*

They ask: *Why does this situation exist? How did it happen? What caused it? Where and when did it first occur? Who is involved in it? What are the different ways that we could solve this problem? Of all the different ways, which solution seems to be the most acceptable, all things considered?*

The very act of *questioning* opens your mind and expands your options. It increases your creativity and stimulates your imagination. Questioning enables you to think more effectively about the problem, and ultimately reach a better decision.

■ JUMPING TO CONCLUSIONS

People with *mechanical* mind-sets tend to jump to conclusions. They see a problem and they immediately decide on a solution. When two events happen close together, they assume that one event is the reason for the second event. *They confuse correlation with causation.* Once they have made a decision, they look for evidence to confirm what they have already decided. Their egos quickly become involved, and they then become reluctant to change their minds.

There seems to be a direct relationship between the quantity of ideas and approaches you develop to solve a problem and your likelihood of coming up with the best idea that will solve the problem in the very best way. For this reason, you must discipline yourself to resist the temptation to jump to conclusions, or to rush to judgment. You must proceed more slowly, like a genius, and keep asking questions. You must keep your mind open.

■ CREATIVITY IS YOUR BIRTHRIGHT

If the truth were known, you are an *idea-generating organism.* Creativity is your birthright. You are a highly intelligent individual with a continuous flow of good ideas that you can use to accomplish goals and improve your life. In fact, even if you have not used your creativity for a long time, and most people have not, you can stir it up, like sugar that has sunk to the bottom of a cup of coffee, by stimulating your mind with methods that we will talk about in the next chapter.

There is a Law of Probabilities that applies to creative thinking and tapping into the powers of your mind. This law says that the more ideas that you are exposed to, the more likely it is that you will be exposed to the right idea, exactly when you need it.

The most successful people today are those who are constantly exposing themselves to new ideas from a variety of sources. Unsuccessful people, in contrast, are those who continue to recirculate the same tired old ideas with little imagination or creativity.

■ LOOK FOR IDEAS EVERYWHERE

When you attend a seminar or a lecture given by an expert who is sharing some of the most current ideas in his or her field, you will often receive a bombardment of new insights that you can use to improve parts of your life. Many people's lives have been completely changed as the result of attending a single lecture given by a single intelligent person who gave them a single insight that was the key to their future.

Imagine what would happen if you attended courses, seminars, and lectures on a regular basis. You would be continually bombarding your mind with new ideas that would keep your mind alert and aware, and keep your creative juices flowing.

Creative people are constantly reading, not only in their own fields but in other fields as well. They read primarily nonfiction. They subscribe to a variety of magazines and newspapers. They are continually scanning through the tables of contents and through the critical articles.

Always read with a pen or highlighter in your hand. Even better, learn how to speed-read so that you can scan material at a thousand words a minute, or faster. Speed-reading is a skill, like riding a bicycle, that anyone can learn with a few hours of application. Forever after, you will be able to process more information than perhaps you ever imagined possible.

■ GET AROUND THE RIGHT PEOPLE

Effective people make a habit of associating with other positive, creative people. They are constantly sharing ideas and experiences, learning from each other. They cut clippings out of magazines and newsletters, and pass them on to their friends. They recommend books they have read and audio programs they have listened to. Their friends do the same for them. Sometimes one good idea that you get from someone else can change the direction of your life.

■ A FOOLISH CONSISTENCY

The second major factor that holds people back is *homeostasis*. This is defined as a "striving for constancy." It is a deep desire to remain consistent with what you have done and said in the past. Ralph Waldo Emerson wrote in his essay "Self-Reliance," "A foolish consistency is the hobgoblin of little minds."

He was referring to the natural tendency of individuals to try to remain consistent with previous opinions and behaviors. This form of rigidity blocks off almost all possibilities for growth in the future. To resist the tendency toward homeostasis, you should be willing to abandon your old ideas when someone can prove that there are newer, better ideas available.

One way to escape the mental trap of homeostasis is for you to *be willing to admit that you are wrong*. The mark of the superior person, in a time of rapid change, is to always remain open to the possibility that one's most cherished ideas are incorrect. This takes tremendous courage and maturity. But it stimulates more ideas and insights.

■ WRONG DECISIONS

According to the American Management Association, at least 70 percent of your decisions will turn out to be wrong in the fullness of time. This 70 percent figure is an average. Some people will be wrong even more often. But you can assume, as a rule of thumb, that 7 out of 10 decisions that you make regarding your life and work will turn out to be wrong in the long run.

Here is a question for you. If 70 percent of the decisions that managers and executives make turn out to be wrong, how can the world continue to function? The answer is simple. Superior people—those who rise to the top of any organization—are those who are willing to cut their losses. They are willing to admit quickly that they have made a mistake and rectify the situation rather than persisting until it gets worse.

Unfortunately, the vast majority of people fall in love with their past decisions, and once having made them, they are reluctant to give them up, even if all the evidence is against them. Don't let this happen to you. Instead, resolve to be the very first to recognize that a decision that you have made or conclusion that you have come to has been invalidated or disproven by new information. Be prepared to drop the old decision and embrace a new solution or new way of doing things.

■ FLEXIBILITY GIVES YOU STRENGTH

According to the Menninger Institute, the most important quality that you will need to be successful in the twenty-first century is the quality of flexibility, especially in the way you think. Flexibility refers to your willingness to change and try new things. It especially means that you have the ability to continually abandon old, outmoded ideas in favor of new, more effective ideas.

Many people spend much of their time arguing, rationalizing, and justifying their behaviors. They are determined to continue doing things the same old way even when it is perfectly clear that the old way no longer works. The way to avoid this tendency is to remain flexible, especially when you are most convinced that you are right.

■ THE MIRACLE OF PERSONAL DEVELOPMENT

One of the great turning points in my life came when, as a young man in my early twenties, I discovered the miracle of personal development. My life has never been the same. I learned that through personal development you can indeed pull yourself up by your own bootstraps. I learned that, by learning what you need to learn to achieve the goals you have set for yourself, there are virtually no limits on what you can do, have, or be.

The truth is that *the future belongs to the competent.* You could lose all of your money tomorrow, but as long as you still had your ability to think and reason, you could make it all back and more besides. The future belongs to those who are better informed. The future belongs not to those who *have more* versus those who *have less*, but to those who *know more* versus those who *know less*.

■ RAPID OBSOLESCENCE

Knowledge and information in your field are doubling every two or three years. Whatever information base you have is rapidly becoming obsolete. You must be in the process of continually taking in new information and ideas just to stay even.

Fortunately, there is a simple, three-part program that you can use to keep yourself ahead of the pack. I have used it and taught it to many thousands of people, and I have files full of letters from people whose entire lives have been changed as a result. The three keys to continuous personal and professional development are *continuous reading, continuous listening to audio learning programs*, and *continuous training*.

■ READ EVERY DAY

In order to stay on top of your job, you should read in your field at least one hour per day, underlining and taking good notes. Anything less than one hour per day will put you in danger of being passed by your competitors. My friend Jim Rohn advises, *"Work at least as hard on yourself as you do on your job."*

At the very least, you should get up every morning and read 30 to 60 minutes in something educational. Take careful notes. Review your notes on a regular basis. Reflect on what you have learned, and think about how you could apply the new ideas in your daily life.

Use your powers of visualization to imagine yourself using the new information in some way. This will dramatically increase the speed at which you learn and retain the new ideas, and increase the likelihood that you will use them at the first opportunity.

If you read just one hour per day, that will amount to about one book per week. One book per week will amount to about 50 books per year. Fifty books per year will total about 500 books over the next 10 years. At the very least, you will need a bigger house just to hold your books, and you will probably be able to afford it as well.

■ GIVE YOURSELF THE EDGE

According to the American Booksellers Association, fully 70 percent of American adults have not visited a bookstore in the last five years. The average American reads less than one book per year; 58 percent of adult Americans never read another book from cover to cover after they leave high school.

Meanwhile, in the information age, if you are not reading continuously you are in serious danger of being made obsolete by the passage of time. However, if you read one hour per day, one book per week, you will be getting the equivalent of a Ph.D. in your field every year. You will become one of the smartest, best-informed, and most productive people in your business.

■ BEATING THE DRUM

Some years ago, I had a good friend who read very little. He was not convinced that reading would make any difference to his life or income. He had gotten out of the habit of reading after he left school. He argued with me that reading wasn't that important. Meanwhile, he struggled to make a living. He was continually frustrated. He was continually losing business to his better-informed competitors.

For almost three years, I kept at him, encouraging him to begin daily reading. Finally, he gave in and began to read each morning, just for a few minutes. He was amazed at how helpful the reading was, and how much more knowledgeable he was when he spoke to his clients.

He soon began reading, as I had recommended, an hour per day, one book per week. Within a year, his income had doubled. After two years, his income doubled again. Today he is one of the highest-paid people in his field. And he is proud to tell me every time I see him that he very seldom meets a client who is as well informed as he is about their business. And the more he reads, the more competent and confident he becomes.

■ TO EARN MORE, YOU MUST LEARN MORE

The rule is that *to earn more, you must learn more.* You cannot move ahead in your field further or faster than you are doing today except to the degree to which you learn and practice something new.

The second part of your personal and professional development program consists of audio learning programs. If you travel in your work, you spend between five hundred and one thousand hours per year in your car. If you turn this driving time into learning time, you will get the equivalent of three to six months of 40-hour weeks of additional education, just driving from place to place. I have met countless people who have doubled, tripled, and quadrupled their incomes by the simple act of listening to audio learning programs as they drive around.

■ TAKE ALL THE TRAINING YOU CAN GET

The third key to continuous learning, and to unlocking your mental potential, is for you to take all the training you can get. If a training program is offered in the public arena, it has already been proven to be highly effective. The person presenting the program has probably acquired many years of experience, and may have spent hundreds of hours assembling the program that you can take in a half or a full day. You can sometimes save yourself weeks, months, and even years of hard work by attending a seminar given by an expert who explains to you state-of-the-art ways to get your job done faster and easier.

■■■■■

When you combine these three: regular reading, regular listening to audio learning programs, and regular and continuous training, you have a dynamite combination that can propel you forward at a greater speed than you ever could without them.

■ KNOWLEDGE IS POWER

As mentioned earlier, Francis Bacon said that *knowledge is power.* This is only partially true. In fact, only knowledge that can be applied to practical purposes for someone else is actually power. The libraries are full of knowledge that does no one any good.

To change your thinking in a positive and constructive way, you must continually feed your mind with new ideas. You must stay current with your field. You must regularly associate with other leading people in your area of specialization. You must be continually looking for ways to do your work better, faster, cheaper, and easier. You must be continually seeking ways to serve your clients and customers better. You must stay on the cutting edge of your field so that you are, and you continue to be, one of the most valuable people in your business.

■ NO-LIMIT THINKING

In the information age, knowledge is everything. And the amount of knowledge that you can gather and apply to your life is limited only by your own personal ambition. There are really no limits on what you can accomplish except for the limits you set for yourself.

The more you learn, the more you earn. The more knowledgeable you become about your field, the more courage and confidence you will have to implement your skills in your work. The more courage and confidence you develop, the higher will be your self-esteem and your sense of personal power. You will become virtually *unstoppable* in everything you do.

ACTION EXERCISES

1. Begin today to create your own personal library of books in your field. Read 30 to 60 minutes each day, underline, and take careful notes.

2. Examine your recent unexpected successes and failures in your business. Could they be indicative of a trend that you can take advantage of?

3. Approach each problem in your life systematically. Imagine that the solution is exactly the *opposite* of what you are currently doing.

4. Continually expose your mind to new ideas and viewpoints. Ask lots of questions. Consider the possibility that you could be wrong.

5. Listen to educational audio programs in your car. Turn your car into a mobile classroom, a "university on wheels."

6. Select an area where expertise can help you to move ahead in your career. Develop a plan to study and learn everything you possibly can in that area. Be the best at what you do.

7. Associate only with positive, optimistic, creative, happy people who are going somewhere with their lives. Get around winners if you want to be one.

Chapter 9

Unleash Your Mental Powers

The potential of the average person is like a huge ocean unsailed, a new continent unexplored, a world of possibilities waiting to be released and channeled toward some great good.

—Brian Tracy

Every change in your life will come about as the result of your mind colliding with a new idea. Ideas are the keys to the future. Ideas contain the answers to all of your problems and the ways to achieve all of your goals. Your need is to become an idea generator, so that you are continually coming up with new and better ideas to deal with the continuous changes and opportunities taking place around you.

Fortunately, you are naturally creative. It is an innate quality. You are born with it. But creativity is subject to the Law of Use, which says, *"If you don't use it, you lose it,"* at least temporarily. The good news is that you can reignite your creativity by practicing the specific methods and techniques discussed in this book.

■ PROJECT FORWARD AND THINK BACKWARD

Changing your thinking requires that you expand your ideas and imagination about the person you could be, the things you could do, and the things that you could have. Every person who accomplishes anything worthwhile in life begins with a big dream or a vision of what is possible for him or her. They rise above their current surroundings, their existing limitations and problems, and instead they imagine themselves sometime in the future living the kind of life they would like to live. You need to practice this way of thinking as well.

Earlier, we talked about your *ideal future vision*. You create this by projecting forward five years and imagining that all of your dreams have come true. What would your life look like if it were ideal in every way? Where would you be? Who would be there with you? What would you be doing? How much would you be earning? And so on.

You then return to the present day and your current situation. You think of specific steps you could take to capitalize on your opportunities and to overcome your limitations and obstacles. This is the primary use of creative thinking. It is to solve your problems and trigger mental breakthroughs that you can use to move faster toward achieving the goals that are most important to you.

■ THREE MINDS IN ONE

You think and operate your life with three different minds. The first is your *conscious* mind. You use your conscious mind to take in new information, compare it with your current knowledge, analyze it in terms of its value or relevance to you, and then decide to act or not to act. This is the mind with which you direct your life. This is often referred to as the *objective* mind.

The second mind you use is your *subconscious*. Your subconscious mind is a huge data bank that records every thought, idea, emotion, or experience that you ever have throughout your life. This is called the *subjective* mind. Its role is to keep all of your words and actions consistent with your self-concept and with your current attitudes, beliefs, fears, and prejudices. Your subconscious mind does not reason; it only obeys your commands.

Your subconscious mind is also responsible for the operation of all of your bodily functions. It controls your autonomic nervous system and your heart rate, breathing, digestion, basic memory, and so on. It is like a huge computer, so powerful and precise that it can process a hundred million commands per second. It maintains a precise balance of hundreds of chemicals in each one of your billions of cells, 24 hours a day.

Your third mind is your *superconscious* mind. This mind is your direct connection with infinite intelligence. It contains all knowledge, and can bring you all the ideas and answers you will ever need to achieve any goal that you can set for yourself. This mind is the source of all inspiration, imagination, intuition, and hunches. It operates 24 hours a day, and will bring you exactly the right answer to your problem or question, exactly when you are ready for it. It is stimulated by clear goals, vivid mental pictures, and clear, positive commands in the form of affirmations.

When you use all three minds in harmony, with each mind performing the functions for which it was designed, you will accomplish more of your goals, faster than you have ever imagined. The proper utilization of your three minds is central to your changing your thinking and changing your life.

■ THREE TRIGGERS TO CREATIVITY

There are three main factors that trigger creativity. You can use each of them regularly, in everything you do. They are: first, *intensely desired goals*; second, *pressing problems*; and third, *focused questions*. When you use them all, you begin to generate ideas at a rate that will amaze you.

By using these three methods of mental stimulation—goals, problems and questions—you activate all three of your minds simultaneously and you begin to function at much higher levels than the average person.

■ INTENSELY DESIRED GOALS

The first factor is a clearly defined, *intensely desired goal*. You must know exactly what you want, set a deadline, make it measurable, and develop a plan for its achievement that you work on every day. There is a direct relationship between how clear you are about your desired goal and how many ideas you will come up with to achieve it.

One of the most powerful ways to harmonize the activities of your three minds, and to activate your creative powers, is for you to rewrite your goals in the present tense each morning.

Get a spiral notebook. Each morning, after your daily reading, take a few minutes and rewrite your major goals in the present tense, exactly as if they already existed. Take a few seconds after rewriting each goal to visualize it as though it were already accomplished. See each goal in your mind as if it already existed. Then, smile, relax, and let go.

This method of rewriting your goals each morning, visualizing them as if they had already been achieved, and them letting them go with complete confidence is a vital part of creating the mental equivalent of the things you want.

By using this method, you will help your goals to materialize exactly when you are ready for them. By writing and rewriting your goals, you burn them deeper and deeper into your subconscious mind. At a certain point, you activate your superconscious mind. At that point, you begin attracting into your life people and circumstances that can help you to achieve them.

■ GET THE FEELING

Emotion is the key. The more intensely you desire a goal, the more rapidly it materializes. Combining your idea of your goal with the intense emotion of desire or excitement is like stepping on the accelerator of your mental potential. Your mind will speed up and generate ideas for goal accomplishment. The more positive, excited, and enthusiastic you are about achieving anything, the more rapidly your mind goes to work to bring it into your life.

Think about how you would feel if you had achieved your goal. Would you feel proud, happy, relieved, joyous, or exhilarated? Whatever the emotion would be, you should confidently and happily imagine yourself enjoying the exact feeling that you would have if your goal were already a part of your life.

If you want to earn more money and achieve a higher standard of living, imagine that you are already there, living the life you desire. Imagine how you would feel. Close your eyes and *get the feeling* of happiness, joy, and inner satisfaction.

When you can combine a clear mental picture of your goal with the same emotion that you would have if it were achieved, you activate your higher powers of mind. You trigger your creativity. You get insights and ideas that will help you to achieve your goal far faster.

■ PROBLEMS AS OPPORTUNITIES

The second factor that triggers your creativity and activates your positive mind is *pressing problems*. It is only when you are experiencing the pressure of problems and obstacles that you are motivated to perform at your mental best. Facing and solving the inevitable problems and difficulties of life make you stronger and smarter, and bring out the very best in you.

Most people do not understand the nature of problems. Problems are a normal and necessary part of life. They are inevitable and unavoidable. Problems come in spite of your best efforts to avoid them. Problems, therefore, come unbidden.

The only part of a problem over which you have any control is your *response* to your problems. Effective people respond positively and constructively to problems. In this way, they demonstrate that they have developed high levels of "response-ability." They have developed the ability to respond effectively when unexpected or undesired difficulties occur.

Problems of all kinds bring out your very best qualities. They make you strong and resourceful. The more pressing your problems, and the more emotion you invest in solving those problems, the more creative you will become. Each time you solve a problem constructively, you become smarter and more effective. As a result, you prepare yourself for even bigger and more important problems to solve.

■ THINK ON PAPER

One way to improve your ability to solve problems, and to trigger your creativity, is for you to think on paper. Take a few moments to ask, *"What exactly is the problem?"* Then write the answer down in such a form that it describes the problem exactly.

You can then ask, *"What else is the problem?"* You should beware of any problem for which there is only one definition. The worst thing you can do is to solve the wrong problem. The more different ways that you can state a problem, the more amenable it becomes to a solution.

Whatever difficulties, obstacles, challenges, or factors that are hindering you or holding you back in any way, define them clearly in writing. As they say in medicine, *"Accurate diagnosis is half the cure."*

Sometimes, when you begin to define a problem, you will find that it is actually a "cluster problem." That is, it is a single large problem surrounded by several smaller problems. Most problems you deal with will be composed of several smaller problems. Often in a difficult situation, there is one large problem that must be solved before any of the smaller problems can be solved.

The best approach to this type of situation is for you to determine the main problem and then define the individual parts of the problem separately. You identify the core problem that must first be solved and then deal with the smaller problems in order. Sometimes solving one part of the problem leads to the resolution of the entire situation.

■ GOALS ARE JUST PROBLEMS

A goal that you have not yet achieved is merely a problem that you have not yet solved. This is why success has been defined as *the ability to solve problems*. If you are not earning the kind of money that you would like, that is an unsolved problem. If you are not enjoying the levels of health and fitness that you desire, this is just a problem that you must solve. An obstacle that stands between you and your goal is merely a problem waiting for a solution. Any limitation that is holding you back is just another problem waiting for you to solve.

In every case, your job is to not let the problem get on top of you, but rather for you to get on top of the problem.

■ YOUR JOB DESCRIPTION

If I asked you what you did for a living, you would tell me the name of your current position or job description. But whatever your title, your real job is "problem solver." This is what you do all day long. It is this ability that makes you valuable. You are a professional problem solver. Your success in your career is determined by how effectively you solve the problems and achieve the goals of your position.

Never complain about your problems at work. You should be grateful for them. If you had no problems at work, you would have no job. When people become unable to solve the problems that arise in their work, they are quickly replaced by people who can. When you become an excellent problem solver, you are quickly promoted to solving even bigger and more important problems.

From now on, see yourself as a problem solver. The only question is, *how good are you at your job?* Your goal is to become absolutely excellent at solving any problem that the world can throw at you.

■ ASK FOCUSED QUESTIONS

The third way to activate your creativity is by asking *focused questions*. Well-worded, focused, provocative, challenging questions activate your mind and stimulate your thinking. The very best consultants often describe themselves as "insultants." They don't give answers. They instead force their clients to ask and answer tough questions.

To trigger your own creativity, you have to ask yourself some tough questions as well, and then question your answers.

Remember zero-based thinking? Keep asking yourself, "If I were not now doing this, would I start it over again today knowing what I now know?" You will be amazed at how creative you become when you examine every aspect of your life as though you could choose to start it again, if you wanted to, based on your present knowledge and experience.

Often, the answer to your biggest dilemma is simply to *discontinue* an activity altogether. If it's not working out, sometimes the smartest thing you can do is to simply abandon a particular course of action. Always ask, *"What is the simplest and most direct solution to this problem?"*

■ CLARITY IS EVERYTHING

There are additional questions that you can ask to trigger your creativity—for example, *"What am I trying to do?"* Be absolutely clear about your answer to this question.

Whenever you experience any frustration or resistance in achieving a goal or getting a result, ask yourself, *"How am I trying to do it?"* and *"Could there be a better way?"* Don't fall in love with your current methods.

What are your *assumptions*? What are your obvious assumptions and what are your unconscious assumptions? What are you assuming to be true that if it were not true, your thinking would change altogether? Alex McKenzie wrote, "Errant assumptions lie at the root of every failure."

■ THE REAL PROBLEM

I often work with companies that are trying to market a new product or service and they are having difficulties in the marketplace. When we seek the reasons for their business problems, they usually give me long lists of difficulties with advertising, promotion, people, sales, distribution, delivery, and service. However, the core problem is always that their *sales are not high enough*.

I then ask them three questions. They are questions that you can ask when considering any potential product or service for any market.

The first question is, *"Is there a market?"* Are there people who can and will buy this product or service in competition with other products and services currently being offered? Many people start businesses without realizing how hard it is to attract a customer away from another supplier if the customer is currently happy with the other vendor.

If the company's answer is, "Yes, there is definitely a market for what we sell. There are people who want it and are willing to buy it from us," my next question is then, *"Is the market large enough?"* Many a product or service is good, valuable, and worthwhile, but there is not a large enough market to justify investing all the time and energy necessary to bring it to the market. There are better and more profitable uses for the money.

■ WHY COMPANIES FAIL

Many people go broke, especially in entrepreneurial ventures, because the market is simply not large enough for them to sell enough to justify the trouble and expense of producing the product or service in the first place. Every investment must be compared with other possible investments that are available at the same time. There may be better places to put your time and money.

This principle applies to you personally, as well. Your job is to invest *yourself* so that you are getting the highest "return on energy." There are a thousand different ways that you can spend your time and your life. You yourself are your most valuable resource, and you must always invest this resource where you can get the highest return.

The third question I ask my clients is, *"If there is a market, and the market is large enough, is the market concentrated enough so that you can advertise and sell to it in a cost-effective way?"*

This final question is what often sinks a new product idea. Yes, there is a market, and yes, the market is large enough, but the market is spread over such a wide geographical area that it is virtually impossible to sell to it effectively.

■ CONSIDER THE CONSTRAINTS

A good way to trigger creative solutions to your problems is to apply the "theory of constraints." This theory says that, in every process or series of activities, there is a *limiting factor*. There are constraints or bottlenecks that determine the speed at which you get from where you are to where you want to go. The very act of identifying the critical constraints in your environment often triggers ideas and insights that help you to alleviate them.

For example, let us say that your goal is to double your income over the next three to five years. You begin identifying the constraints on achieving this goal by asking, *"Why isn't my income twice as high already?"*

Be honest. Ask yourself the brutal questions: Why aren't you *already* earning twice as much as you are earning today? What is holding you back? Of all the things that are holding you back, what is the major limiting factor that will determine how fast you achieve your goal?

■ APPLY THE 80/20 RULE

The 80/20 Rule seems to apply to constraints, but in a special way. In this context, this rule says that 80 percent of the constraints that are holding you back from achieving your goal are *inside* yourself. They are contained within you, rather than in your environment.

Only 20 percent of the factors that are holding you back are in the *outside* world. This discovery is a shock to most people. The vast majority of people think that their major problems are created or caused by situations and people around them. But this is usually untrue. Most of the reasons why you are not moving ahead have to do with your own lack of skills, ability, or good personal qualities.

■ DOUBLE YOUR INCOME

Let us say that you are in sales. You want to double your income in the next three to five years, if not sooner. The first critical constraint you will identify is the amount of your product or service that you have to sell. If you could resolve this problem, you would achieve your goal.

Once you have identified this main constraint, you then ask, "What is the constraint behind that?" Your next constraint could be the number of prospects that you have to find. If you could speak to enough prospects, you could probably double your sales and double your income.

You then look behind that constraint and ask what is the constraint that is causing this limitation. This actual constraint may be your ability to prospect, something that is inside of you rather than in the marketplace.

■ LOOK AROUND YOU

One good way for you to determine whether the constraint is internal or external is to look around you and see if anyone else is accomplishing the same goals that you want to accomplish. Is anyone else already earning twice as much as you are earning selling the same product or service in the same market? If someone is already doing it, then the constraint is *internal*, not external. It is something inside you. It is the lack of a particular ability or attribute that you need to overcome.

It has been said, *"When a man's fight begins with himself, he is really worth something."* The superior person always asks the question, *"What is it in me that is holding me back?"* Superior people always look to themselves first. It may very well be that there is something in your outside world that is acting as the brake on your potential, but the place to start looking is inside. The odds are you'll find it there.

■ PULL THE TRIGGERS

When you pull these triggers regularly, you will be stimulating your creative ability and switching on your mental lights, like turning up the lights in a dark room with a dimmer switch.

When you set clear goals that you have a burning desire to achieve, you activate your creative mind. When you combine your goals with pressing problems, clearly defined, you generate more ideas. When you continually ask focused questions that provoke your thinking, you see more and better possibilities in every situation. And when you identify your key constraint to achieving any goal or solving any problem, you begin to perform like a genius. You put yourself onto the high road of success and great achievement.

■ USE ALL YOUR INTELLIGENCE

You have at least 10 different forms of intelligence, according to the research of Howard Garner at Harvard and the work of Charles Handy in England. Throughout your schooling, you were tested only on the basis of your verbal and mathematical intelligences. But research in the past few years indicates that you have a variety of intelligences, in any one of which you could be a genius; in combination, they enable you to accomplish extraordinary things. Your first job is to identify your *predominant* intelligence or intelligences; you then apply yourself using more of that intelligence in whatever it is you are trying to achieve.

■ VERBAL INTELLIGENCE

Your first intelligence is *verbal*. This is your ability to speak, your command of language. The ability to understand and to use language well is closely associated with success in any field that involves communication with others. In every society, there is a direct relationship between your level of fluency in your language and your income. You can actually increase your prospects and your rate of promotion just by learning and using more words.

Each word is actually a tool for the expression of thought. The more words you know and understand, the more complex thoughts and ideas you can form. The better your vocabulary, the more respected and listened to by others you will be. This is why language skills are considered a key measure of intelligence.

■ MATHEMATICAL INTELLIGENCE

The second intelligence used to measure IQ is *mathematical*. This is your ability to use numbers skillfully, to add, subtract, divide, and multiply. In business, this is your ability to read financial statements and develop financial projections. The more knowledgeable you are about prices, costs, expenses, and financial ratios, the better decisions you can make, and the more valuable you become.

Many people feel that they have no ability for numbers. They therefore avoid any area or activity where financial fluency is necessary for success. This can be fatal if one of your goals is to achieve financial independence. Fortunately, you can learn to understand the critical numbers in your business with a little study and application. As a result, you will be far more competent and capable of making good decisions for the rest of your business life.

■ PHYSICAL INTELLIGENCE

Your third area of potential genius is *physical* intelligence. This is the kind of intelligence enjoyed by top athletes who have extraordinary abilities of timing and coordination in the movement and use of their bodies. A person could fail in school on verbal and mathematical tests and still be an extraordinary success athletically, even though it would never show up on a report card.

Many people sell themselves short by believing that they are not particularly capable at sports or certain physical activities. The good news is that with proper instruction and practice you can perform quite well in a variety of sports, such as swimming, skating, or skiing. It is really only a question of desire on your part. You have far more physical ability than you have ever used before.

■ MUSICAL INTELLIGENCE

Your fourth form of intelligence can be *musical*. A Mozart or a Beethoven could have been poor at sports and poor in school and yet capable of composing some of the most beautiful classical music of all time. Many of the top musicians and popular singers today did poorly in school but turned out to have an exceptional ability to create and express music. They were able to perform at outstanding levels musically.

■ VISUAL-SPATIAL INTELLIGENCE

Your fifth area of mental potential is *visual-spatial* intelligence. This is the ability to see and create shapes, forms, and patterns. An architect, an engineer, a painter, or a person who has developed the capacity to visualize very clearly would have this intelligence.

An architect, for example, might be able to develop, first in his or her mind and then on paper, beautiful buildings that then people with mathematical intelligence would be able to convert into blueprints and exact dimensions for construction.

This is also the intelligence you use for visualizing and seeing your goals in your mind's eye before they emerge in your reality. This is an intelligence and an ability that you can develop with practice.

■ INTERPERSONAL INTELLIGENCE

Your sixth form of intelligence is *interpersonal*. This is the highest-paid form of intelligence in the United States. It is the ability to communicate, negotiate, influence, and persuade other people. It is characterized by a high degree of sensitivity to the thoughts, feelings, motivations, and desires of others. A person with high interpersonal intelligence has the ability to interact with people effectively to get things done.

Successful managers, team leaders, and even military officers usually have interpersonal intelligence developed to a very high degree. As a result, people want to work and cooperate with them in the accomplishment of group goals.

The highest-paid salespeople are those who are excellent at persuading others to purchase their products and services. The most effective businesspeople, consultants, and professionals demonstrate this intelligence constantly. It is the most important single ability of the successful politician. This may be your particular area of genius, as well.

■ INTRAPERSONAL INTELLIGENCE

Your seventh form of intelligence is *intrapersonal*. This is the ability to be aware of yourself—who you are and who you are not. With this intelligence, you know exactly what you want and what you don't want. You are capable of setting goals for yourself and making plans for their accomplishment. People with high levels of intrapersonal intelligence are good at introspection. They reflect on how they are thinking and feeling. As a result of understanding themselves better, they are more effective in dealing with others.

The greater your level of self-awareness, gained through thought and introspection, the greater your level of *self-understanding*. The better you understand yourself and why you think and feel the way you do, the greater will be your level of *self-acceptance*. The more you accept yourself as a valuable and worthwhile person, the more you like and respect yourself. And the more you like yourself, the more you like others and the more they like you. Intrapersonal intelligence is very important to a happy and successful life, and you can develop it with practice.

■ ENTREPRENEURIAL INTELLIGENCE

Your eighth form of intelligence is *entrepreneurial*. This is the ability to see market opportunities and then to bring the various resources together to produce products and services that can be sold at a profit. Entrepreneurial intelligence is one of the highest-paid forms of intelligence in our society today, and is the foundation of all successful, fast-growing businesses.

Most self-made millionaires and many self-made billionaires started with nothing and made their money by applying their entrepreneurial intelligence to market opportunities that appeared before them. Bill Gates dropped out of Harvard to start Microsoft with an idea to develop software for the emerging market in personal computers. Michael Dell began assembling personal computers in his dorm room at college. They had high levels of entrepreneurial intelligence. You probably do as well.

■ INTUITIVE INTELLIGENCE

Your ninth form of intelligence is *intuitive*. This is the ability to sense the rightness or wrongness of a situation, to judge people quickly and accurately, and to come up with ideas and insights separately from your logic or training.

Many people are great judges of character. They seem to know an enormous amount about a person within just a few seconds of meeting them or even just hearing their voices.

Women's intuition is more respected than men's. But when men and women are tested and given intuition-dependent questions to answer, men and women score equally well. Why then do we respect women's intuition so much? It is because women themselves listen to and trust their intuition more than men do.

Fortunately, your intuitive intelligence is inborn and can be increased with use. The more you listen to and trust your intuition, the sharper and more accurate it becomes. As you use your intuition more, you will receive more and better answers from it. Author Jane Ponder said that *"men and women begin to become great when they start to listen to their inner voices."*

■ ABSTRACT INTELLIGENCE

Your tenth form of intelligence is *abstract,* or conceptual intelligence. This is the kind of intelligence possessed by an Einstein who could see himself riding on a beam of light and as a result was able to formulate the theory of relativity, which completely revolutionized the field of physics.

The scientist F. A. Kekule saw a great snake curling back on itself and grasping its own tail. He recognized it as a clue to the ringlike structure of the benzene molecule, a critical discovery for our century.

Often in your life, you will get a sudden idea or picture that combines several factors into a new synthesis. This can turn out to be a new business idea, such as Ray Kroc had when he observed the mass production methods for cooking hamburgers and french fries developed by the McDonald brothers of San Bernardino. With that insight, he started the 30,000-unit McDonald's Corporation.

■ YOUR INTELLIGENCES MAKE YOU UNIQUE

Your combination of intelligences makes you a potential genius, and also makes you different from anyone else who has ever lived. Think of yourself this way: Imagine that these 10 intelligences are like the 10 digits from zero through nine. If you take any large city, you will find that there are hundreds of thousands of people with different telephone numbers, even though all of their telephone numbers are made up of an area code plus seven digits.

If you give yourself a score from zero to nine in each of the 10 intelligences, you will have a 10-digit number that describes your personal combination of intelligences. This unique combination of intelligences forms a kind of *personal* intellectual telephone number. Your private mental code number makes you different from every other person who has ever lived. Like DNA, the likelihood of someone else having the same intellectual formula as you is billions to one.

■ APPLYING YOUR INCREDIBLE MIND

By developing and exploiting your unique combination of intelligences, you can perform at extraordinary levels. You need to first evaluate your intelligences and then grade yourself in each one.

Next, you identify the special areas of intelligence that you enjoy the most, the ones that you have used most successfully in the past. Finally, you look around you and think about what kind of work you could do that would enable you to use your special combination of intelligences at the highest level.

Above all, you must develop a greater respect for yourself and your potential brainpower. The psychologist Abraham Maslow estimated that not more that 2 percent of adults were doing all that was possible for them based on their special talents. You must therefore develop a higher level of faith and confidence in your ability to use your mental powers to overcome any obstacle and to achieve any goal that you can set for yourself.

■ THREE WAYS OF LEARNING

You have three ways of learning: auditory, visual, and kinesthetic. You can learn by *listening*, learn by *seeing*, or learn by *feeling and movement*. Each person uses all three modalities to learn, but each person also has what is called a *preferred* learning style.

➤ The Visual Learner

Visuals like to see things clearly in front of them. They process information with their eyes. They have acute senses of sight and like to meet friends and business associates personally. If you give them verbal information on business results, they will ask, "Do you have that in writing?"

They are avid readers. When you quote a book or a magazine, they will want to get a hard copy to read personally. They like to take photographs, and like to see things rather than to talk about them. Visuals represent about 50 percent of the population.

➤ The Auditory Learner

An auditory learner likes to listen to others, to educational audio programs, audio books, music, lectures, speeches, and seminars. They are active conversationalists and prefer to have new ideas and concepts explained to them. If you hand them a written report, they will glance at it and ask, "What does it say?"

Auditories say things like, "That sounds good to me," and "I hear what you're saying," or "That doesn't sound right."

They are also sensitive to music, and enjoy high-quality stereo equipment, concerts, CDs, and other sound reproductions. Auditories represent about 40 percent of the population.

➤ Learning by Doing

The third preferred learning style is kinesthetic, or learning by doing and touching. *Kinesthetics* have a hard time just sitting around. They want to be active, to try things out, often ignoring the written instructions (visual) or verbal instructions (auditory).

You find kinesthetics in any type of work that requires manual dexterity, such as carpentry, mechanics, construction, and even driving trucks or cars. Athletes are kinesthetics as well.

■ YOU ARE TRULY UNIQUE

What is your preferred way of learning and dealing with the world? You will be happy and fulfilled only when what you are doing on the outside is in harmony with the unique and special person you are on the inside.

When you combine your dominant intelligences with your preferred method of learning, you can create a combination of intelligence and ability that will enable you to achieve extraordinary things with your life.

■ UNLOCKING THE FLOODGATES OF YOUR MIND

There are two powerful methods that you can use to unlock your brainpower and generate more ideas for goal attainment. These methods are called *"mindstorming"* and *"brainstorming"*. The first will make you rich personally, and the second will make you successful by enabling you to tap into the brainpower of other people. These methods are responsible for the creation of many self-made millionaires. You can use them almost anytime and anywhere.

■ MINDSTORMING FOR IDEAS

The process of "mindstorming" is often called the "20-idea method." It is so powerful in generating ideas that when you begin using it your entire life will change. I have taught it to many tens of thousands of people all over the world. Everyone who uses it sees immediate profound improvements in each part of their lives to which this method is applied.

The method is simple, which is probably why it is so powerful. All you need is a blank sheet of paper. At the top of the page, write out your current problem or goal in the form of a question.

Let us say that your goal is to double your income over the next two years. Make the question on this goal as specific as possible. The more specific the question, the better your mind can focus on it and the better quality of answers you will generate with this exercise.

So instead of writing, "How can I make more money?" you would write instead, "What can I do to double my income over the next 24 months?" Remember, you write this question at the top of the page.

■ GENERATE 20 ANSWERS

You then discipline yourself to generate at least 20 different answers to that question. Force yourself to write out 20 different things that you could do that would help you to double your income. You can write more than 20 answers, but you must write a minimum of 20.

Your first answers will probably be simple and obvious. You could write, "work harder," "work longer," "upgrade my education," "improve my skills in specific areas," and so on. They will be easy. The next 5 to 10 answers will be harder. The last 10 answers will be excruciatingly difficult, like squeezing water out of a stone.

But to get the most out of this exercise, you must force yourself to continue writing until you have answered the question 20 different ways. You can play with these answers if you like. For example, you can write the exact opposite of one of your earlier answers. You can also generate ridiculous answers as well.

■ THINK OUT OF THE BOX

For example, you might write, "work harder at my current job." Your next answer might be, "work less at my current job." Or, "work harder at a different job." Or it may be to create your own job. Or it may be to get a second-income job, or to work part-time in another field.

If your income depends on selling and your success in selling depends on prospecting, your answer could be to *double* the number of qualified prospects you see each week. Or it could be to see higher-potential prospects who have the ability to buy twice as much of your product. Or it could be to sell a different product with a higher commission per sale.

In any case, the potential answers are limited only by your imagination, and your capacity to generate ideas to help you is, to all intents and purposes, infinite.

■ THE IMPORTANCE OF ACTION

Once you have answered your question with at least 20 answers, go back over your answers and select at least one answer that you are going to take action on immediately. This step is very important! It is your taking action of some kind that keeps the torrent of ideas flowing through your mind. As you take action on one idea, another idea for another action will come to you.

Here is an exercise you can use to double and triple the impact of the 20-idea method. Once you have generated at least 20 ideas and selected the one idea you are going to implement immediately, you can then perform the 20-idea method on *that* new idea, generating 20 different ways to put that idea to work.

■ FIRST THING IN THE MORNING

If you generate 20 ways to achieve your major goal in the morning before you start out, you will find yourself thinking creatively all day long. Your mind will be sharper and more alert. You will see solutions to problems and obstacles as fast as they come up. You will activate the law of attraction and begin drawing into your life people and resources that can help you to achieve your goal.

If you practice this exercise each day for five days, you will generate 100 new ideas to help you achieve your goals in the next week. If you then select one idea per day, you will be initiating five ideas per week. That is more ideas than the average person generates in a month, or even a year.

If you generate 20 ideas per day, 5 days per week, 50 weeks per year, you will come up with an astounding total of 5,000 new ideas to improve your life and work each year. If you implement only a single new idea each day, 5 days per week, 50 weeks per year, you will be using 250 ideas per year to help you solve your problems and achieve your goals.

The average person lives with very little creativity. He is usually a victim of *psychosclerosis* and *homeostasis*, content to keep on doing the same things in the future that he has done in the past, whether doing so is working or not. When you practice mindstorming on a regular basis, you will soon have so many good ideas that there will not be enough hours in the day to carry them out.

More people have become rich using this 20-idea method than any other method of creative thinking ever discovered. All that is necessary for this method to work is for you to practice it regularly in your own life. All that is required is your willingness to use mindstorming regularly, and then to try out the ideas you generate until this process becomes a normal part of your life.

■ BRAINSTORMING WITH OTHERS

Mindstorming is an exercise that you can do by yourself. Brainstorming is something that you do with others. Brainstorming is a form of mindstorming done in a group, but it has slightly different rules.

Brainstorming was originally developed by advertising executive Alex Osborn, and was first described in his 1946 book, *Applied Imagination*. It has since proliferated and is used all over the world, in every type of organization and situation, to generate ideas for a variety of reasons. It is a very simple process to learn and use.

➤ Six Steps to Brainstorming

Step One: Assemble the group. The ideal number of people in a brainstorming session is four to seven. Below four, you don't have enough minds to generate a large enough variety of different solutions to the problem. With more than seven people, the group becomes too large for participants to get sufficient opportunity to contribute.

Step Two: Do not permit criticism or ridicule. The essential part of brainstorming is that no evaluation of the ideas takes place during the brainstorming session. The entire focus of the brainstorming session is on generating the greatest *quantity* of ideas possible within a short period of time.

Nothing kills a brainstorming session faster than the tendency of people to criticize the ideas as they are generated. As soon as one person's ideas are criticized, the brainstorming session comes to a halt. No one wants to be criticized. No one wants to be humiliated or ridiculed in front of others. That is why you must concentrate on the quantity of ideas and leave the evaluation of them to another time, or to other people.

Step Three: Set a specific time limit. The ideal length for brainstorming sessions ranges from 15 to 45 minutes. One of the jobs of managers and team leaders is to sit their staff down on a regular basis to brainstorm certain problems. Call everyone together and announce that you are going to brainstorm a particular goal or situation for 15 minutes and then everyone is going to go back to work. You'll be amazed at the results.

Step Four: Select a leader for the group. The leader's job is to encourage everyone to contribute as much as possible. One of the best ways to lead a brainstorming session is to go around the table and encourage each person to contribute an idea—almost like playing cards, where you encourage each person to bet or pass. Once you have gone around the table a couple of times, people will start generating ideas at a rapid rate.

Step Five: Select someone to keep track of the ideas. A key function in a brainstorming session is that of the *recorder*. This is the person who writes down the ideas as they are generated.

Step Six: Be punctual. Start and stop the brainstorming session exactly on time, no matter how well it is going. At the end, you gather up all the ideas and take them away to be evaluated at a later time.

■ IDEAS ON INDEX CARDS

In another type of brainstorming session involving dozens of people, we break the group up and distribute index cards to each subgroup. Each of the smaller groups is assigned to generate ideas in answer to the question or problem. Afterward, the index cards containing the ideas are collected. They are then shuffled and handed out to the subgroups again, completely mixed up.

In the second phase of the exercise, each subgroup is asked to take the ideas on the cards that they have received and evaluate them, rating them in terms of their value prior to reporting back to the overall group.

In a session with 20 or 30 people, two or three hundred ideas will be generated in 30 minutes. When those ideas are gathered, distributed, evaluated, and reported back to the overall group, the results are absolutely astonishing! I have worked with companies that have come up with so many solutions to problems that had been stumping them that they did not have enough hours in the day, or enough people, to take action on more than a small number of them.

■ THE HOME TEAM

If you are in a good relationship with another person, the two of you can form an excellent ongoing brainstorming team. A husband and wife, or any two people, together can generate a continuous flow of ideas, as long as they do not attempt to evaluate or criticize the ideas at the same time they are generating them.

■ IDEAS ENERGIZE YOU

There are two parts to unlocking your mental potential and harnessing the genius that lies within you. The first is to accept that you are extremely intelligent in your own way. The second is for you to use the methods and techniques described in this chapter until they become second nature to you. Like a muscle that grows and becomes stronger with use, your mental muscles grow and become stronger every time you practice one of these exercises.

There is something exciting and uplifting about generating ideas that help you to achieve your goals. The more ideas you generate, the more energy and enthusiasm you have. The more energy and enthusiasm you have, the more confident you become that you can achieve any goal you can set for yourself. The more ideas you generate, the faster you change your thinking about what is really possible for you. Eventually, you will reach the point in your own thinking where you will be *unstoppable*.

ACTION EXERCISES

1. Define your most important goal or problem in the form of a question and write it at the top of a page. Then, generate at least 20 answers to your question.

2. Make a list of your most pressing problems or obstacles to achieving your goals. What is the simplest and most direct solution to each one?

3. Think of your most important goal and ask, "Why have I not achieved that goal already?"

4. Identify the constraints or limiting factors that determine how fast you increase your income. What can you do right now to alleviate these constraints?

5. What are the *intelligences* that you seem to be better at than others? How could you organize you life and work so that you are capitalizing more on these intelligences?

6. What have you been good at in the past? What activities give you your greatest feeling of importance?

7. What parts of your work give you the highest *return on energy*? How could you structure your work and your life so that you are spending more time in these areas?

Chapter 10

Supercharge
Your Thinking

**Each problem has hidden within it an opportunity so
powerful that it literally dwarfs the problem. The greatest
success stories were created by people who recognized a
problem and turned it into an opportunity.**

—Joseph Sugarman

The way you think about yourself and your life determines almost
everything that happens to you. Your primary responsibility is to
take full control over your thinking and to keep your words and
thoughts clearly focused on the things that you really want. Simultaneously, you must refuse to think about the things that you don't
want. This simple formula is the real key to health, happiness, and
personal prosperity.

This chapter is about "possibility thinking." This is the process
of looking at everything that is going on around you in terms of possibilities and opportunities rather than as difficulties or problems.
Your goal is to make this a habitual way of thinking, and, like all
habits, it is learnable. You can develop it with constant repetition.
Eventually, you will become a completely positive and constructive
person in everything you do.

■ POSITIVE MENTAL ATTITUDE

A positive mental attitude is closely associated with success in every area of life. The kind of people we like the most and want to associate with tend to be people who are generally cheerful and optimistic about their work and personal lives. No one wants to spend time with a negative, pessimistic, complaining person.

Unfortunately, it is easy to slip into the habit of criticizing and complaining. We are bombarded continuously with negative information, from radio, television, newspapers, and magazines and in our daily interactions with others. It may not be easy to rise above the flood of negativity that engulfs you, but it is absolutely essential to do so if you want to keep your spirits up and your mind clear and positive.

■ RESPOND CONSTRUCTIVELY TO STRESS

A positive mental attitude can be defined as a *constructive response to stress*. It doesn't mean that, no matter what happens, you are happy and cheerful all the time. Having a positive mental attitude instead requires that you deal with the inevitable problems of your daily life in a more effective way than the average person.

Stress is inevitable. Problems are never ending. Failures and disappointments happen to everyone, all the time. The only thing over which you have any control is how you respond to these stressful events. If you respond in a positive, constructive way, you will maintain a generally positive attitude. When your mind is calm and clear, you will be more creative and alert. You will be more likely to see more ways to solve your problems, and to keep moving toward accomplishing your goals.

When you respond in a negative or angry way to a problem or difficulty, you trigger a series of nervous reactions that shut down the most creative parts of your brain. Instead of going into a "react and respond" way of thinking, you develop a "fight or flight" mentality.

■ FIVE STEPS TO PERSONAL POWER

There is a five-step power process that you can use to keep yourself positive and to achieve your goals faster. This five-step process brings together several of the very best techniques ever discovered for permanent mind change. It contains and illustrates all of the key principles that you need to know to become a highly effective, positive "possibility thinker" in your own life.

The five steps are: first, to *idealize*; second, to *verbalize*; third, to *visualize*; fourth, to *emotionalize*; and fifth, to *realize*. Let me explain how they work one at a time, and then, altogether.

■ IMAGINE YOUR PERFECT FUTURE

Perhaps the biggest obstacle to creating a wonderful life is "self-limiting beliefs." Everyone has them, and some people have so many of them that they are almost paralyzed when it comes to taking action.

A self-limiting belief is an idea you have that you are limited in some way, in terms of time, talent, intelligence, money, ability, or opportunity. As a result of these beliefs, most of which are probably not true, you hold yourself back from taking the steps necessary to create the kind of life you really desire.

The way you free yourself from these negative brakes on your potential is to change your thinking about who you are and what is truly possible for you. You put aside any thought of limitation and begin to idealize and imagine the kind of life that you want to have a week, a month, a year, and five years from now, as if anything was possible.

In *idealization*, you consider each of the key areas of your life and imagine what each would look like if that area of your life were exactly as you would want it to be, in every respect.

■ SHOW ME THE MONEY

Start with your income. How much do you want to be earning one, two, three, and five years from today? Look around you and ask, "Who else is earning the kind of money I want to earn, and what are they doing differently from me?" If you don't know or you aren't sure, go and ask them. Do your homework.

What knowledge, skills, and abilities would you have to have to be able to earn that amount? What kind of work would you, or could you, be doing to achieve that kind of income? What position will you have in your company? How high up will you have to be in your field or profession? If you are in sales, how much will you have to be selling, and to whom?

■ DESIGN YOUR PERFECT LIFE

Imagine your perfect lifestyle. If you had no limitations at all, how would you like to live, day in and day out? If you were financially independent, what kind of home would you like to live in? What kind of car would you want to drive? What kind of life would you like to provide for your family? What sort of activities would you like to engage in throughout the week, month, and year?

How much time would you want to take off on vacation, and where would you like to go? What would you like to do? What sort of activities do you most enjoy? If you were forced to take a month off from work and you had all the money you needed, how would you spend that time?

■ FAMILY PLANNING

Involve your family in your design of an ideal lifestyle. Make this an ongoing part of your relationships. The more people get a chance to discuss a course of action, the more committed they will be to whatever is finally decided.

Some time ago, a good friend of mine sat down with his wife and children to discuss the fact that he was working too much and not spending enough time with the family. They imagined how they would spend their time as a family if they had no limitations. Everyone contributed ideas, including the young children.

As a result of this exercise, they made some decisions about both time and lifestyle. They decided to move out of the city to a larger home with a bigger yard in the country. He reorganized his workweek so that he worked four days per week in the city, 10 to 12 hours per day, and then worked only three or four hours on one day in his office at home in the country. He ended up spending much more time with his family and getting far more satisfaction out of life. The best part was that both his results and his income actually increased with this new plan.

■ TURN YOUR IDEAL INTO REALITY

When you sit down and design your ideal lifestyle, you can then compare it to what you are doing today and notice the differences. You can then start thinking about how you could bring your *real* or current lifestyle closer to your *ideal*.

When you idealize your income and your lifestyle, you develop a vision for your life. You begin to practice a key quality of personal leadership. You begin projecting into the future and making plans to turn your future dreams into a current reality.

■ HEALTH AND FITNESS

You should idealize about your health, as well. Imagine your health was perfect in every way. How would you be different from today? Exactly how much do you want to weigh, and what level of fitness do you want to enjoy? How does that compare with where you are today? What steps will you have to take, and what changes will you have to make in your health habits in order to become the ideal person that you desire to be personally? This description then becomes your ideal future vision for yourself.

■ THE PERSON YOU BECOME

Create an ideal future self in terms of your personal and professional development. What kind of a person do you want to be in the future? What additional knowledge and skills do you want to acquire? In what areas would you like to become absolutely excellent? What subjects would you like to master? What do you need to learn to move to the top of your field? What is your growth plan to get from where you are to where you want to go?

■ YOUR MISSION STATEMENT

When you conduct personal strategic planning for yourself, you always begin with a *mission statement*. This is clear definition of exactly what you want to be and accomplish at some future date. To develop your mission statement, you project forward and imagine that you have been completely successful in achieving all your goals in a particular area. You then describe your life and activities in this area exactly as if they were already true today.

For example, your personal mission statement could be something like: *"I am a happy, healthy, positive person who does excellent work, is paid extremely well, is highly respected by his customers and coworkers, and is deeply loved by his family."*

This kind of mission statement can then serve as an organizational blueprint for your life. You can use it to make decisions by comparing what you are about to do to see if it is consistent with your mission. If it is not consistent with your mission, or with your ideal image of the very best person you could possible be, you would not do it.

■ A BENCHMARK FOR DECISION MAKING

I conducted a strategic planning session for a large corporation not long ago. The executives had more than 250 potential projects on their drawing boards. After we had defined the values, vision, and ideal mission of the company, they were immediately able to discard more than 200 of those potential projects. It was clear to everyone at the meeting that these projects were not consistent with who they were as a company and where they wanted to be in the future. This can work for you as well.

One of your problems today is that you are overwhelmed with too much to do and too little time. You have too many things to think about. You are swamped by too many problems, possibilities, and opportunities. When you idealize and become crystal clear about what your perfect life would look like sometime in the future, you will immediately start to make better choices in your day-to-day activities. You will immediately begin eliminating activities that are not consistent with where you really want to end up.

■ A KEY TO HAPPINESS

A clear definition of your ideal, in any area of your life that is important to you, is the starting point of making better decisions in the present that will lead to greater success and happiness in the future. As you feel yourself moving toward the achievement of a worthy ideal, you will feel happier and more confident. The more progress you make toward a clear goal or set of ideal conditions, the more energy and enthusiasm you will have.

■ THE DEFINITION OF INTELLIGENCE

Some years ago, the Gallup organization interviewed 1,500 very successful men and women in a search for some of the common denominators of success. But when they asked them to define "intelligence," they got an unexpected answer.

The top people in the survey defined intelligence not so much as IQ or good grades in school, but more as *a way of acting*. Intelligent behavior was defined as doing only those things that moved them toward their goals. They defined intelligence as the ability to systematically eliminate those time-consuming activities that did not help them to achieve their goals, or even worse, moved them *away* from their goals.

■ GET SMART

Whenever you are doing something that is moving you in the direction of your own self-professed goals and ideals, you are acting intelligently. This is true irrespective of your education or your IQ. This is why there are many people of average intelligence or who did poorly in school who are accomplishing far more than people with university degrees. These high achievers focus more and more of their time and energy on activities aimed at accomplishing only those goals that are most important to them.

■ PUT IT IN WORDS

The second part of this five-step process is for you to *verbalize* clearly the person you want to be, the things you want to do, and the goals you want to achieve. You verbalize with positive affirmations. Because you can completely reprogram your subconscious mind with affirmations, by using them repeatedly you will find that your potential is unlimited.

The Law of Subconscious Activity says that whatever you repeat over and over to yourself in your conscious mind will eventually be accepted by your subconscious mind. Once your subconscious mind accepts your conscious thoughts as commands, it passes them on to your superconscious mind, which then works 24 hours a day to bring those goals into your life.

With positive affirmations, you can take full control over the content of your conscious and subconscious minds. You can activate all your mental powers. You can tap into a great universal mind that can help you to move more rapidly toward your goals of higher income, better health and relationships, and greater success in your field.

■ THE THREE Ps OF POSITIVE PROGRAMMING

A positive affirmation is phrased using the "three Ps." This means that for maximum effectiveness, an affirmation should be *personal*, *positive*, and stated in the *present tense*.

Your subconscious mind is like a special computer. It can be accessed and activated only with words and commands that are presented in a specific language. It accepts only positive commands that are phrased in the personal, present tense, as though the goal has already been achieved. It knows no past or future tense.

My favorite affirmation is, *"I like myself!"* repeated over and over again in a spirit of complete confidence. When you repeat, "I like myself!" several times per day, you send this message deep into your subconscious mind. The more you like yourself, the higher will be your self-esteem. The higher your self-esteem, the better you will perform in every area of your life. The more you like yourself, the better you will do, and the better you do, the more you will like yourself.

■ BECOME YOUR OWN CHEERLEADER

To improve your performance in your work, or in any other area requiring skill or ability, continually repeat the words, *"I'm the best, I'm the best, I'm the best!"* By talking to yourself as if you were already the person you want to be sometime in the future, you become your own cheerleader. You will then find yourself doing better and better at whatever you attempt.

Another powerful affirmation you can repeat every morning before you start off is, *"I love my work!"* Sometimes when you wake up in the morning, you won't feel particularly excited about the coming day. But you can take control over your mind and emotions by repeating, "I love my work!" until it actually feels true.

Even better, you can start every day with the words, *"I like myself and I love my work!"* This affirmation, repeated enthusiastically several times every morning, will rev you up and get you excited about getting to your job.

■ CONTROL YOUR SELF-TALK

Fully 95 percent of your emotions are determined by the way you *talk* to yourself. Dr. Martin Seligman's book *Learned Optimism* says that your "explanatory style" is the critical factor in determining whether you are a positive or negative person.

Your explanatory style is defined as *how you explain things to yourself.* If you explain or interpret things to yourself in a positive way, you will be positive. If you explain them in a negative way, you will be negative. What Seligman concluded is that optimistic people, when something goes wrong, always explain the event or experience to themselves as though it were a temporary, specific situation, rather than a long-term, general condition.

Imagine that you make a sales call and the prospect is not interested in what you are selling. It didn't work out. It was a waste of time. If you are a *positive* person, you will say something like, "Well, it's just one sales call." This makes it temporary. You will say, "The customer is probably having a bad day." This makes it specific. You then say, "I'll be more successful on the next call." This focuses you on the future. When you dismiss temporary setbacks in this way, you keep your mind positive. You remain confident and optimistic.

■ DON'T TAKE THINGS PERSONALLY

When *negative* people experience problems, setbacks, or difficulties, they interpret them differently from confident, optimistic people. When they fail temporarily, which is inevitable, they immediately interpret this as a personal statement about their deficiencies. If the sales call is not successful, they say, "I must be a terrible salesperson. The product is no good. Customers are not interested in what we have to sell. I'll never succeed in this field."

In other words, they overgeneralize and overdramatize a small failure rather than dismissing it as a temporary setback and going on to the next call. They interpret the experience negatively. It then has a negative effect on their self-image: "I'm no good." Their work performance declines and they do even worse next time.

The good news, however, is that how you interpret an event is under your control. It is a matter of choice. You determine how you are going to feel and react by how you choose to explain a situation to yourself. Choose to put a positive spin on it, whatever it is. You are in charge.

■ MAKE IT SIMPLE

When you verbalize your goals in the form of positive affirmations, you should use words that your subconscious can easily understand and go to work on. Make your statements simple and practical. For example, "I like myself" is personal. "I'm the best" is personal and positive. And "I love my work" is personal, positive, and in the present tense.

These are the kinds of affirmations that are immediately accepted by your subconscious mind as commands. They have an immediate impact on how you think and feel about yourself. They instantly boost your self-esteem and self-confidence. To remain optimistic, you must be continually talking to yourself in terms of the way you *want to be* rather than the way things are at the moment.

In neurolinguistic programming, the way that you talk to yourself about what is happening to you is called your "interpretive style." The way you interpret things is a key part of changing your thinking. The question is always whether you interpret things that are happening around you in a positive or negative way. Remember, the optimist sees the glass as half full while the pessimist sees the glass as half empty. Choose to be an optimist.

■ BECOME AN INVERSE PARANOID

The multimillionaire W. Clement Stone started off selling newspapers on the streets of Chicago at the age of 12. He went on to build Combined Insurance Company of America, and died recently at the age of 100 worth more than $800 million. He was a great inspiration to thousands of people, and was famous for his habit of being an "inverse paranoid."

A paranoid is someone who believes that people are conspiring against him or her. An *inverse* paranoid, in contrast, is a person who is convinced that the world is conspiring to make him or her *successful*. An inverse paranoid insists upon interpreting everything that happens as part of a great plan leading to success. W. Clement Stone used to respond to every difficulty with the emphatic statement, "That's good!" Then he would concentrate his attention on finding out what was good about the situation. And he always found something, even if it was just a valuable lesson.

If you change the definition of a problem to a *situation*, a *challenge*, or an *opportunity*, your response to the problem will be positive and constructive, rather than negative and angry. If you look at every problem as a potential opportunity, you will almost always find within the problem an opportunity or benefit that you can take advantage of.

Norman Vincent Peale used to say, "When God wants to send you a gift, He wraps it up in a problem." The bigger the problem that you have, the bigger the gift—in the form of valuable lessons, ideas, and insights that it probably contains. Is the glass half full or is it half empty? It's up to you.

■ YOU WILL BELIEVE IT WHEN YOU *SEE* IT

The third part of the five-part process of supercharging your thinking is *visualization*. You already know how powerful this can be in helping you to achieve your goals. It is only when you learn to use visualization on every goal and activity that you will truly tap into its amazing power for good in your life.

As it happens, everyone visualizes, all the time. The difference is that successful people visualize the things they want, and unsuccessful people visualize the things they don't want. Prior to every new experience, a successful person will take a few moments to recall and relive a previous successful experience in that area. Unsuccessful people, in contrast, prior to a new experience will recall and relive a previous failure experience.

In each case, people are creating a predisposition to succeed or fail. When they visualize, they send a command to their subconscious minds. The subconscious mind then coordinates their words and actions in the upcoming situation so that they perform consistent with that picture.

■ IMAGINE A PERFECT OUTCOME

In visualizing, you project your mind forward and create a clear picture of your ideal future goal. You imagine what it would look like if it were already achieved. You make your picture as vivid as possible. You repeat this mental picture over and over, as often as you possibly can during the day, and for as long as you can.

There is a direct relationship between how clearly you can see your goal or performance on the inside and how rapidly it comes into your reality on the outside. Visualization is one of the most powerful faculties available to you to become a possibility thinker, to change your thinking about your life and your future. With visualization, you can make your current dreams into future realities. You can change your thinking completely by changing your mental pictures.

■ PROGRAM YOUR MIND

There are three techniques combining verbalization and visualization that you can practice to achieve your goals faster. These are often referred to as "mental programming techniques." They are amazingly effective in preparing yourself and your mind for an upcoming event.

The first of these methods is what is called the *quick programming technique*. Here is how it works. Prior to any nonrecurring event of importance, like a sales call, a meeting, or an interview, you take a few moments to prepare mentally, like an athlete would warm up for a competition.

First, take a few deep breaths. This relaxes you and drops your mind into the alpha state. In this state, your subconscious mind becomes highly receptive to any incoming command. Second, you visualize the ideal outcome of the upcoming situation. You imagine it as turning out perfectly for you in every respect. For example, if you are making a sales call, visualize the client responding to you in a positive, receptive way. Especially, visualize the client signing the check or sales order at the end of the conversation.

One of my good friends has used this technique for many years to become one of the highest-paid people in his industry. He says it is absolutely amazing how many times the sales situation works out exactly as he visualized it before he went in. Try it for yourself and see.

➤ Affirm and Visualize

The third and last part of the quick programming technique is for you to verbalize or create a positive affirmation that is consistent with your mental picture. A simple affirmation would be "This sales call goes extremely well and concludes satisfactorily for everyone involved." This command instructs your subconscious mind to give you the words, feelings, behaviors, and body language consistent with achieving your goal of a successful sales call.

We teach this "quick affirmation" technique to applicants who are going on job interviews, speakers giving public talks, performers in the arts, and even to politicians. It is an extraordinarily effective technique, and it only takes a few seconds prior to each event.

■ WRITE AND REVIEW YOUR GOALS

The second method you can use to bring about rapid internal changes to your thinking and your life is called the *standard affirmation technique*. This technique requires that you write out your major goals in the form of present, positive, personal affirmations on three-by-five index cards, one goal per card. You can work on 10 to 15 goals at a time using this method.

Carry these cards around with you. At the beginning of each day, take a few minutes by yourself to review each goal.

Take the first card and read it. Perhaps the first card says, "I earn $50,000 per year." Read the card and let your eyes focus on the message so that it is imprinted on your subconscious mind. Then, close your eyes, take a deep breath, and repeat the affirmation five times. As you affirm, visualize your goal as already achieved. See it. Feel it. Then open your eyes, relax, exhale deeply, and read the next card.

■ PREPARE FOR THE DAY

This entire exercise, with 10 to 15 goals, takes about 10 minutes. It programs your subconscious mind at a deep level, and prepares you to perform at your very best for the rest of the day.

If you practice this each morning before you start out and each evening before you go to bed, you will be absolutely amazed at how quickly your goals begin to materialize.

Your subconscious mind is the sending and receiving station for the power of attraction in your life. The more you feed your subconscious mind with words and pictures consistent with what you want to accomplish, the more you magnetize your goals. You become a *living magnet*. You begin to attract people, opportunities, ideas, and resources into your life that make achieving your goals a possibility.

■ PRACTICE MENTAL REHEARSAL

The third mental programming technique that you can use to perform better and achieve your goals faster is often called *mental re-*

hearsal. It is taught and used extensively in sports of all kinds. The process is both simple and powerful.

First, you sit or lie down, completely relaxed, with your eyes closed, and breath deeply until your whole body is calm and quiet.

Second, you clearly visualize an upcoming event, or a goal that you desire. You allow yourself to enter into the experience and see it clearly in your mind. You imagine yourself actually doing and saying the things you would if the upcoming situation is perfect.

One of the very best times to practice mental rehearsal is just before you go to sleep. By verbalizing and visualizing your ideal goals or activities for the coming day immediately prior to sleeping, you program your subconscious mind to work on those goals all night long. Then, when you wake up in the morning, you will often have insights and ideas that you can use to make those goals a reality. It is an amazing technique and is extremely effective.

■ PREPROGRAM FOR PEAK PERFORMANCE

You can use this technique to preprogram your mind for a variety of things. For example, let us say you have a problem that you are worried about. Just before you go to sleep, turn this problem over to your superconscious mind and ask for a solution. Then, forget about it and go to sleep. Very often, when you wake up in the morning the solution will occur to you. It will be crystal clear and perfect in every respect.

You can use this method of mental programming to assure that you wake up feeling positive and energetic. The process is both simple and effective. Just before going to sleep, say to yourself, "When I wake up in the morning, I feel terrific!" Repeat this several times. Imagine yourself getting up the next morning feeling happy and full of energy. Especially when you go to bed late and you need to be at your best the next day, use this technique to wake up feeling refreshed. It works every time.

■ WAKE AT A CERTAIN TIME

You can use mental rehearsal and preprogramming to wake up at the desired time without an alarm clock. No matter where you are, or in what time zone, you can "set your mind" on a certain time before you go to sleep, and you will wake up at exactly that minute.

Before you fall asleep, you say, "I wake up tomorrow morning at seven o'clock sharp." You can then fall to sleep without worrying. The next morning, your heart rate will gradually speed up, waking you at your preset time. You will be unable to go back to sleep. You can even travel great distances and wake up in different time zones on schedule using this method.

■ GET THE FEELING OF SUCCESS

The fourth element in mental programming is *emotionalization*. This requires that you create the feeling that would go with successful accomplishment of your goal. This is the part that makes idealizing, verbalizing, and visualizing really work for you. Your emotions are the energy source, the jet fuel that drives you toward your goal.

You have heard it said that humans are 10 percent logical and 90 percent emotional. The fact is, however, that you are initially 100 *percent* emotional. You decide emotionally, and then justify logically. Everything you do is governed and controlled by your emotions, in some way. The only question is, "What emotion is in charge?"

■ MASTER OR SLAVE?

Many people are slaves to their emotions. With very little control over their feelings, they continually react and respond to other people and situations. They have no minds of their own.

One of your chief responsibilities to yourself is to get your emotions under control. Take charge of your positive emotions rather than allowing yourself to be dominated by your negative emotions. By using your emotions deliberately and purposefully, especially by keeping them positive and focused on what you want, you can put enormous power behind your visualizations, verbalizations, and idealizations.

■ IMAGINE YOUR IDEAL OUTCOME

One way to unlock the energy and power contained in your emotional nature is for you to get the feeling that you would enjoy if you had already achieved your goal. See it in your mind's eye and create within you the emotions you would experience if your dream came true this very minute.

Imagine, for example, that your goal is to earn a certain amount of money. Project mentally into the future and see yourself earning this kind of money. *See* the larger house, the bigger car, the better clothes, the nicer restaurants, and the more elegant lifestyle that you will enjoy when you are earning this amount of money. Imagine how you would feel if you were already enjoying all these ingredients of success. Imagine the feelings of pride, happiness, satisfaction, pleasure, joy, and gratitude that you would experience once you achieved this goal.

Just like a person soaking in a hot bath, soak your mind in these feelings, exactly as if you were already at your destination. These emotions will then trigger thoughts, desires, and actions consistent with them. Each will reinforce the other.

■ THE COMBINATION IS POWERFUL

When you combine all three—a mental picture, a verbalization, and an emotion—you activate your subconscious mind. Your subconscious mind then passes this impression on to your *superconscious* mind, which works on your goals 24 hours per day. When you practice combining verbalization, visualization, and emotionalization on every goal, you will be absolutely astonished at the things that begin happening to you, and the goals that you accomplish.

Once you activate your superconscious mind, you will receive a continuous stream of insights and ideas that you can use to solve your problems and achieve your goals. This mind will show you how to remove, get around, or climb over any obstacle that appears on your path. It will bring you the information that you need, at exactly the right time for you. It will give you intuitions and hunches that guide you to make the right decisions. Your superconscious mind will give you a steady flow of energy, enthusiasm, and motivation that will drive you toward your goals.

The way you activate this process and unleash all your mental powers is by continually idealizing, verbalizing, visualizing, and especially emotionalizing.

■ DREAMS COME TRUE

The fifth element in this five-step power process is *realization*, to actually achieve your goals and to have your wishes come true.

This is the most important part of the process. But you must be aware that every goal takes a certain amount of time to materialize. Some goals can be achieved quickly. Some require weeks and even months of patient, steady work. Others are long-term goals, requiring several years to bring to fruition. Your attitude toward the time required for goal attainment has a major impact on whether and when you accomplish them.

In the realization phase, after you have practiced the first four steps, you simply relax and let go of the process. You allow your goal to appear in its own time. Exactly the things that you want and need will come to you at exactly the time that you are ready for them.

Successful people eventually develop an attitude of calm, confident expectation. They are never rushed or hurried. They are relaxed and confident, and they absolutely believe that everything is conspiring to bring them exactly what they want, at exactly the right time for them. This must be your attitude as well.

■ MULTIPLY YOUR POWERS

You can get even greater benefit from this five-step process for achieving your goals by using special techniques in response to the things that happen to you each day.

First of all, no matter what happens, *look for the good* in every situation. Seek the valuable lesson. Look for what you can gain from any temporary setback or obstacle.

Napoleon Hill studied and interviewed successful men and

women for 25 years. He found that they had one characteristic in common. Each of them had developed the habit of continually looking into every difficulty for the seed of an equal or greater benefit or advantage. They constantly looked for the silver lining of even their darkest cloud.

When you are looking for something good to come out of every problem situation, you will respond to difficulties in a more positive, creative, and constructive way. You will be more optimistic and confident. If you think that you are going to benefit from everything that happens to you, you will develop the attitude of the possibility thinker. As a result, no matter what happens, you will almost always find something good that you can turn to your benefit or advantage.

■ THE RUDDER OF THE DAY

Just as you become what you eat, you also become what you feed into your mind. Your mind is most receptive to new ideas first thing in the morning. You can accelerate the process of changing your thinking by starting off every morning by reading for 30 to 60 minutes in something uplifting and inspirational before you start your day.

Just as vigorous physical exercise in the morning will prepare you to be stronger and more resilient *physically* during the day, positive mental exercise in the form of inspirational reading will prepare you to be more *mentally* fit during the day.

The first hour of the morning is called the "rudder of the day." Whatever you put into your mind in this "golden hour" sets the tone of your thinking for the rest of the day. When you get up in the morning and, instead of reading the newspaper or watching television, you read something positive, constructive, and inspiring, you preprogram your mind for the hours ahead.

Throughout the day, things will go better for you. You will be calmer, more creative, and more alert. You will be more resilient in the face of difficulties. You will respond more effectively when you face the inevitable ups and downs of your daily life. Your early-morning reading will have prepared you mentally to perform at your best.

■ LEAVE NOTHING TO CHANCE

You can become a more optimistic person by planning each day in advance. This exercise frees your mind from the stress of trying to remember what you have to do. It gives you a sense of control over your work and your life. It puts you in charge. You become proactive rather than reactive. And all it takes is a list!

The ideal time to plan is the night before. Make a list of everything you have to do the following day. Go over the list and organize your work by priority. Select your most important task so that you can start in on it first thing. You will be amazed at how much better you sleep and how much better you feel when you awaken if you have already preplanned your day so that you know what you are going to do and in what order.

■ START YOUR DAY RIGHT

Start your day with healthy, nutritious food. Eat more fruits, vegetables, and high-quality protein foods, such as eggs. Drink more fruit juice and water. Eat whole-grain breakfast cereals, muffins, and yogurt. Avoid fatty foods that are hard to digest, and which tire you out.

The standard American breakfast of bacon, eggs, and toast, is one of the very worst combinations you can eat in the morning. Within an hour after eating these foods you will start to become drowsy again. All the blood in your brain will rush to your stomach to try to break down these heavy, fatty, overcooked proteins, fats, and starches. You will then compensate by drinking coffee all morning to wake up.

But when you start each day with a light, healthy, nutritious breakfast, you will have more energy. You will be more alert and cheerful. You will be more eager to get on with the day. You will be more creative because more of your blood is available to your brain. You will be brighter and sharper. You will see more possibilities in everything that is going on around you. You will be a more optimistic person.

■ GET LOTS OF REST

In addition to good mental and physical nutrition, you need to get plenty of rest. Vince Lombardi, the legendary Green Bay Packers football coach, once said, "Fatigue doth make cowards of us all." When you are not getting enough rest, you are far more likely to be negative, irritable, and lacking in self-confidence.

But when you are fully rested and eating well, when you are feeding your mind with positive messages continually, when you are reading inspirationally and constantly visualizing your goals as a reality, you become a more positive, optimistic, and cheerful human being.

You will wake up in the morning with the feeling that there is nothing that you cannot do if you put your mind to it. If you hold that thought long enough and hard enough, it will become true in your life. You will begin to feel *unstoppable*.

ACTION EXERCISES

1. Resolve today to talk to yourself positively, using affirmations phrased in the positive, personal, present tense. Be your own cheerleader.

2. Make a set of three-by-five index cards with each of your goals written out in the form of an affirmation. Review these cards twice a day, morning and evening.

3. Look for something good in every problem or difficulty. Practice being an inverse paranoid, convinced that there is a vast conspiracy to make you successful.

4. Create a mental picture of your most important goal, exactly as if it were already a reality. If possible, cut pictures of your goal out of magazines and study them regularly to program them into your subconscious mind.

5. Get the feeling that would go with the success or the goal that you desire. Imagine that you have to pretend the emotion of joy, happiness, or satisfaction in an audition for a role in a movie. Fake it until you make it!

6. Imagine that your life was perfect in a particular area. What would it look like? How would you feel? How would you describe it?

7. Before falling asleep each night, mentally rehearse the key events of the coming day. Visualize and emotionalize them turning out perfectly in every way. Then go off to sleep with a smile on your face.

Chapter 11

Create Your Own Future

The miracle, or the power, that elevates the few is to be found in their industry, application, and perseverance under the promptings of a brave and determined spirit.

—Mark Twain

There can be no great courage where there is no confidence or assurance, and half the battle is in the conviction that we can do what we undertake.

—Orison Swett Marden

Every successful person has experienced countless temporary setbacks, obstacles, and even outright defeats, in the course of his or her life. But it has been the ability to respond positively and constructively to these defeats and to bounce back that ultimately has assured success. This quality of bouncing rather than breaking will determine your success as well.

Dr. Abraham Zaleznik of the Harvard Business School did a study some years ago on the role that *disappointment* plays in life. Many people had researched and written on motivation and its relationship to success. But Zaleznik was the first person who looked at the other side of the coin.

■ THINKING AHEAD

If you are a normal, intelligent person, you will organize each area of your life to avoid failure and disappointment as much as possible. You will think ahead and anticipate what could go wrong. You will then take the necessary precautions to guard against setbacks and problems. You will weigh and balance different options. You will select the course of action that offers the greatest likelihood of success.

Nonetheless, no matter how well you think and plan, things will not always turn out the way you expect. Murphy's Law says: *"Whatever can go wrong will go wrong. Of all the things that can go wrong, the worst possible thing will go wrong at the worst possible time and cost the most amount of money."* Cohen's Law then adds: *"Murphy was an optimist!"*

Therefore, disappointment comes unbidden. Disappointment comes in spite of your best efforts to avoid it. Disappointment is inevitable and unavoidable. As sure as the sun rises in the east and sets in the west, you are going to experience disappointments in life. And the more goals you set and the more things you try, the more difficulties and problems you will have.

■ THE ONE THING YOU CAN CONTROL

What Dr. Zaleznik discovered was that successful people *respond* to disappointment differently from unsuccessful people. His conclusion was that the way you deal with disappointment is an extremely good predictor of whether you will achieve success in your field, or in life overall.

Since you can't always avoid disappointment, no matter what you do, the only thing that matters is how you deal with the disappointment when it comes upon you, unwanted and unexpected. Do you let it overwhelm you? Do you blow up, become angry, and blame or attack other people? Or do you roll with the punches, and respond effectively?

Successful people deal with disappointment by taking it in stride. Unsuccessful people allow disappointment to stop them. Successful people recover and continue forward. Unsuccessful people often quit and go back. Motivational speaker Charlie Jones says, *"It's not how far you fall but how high you bounce that counts!"*

■ THE TRIGGER OF NEGATIVITY

Most negative emotions are triggered by *frustrated expectations.* You wish, hope, or plan for something to happen in a certain way, and when it doesn't, you react with impatience and anger. This is quite normal. If you care about a result, you are going to be hurt if you don't achieve it.

The challenge is that emotions are triggered instantaneously. For this reason, you can have very little control over your emotions and reactions at the moment that something happens to you. It is too late. When the disappointment occurs, you will react instinctively and habitually, depending on your previous experiences. When things go wrong, it is too late for you to think of fine and noble thoughts. You simply react.

Epictetus, the Greek Stoic philosopher, once wrote, "Circumstances do not make the man; they only reveal him to himself," and to others, for that matter. It is not the adverse situation that builds your character so much as it *reveals* your character as it exists at that moment.

■ PREPARE IN ADVANCE

One of the best ways to change your thinking, and your life, is to prepare for disappointment in advance. Set yourself up to bounce back quickly by practicing mental prepreparation.

Mental prepreparation enables you to prepare internally for the inevitable disappointments of life and work, even though you do not know what they are or when they will come. This is one of the most powerful of all thinking techniques that you can use to gain and keep control of your emotions, assuring that they are primarily positive and constructive, no matter what happens.

In mental prepreparation, you begin with the premise that you are going to face all kinds of problems and difficulties when you decide to accomplish anything worthwhile in life. In fact, if you set a big, challenging goal for yourself, one that forces you out of your comfort zone, you are going to meet with countless obstacles and difficulties that you cannot now imagine.

This trial by endurance seems to go with the territory. Every time you try to be or do something more or different, problems of all kinds will arise in your path. If you are not prepared in advance, they can discourage you and drive you back into your comfort zone.

Instead of waiting for the inevitable problems to occur, you mentally prepare for these inevitable difficulties before they happen. You say to yourself: *"Today I will face all kinds of ups and downs, difficulties and setbacks, but I will not let them get me down. Once I start toward my goal, I will be unstoppable!"*

■ PRACTICE CRISIS ANTICIPATION

In business consulting, we teach a way of thinking called "crisis anticipation." I encourage decision makers to look six months to a year into the future and ask the question, "What are some of the negative things that could happen that would derail our plans? Of all of them, what are the very worst things that could happen?"

We then make a list of all the different setbacks or unexpected emergencies that could occur that would threaten the enterprise. For example: A competitor could come out with a new product or service that was better and/or cheaper than ours. Interest rates could go up. Government could place new taxes and regulations on our activities. Costs of fuel or raw materials could increase. A key person or persons within the organization could depart for some reason. A key customer or customers could leave and go to a competitor. Competitors could cut their prices below costs in order to take business away. The economy could tip into recession and the overall market could shrink dramatically.

In each of these cases, the ability of the company to respond quickly and effectively could determine its very survival. These possible reversals and setbacks should be thought through in advance. The best rule is "no surprises!"

Royal Dutch/Shell of the Netherlands has one of the most complete forward planning processes of any company in the world. It has developed over 600 scenarios to deal with problems that might occur around the world in areas where it has oil and gas operations. As a result, the company is seldom surprised by anything that happens. It is never caught off guard. It always has a backup plan ready to go. It has also become one of the most continuously profitable and successful companies in the world. Thinking ahead really pays off.

■ LOOK INTO THE FUTURE

What works for large and small corporations can work for you as well. You should practice crisis anticipation regularly in everything you do. Look down the road of your life, like a traveler, and imagine some of the negative things that might happen and how you could respond to them. You will be amazed at how much more positive and confident you will feel when you have already developed alternative courses of action to some of the worst things that could happen in a particular area.

For example, what would you do if you lost your job today? The idea of losing one's job is a major fear for most people, affecting 37 percent of the working population according to one study. I received a letter recently from a gentleman who told me that his fear of losing his job, which he recognized was completely irrational, was so great that it was paralyzing him. It was actually holding him back from doing the kind of work that he had to do in order to *keep* his job. His fear and his lack of alternatives were actually increasing the likelihood that he would be laid off.

■ YOUR NEW JOB

Sometimes I ask people in my audiences, *"What is your next job going to be?"* For most people this question comes as a surprise. They have not even thought about what their next job is going to be. But we know that the world of work is changing at a rapid rate. The fact is that you have already changed jobs several times. It is virtually inevitable that you will change jobs again, and perhaps sooner than you expect. What is your next job likely to be?

When I explain that each person must be preparing for his or her next job, it is a new idea for most people. They either have not thought about it or don't want to think about it. But the only question is this: "What level of knowledge, skills, and ability will you require at your next job in order to continue to earn the kind of money that you want to earn in the future?"

If you don't think about this question in advance, you may be forced to think about it when your time has run out and the question is forced upon you.

■ YOUR NEW CAREER

After audience members have thought about what their next job is going to be, I then ask the second question, *"What is your next career going to be?"* What entirely new field, industry, business, or line of work are you going to be in 5 to 10 years from now?

According to employment experts, a person starting work today will have an average of 14 or 15 full-time jobs, each lasting two years or more, over the course of a working lifetime. He or she will also have as many as five different careers, in completely different fields, each of which will require new kinds of knowledge and different skills.

Much of what you know about your current work will be obsolete within five years. Because of rapid changes taking place in every area, your existing store of knowledge, information, ideas, and skills will be of little value. These will have no relevance or application to the job market and the economy of the future. You will need new knowledge and skills if you want to survive and thrive in an increasingly competitive society.

This is why Peter Drucker said, "The only skill that will not become obsolete in the years ahead is the ability to learn new skills."

■ CONTINUALLY THINK AHEAD

You probably recall the famous comment by hockey star Wayne Gretzky. When he was asked by a reporter for the secret of his success on the ice, he replied by saying, *"Most players are pretty good, but they go to where the puck is. I go to where the puck is going to be."*

This observation is directly relevant to you. Where is *your* puck going to be three to five years from now? Where is your puck going to be 10 years from now? Taking a long-term perspective on your work life enables you to make better decisions in the short term. As strategic planner Michael Kami says, *"Those who do not think about the future cannot have one."*

Look into your future and begin to imagine and anticipate some of the twists and turns that might occur. If you lost your job today, how would you react? What would be your first thought? The great majority of people, when they think about losing their jobs, go into a form of panic. They have no idea what they would do.

However, in my work with many thousands of *successful* people, I have found that they have one particular attitude in common. They all know with complete assurance that if they lost their jobs they could walk across the street and get another job tomorrow. They are so good at what they do, and so confident in their abilities, that job loss to them would be merely an inconvenience. They have lots of options.

As I mentioned in Chapter 6, there is a way to determine how good you are in your field. What is the number of job offers you get on a regular basis? Just as a store or restaurant can measure its success by the number of customers or patrons it attracts, you can measure how valued and respected you are for what you do by counting the number of people who want to hire you and use your services. How are you doing?

■ EXPECT THE UNEXPECTED

Sometimes I ask audiences what they would do if their entire industry disappeared overnight. They shake their heads and they say that can't possibly happen. Then I point out that the defense industry in California literally collapsed in the early 1990s and over 400,000 highly competent defense engineers and executives, with many years of education and experience, were rendered obsolete. Their jobs were not only gone; they were gone forever. Each of these thousands of competent, capable men and women were forced into the position of going out into the marketplace, developing new skills, and going to work in entirely new fields.

The collapse of the dot-com mania wiped out more than 90 percent of the Internet jobs and companies that had sprung up across the country. The collapse in the telecom sector led to layoffs of many thousands of workers. The decline in recent years of the frantic investment activity that had been seen during the 1990s triggered the layoffs and firings of tens of thousands of people in the financial services industries. It goes on and on, and will continue. Only the names of the industries will change. This rapid shift in jobs and industries is going to happen more and more often to more and more people.

■ YOUR FINANCIAL LIFE

The world of finance and investments is constantly changing. The markets are increasingly volatile. The old philosophy of "buy and hold" is no longer relevant to the world of today, and tomorrow. If you have money invested, you should be thinking continually about what might happen if your investments went bad and you lost all your money. You should always be preparing against the worst possible outcome of a particular investment.

There is a direct relationship between how much time you invest in thinking about and planning your financial life and how likely you are to become financially independent. According to Dr. Thomas Stanley's interviews with thousands of self-made millionaires, they share a common characteristic: they spend far more time thinking about financial matters than the average person.

The average adult, even though he or she worries about money much of the time, spends only two to three hours per month actually thinking about his or her finances, usually at bill-paying time. The average *affluent* American, in contrast, spends 20 to 30 hours per month thinking about his or her money. As a result, they make far better spending decisions and more intelligent investments than the majority. They become increasingly skilled in money matters, and eventually pull ahead of their peers.

■ THE STRATEGY OF NAPOLEON

The French general Napoleon dominated the continent of Europe for almost 20 years. He led his armies to victory in dozens of battles, and lost only three battles in his entire career. He lost almost 600,000 men when he invaded Russia, failing to anticipate the cold of the Russian winter. Greatly weakened from the Russian campaign, he subsequently lost the battle of Leipzig, which led to his being exiled to the island of Elba. And finally, he lost at the battle of Waterloo due to a series of miscommunications with his field generals.

It is often forgotten that he won many other battles, small and large, and is considered to be one of the three greatest military geniuses of history. (Alexander the Great and Genghis Khan were the other two.) Napoleon had developed a quality that helped him to achieve victory, which you also can develop. It is called *extrapolatory thinking*. This is the ability to think and plan several moves ahead in whatever you are doing. This way of thinking involves your considering every possible event that could occur, and then making provisions for them, well in advance.

Napoleon personally felt that his thoroughness and depth of preparation, carefully considering every detail, were his key to victory. This quality was demonstrated by his phenomenal ability to arrive onto the field of a potential battle and then to think through every single possible twist and turn of the battle to its logical conclusion—before the first shot was fired.

Once he had completed his preparations, he could take his position at his command center to direct the battle. No matter what news he received from any part of the battlefield, he was always ready with an immediate response. Many people thought that his quickness of response under fire was because he was a brilliant thinker, which he was, but that was not the secret of his success. His secret was that he had thought through every possible eventuality, in advance.

■ EXTRAPOLATE FROM THE PRESENT

This ability, to think through every major situation in your life in advance, is a way of thinking that you can learn with practice. The better you become at anticipating future events based on current facts, the better your life will be. You will be able to minimize reversals and maximize opportunities. Thinking this way will give you an edge over others who simply react and respond to whatever happens.

If you work for a company, you should be thinking through the worst possible things that could happen in the next six months to a year that could affect your job and your security. If you own the company, you should identify the worst possible things that could affect the survival and health of your enterprise. You and your spouse should discuss possible problems and difficulties that might occur in your family life, and then make plans to guard against them.

■ TAKE NECESSARY FINANCIAL PRECAUTIONS

You often read about people who failed to insure properly and consequently lost their cars, their homes, and sometimes all of their possessions. They failed to look into the future and ask what the consequences to their life would be if a fire occurred in their home or if they had a traffic accident and they were not sufficiently insured.

One of the smartest things that you can do to preserve your financial well-being is to develop a regular savings program. Your goal should be to save 10 percent and more of your income, off the top, each month, from each paycheck or income source. There are few things that will give a greater sense of confidence and control than for you to know that you have a cash reserve set aside in the event of an unexpected emergency. In contrast, there is nothing that will cause you more stress and tension than to be living on the edge of your financial resources, unable to deal with a financial emergency or a need of any kind.

W. Clement Stone once said, *"If you cannot save money, then the seeds of greatness are not in you."*

■ LIVE WITHIN YOUR INCOME

Your ability to save money and to discipline yourself to live within your income is a key measure of your ability to succeed in life. If you do not have the *internal* self-control to refrain from spending everything you earn, this suggests that you probably don't have the discipline necessary to succeed in other areas of your life. Although the Bible says that the love of money is the root of all evil, it is far more likely that the *lack* of money is the root of all evil.

Perhaps the greatest benefit of saving your money and building up a cash reserve is that it enables you to take advantage of opportunities when they arise, as they always do. In the movie *Field of Dreams*, a profound idea was expressed: *"If you build it, they will come."* In the financial world, this means that if you accumulate money through hard work and saving, you will attract into your life opportunities to invest that money to earn even more.

■ BECOMING A MONEY MAGNET

The Law of Attraction is very powerful in monetary matters. When you save even a small amount of money and put it in a bank account or a carefully chosen mutual fund, you create a certain force field of energy around that money. This energy somehow begins to attract even more money into your life. As your savings and investments grow, the magnetic power of your money grows even stronger. The more money you accumulate, the more money that will be attracted to you, and the more opportunities you will have to accumulate even more.

When you think about your money and the pleasure it gives you to have money in the bank, you increase the energy field around your money and you attract even more. This force field becomes even more powerful when you love your money. When you think about your growing financial reserves with intense happiness, you intensify the energy around your money and you attract even more.

When people say that *it takes money to make money,* they are right in two special ways. First, your ability to save money and build up a nest egg is a measure of whether you have the ability to earn even more money and whether you can be trusted with money. Second, when you put together even a small amount of money, you will attract opportunities to accumulate an even larger amount.

■ A SUCCESS STORY

A participant came up to me at a seminar recently and asked if I remembered him. I told him that unfortunately I spoke to too many people each year to remember all of them. He reminded me that he had attended my two-day seminar about six years before. He was quite shy so he waited at the lunch break until everyone had left. He then told me about a most remarkable series of events that had happened to him since the seminar.

When he came to my seminar, he was a used car salesman. He had two children and was in his early thirties. He was earning an average income and was up to his neck in debt. He was living in a rented house with his family.

At the seminar, he decided that his biggest source of worry was the fact that he was in debt and had no money in the bank. So he set a goal to get out of debt and to save $30,000 over the next five years. This was a huge goal for him, considering his circumstances and his past. He had not been out of debt since his teens.

■ TAKING ACTION

Nonetheless, in faith, he wrote down his goal, made a plan, and began working on it every day. This decision activated his mental powers. Because of the Law of Correspondence, the Law of Attraction, and the Law of Subconscious Activity, among others, things began to change for him far faster than he had imagined. He actually achieved his financial goal in only three years. He was out of debt and had $30,000 in the bank.

One day, his boss, the owner of the dealership, called him in and asked him if he was interested in a business opportunity. He was quite flattered and asked his boss to explain. His boss said that he had observed how much better he had become as a salesman, and he had also heard that he had saved up some money from his income.

This salesman was shy and cautious, and asked his boss what he had in mind. His boss told him that he had been approached by the automobile manufacturer in Detroit and asked to recommend someone who would be interested in opening a new car dealership in the same city in a growing part of town. The boss said he was willing to recommend him, and back him in this dealership. He would go in with him as a full partner if he were willing to put in his money as well.

The final outcome of this story was that his boss helped him set up the new dealership; he helped him with all the purchasing, inventory, parts, service department decisions, and staffing. After two years, his boss sold the half share back to him, so he ended up owning the dealership 100 percent.

Then he said to me, "And today, I'm a millionaire." He said, "Six years ago I was a used car salesman, and today I am a millionaire." He was one of the happiest people I've ever met. He said if he had not taken that advice from the seminar and begun saving his money and getting out of debt, he would not have been in a position to take advantage of that opportunity when it came along. He said, "Taking your seminar probably saved me 20 years of hard work, and maybe even a lifetime."

This story applies to your life as well. One of the most important actions that you can take to remain positive and optimistic is to prepare mentally, financially, and physically in advance. Think through what might possibly happen and make plans to prepare for opportunities. Make plans and put aside reserves to minimize or escape the consequences of a financial setback. This way of thinking, of planning ahead in every area, is a mark of the superior individual.

■ TWO MAGIC QUESTIONS

Here are two questions that you can ask to turn failure into success. I call these the magic questions because of the incredible power they have to improve your life. You can ask them and benefit from them after every experience.

The first question is, *"What did I do right?"* No matter what you do, or how it turns out, whether it is a success or a failure, you should do an instant mental replay of the event and assess everything that you did right in that situation.

Even if it turns out badly, or was a complete failure, there were always things that you did that were *correct*. If you can isolate the positive parts of your performance and write them down, you will be preprogramming your mind to repeat the things that you did right in the next similar situation.

The second magic question is, *"What would I do differently?"* This is an excellent question because it forces you to think positively about what happened and how you could do better. Ask yourself, if you had to do it over again, how would you *change* or *improve* your performance or behavior in that situation? What would you do more of or less of?

Be sure to write down your answers. This ensures that you capture them before you forget. Each time you try something new or different, immediately sit down with a pad of paper and answer those two questions: "What did I do right?" and "What would I do differently?" Both of these questions are positive and they both require positive responses. Your answers prepare you, consciously and unconsciously, to do even better next time. Both sets of answers keep you focused on improvement rather than regret.

■ POSITIVE VERSUS NEGATIVE THINKING

Both winners and losers examine how they performed after an important event. But underachievers almost invariably rehash the *mistakes* they have made, the expenses they have incurred, and the failures they have experienced. High achievers, in contrast, those who think positively about themselves and their lives, are constantly reviewing the *best parts* of their performance and making plans to repeat those actions the next time.

When you think about what you did right and what you could do differently next time, your mind will be completely positive. Your creativity will be stimulated. You will see all kinds of opportunities and possibilities for improvement that you would have missed completely if you allowed yourself to feel sorry for yourself after an unsuccessful event.

■ BUSINESS AND SALES

If you are in *business*, you should ask these questions regularly of yourself and your key staff: *"What did we do right?"* and *"What would we do differently next time?"* Remember, most things you try will be unsuccessful the first few times. By asking these questions, you extract the greatest value possible from the situation. Treat every experience as an opportunity to learn something that can help you next time.

If you are in *sales*, use this method after every sale. Immediately after a sales call, successful or not, ask the magic questions. This quick review will dramatically increase the speed at which you learn and grow as a sales professional.

Make this instant replay a part of your life. Use this method repeatedly so that it becomes automatic. No matter how disappointing the setback or difficulty may be, you will soon be preprogrammed to learn the most from the situation and to extract every kernel of good that you can possibly get from it.

When you combine this method with mindstorming—forcing yourself to generate 20 answers to each question—you will be absolutely astonished at the number of great ideas and insights for growth and improvement you will come up with. These ideas will dramatically increase the speed at which you become one of the best in your field.

■ THE EDISON APPROACH

Thomas Edison, the greatest inventor of the modern age, was convinced that experimentation was simply a *process of elimination*. He therefore kept accurate records of every experiment. Once he had decided that an invention was possible, he dedicated himself to eliminating the ways that wouldn't work until the only method left standing was the *one way* that would work. As a result, he became the greatest inventor of the modern age and one of the wealthiest businessmen in the country. You should do the same.

From now on, each time you try and fail, shrug it off as a *learning experience* that just moved you one step closer to success. As Henry Ford once said, *"Failure is merely an opportunity to more intelligently begin again."*

■ YOUR RECOVERY RATE

When you experience a disappointment of any kind, your natural reaction is to feel stunned emotionally. You feel as though you have been punched in your *emotional* solar plexus. You feel hurt, let down, disappointed, and discouraged. You occasionally feel like quitting altogether and doing something completely different. These feelings are normal and natural when you experience frustration or failure of any kind. The only question is, how long do they last?

When you go to a doctor or clinic for a complete medical exam, you will often be given a stress test. First, they will take your pulse at your resting heart rate. Then they will ask you to do some aerobic exercises to raise your heart rate. Once your heart rate is up to a particular point, they will measure it again. They will wait one, two, and five minutes after the exercise, and again take your pulse. The mark of how fit you are is how rapidly your heart returns to its resting pulse rate after exercise.

■ BOUNCING BACK

With your personality, it is the same. The mark of how mentally healthy you are can be measured by how quickly you recover after experiencing a disappointment. Of course, a setback or reversal will hurt. It always hurts if what you are trying to do is important to you. But that's not the main point. The main point is how quickly you bounce back. Your recovery rate is everything. If you plan in advance for setbacks and problems, and preprogram your mind the way we have described in this chapter, your recovery rate will be much faster.

Your recovery rate is under your control. It is completely determined by the way you think about what happens to you. It is not the event itself that affects you, but rather the way that you interpret the event to yourself. And this is very much a choice you make.

■ YOUR INNER DIALOGUE

Here are several powerful affirmations that you can use to take immediate mental and emotional control over a negative situation. These words quickly neutralize any negative feelings you might have.

The first thing you say when something goes wrong is the words: "I am responsible!"

Your natural tendency when something goes wrong will be to become angry and upset and either blame someone or something else or make excuses. But the moment you say, "I am responsible!" you stop blaming someone else for the problem. By accepting responsibility, even if it is only for the way you react, you short-circuit your feelings of disappointment, anger, and frustration. The instant you say, "I am responsible!" your mind becomes calm and clear again. You begin to think of positive, constructive things you can do to minimize the damage or to maximize the opportunity.

■ INTERPRET IT POSITIVELY

Here is an affirmation that has been extraordinarily helpful to me over the years. No matter what has happened, and no matter how disappointed I am, I immediately say, *"Every experience is a positive experience if I view it as an opportunity for growth and self-mastery."*

This statement enables you to assert control over your emotions. It forces you to think about how you can learn and grow from this problem. Like the statement "I am responsible," these words give you a sense of control and personal power in any situation. *"Every situation is a positive situation if I view it as an opportunity for growth and self-mastery."*

You then look into the situation and ask yourself what you can possibly learn from what has just happened. How can you grow as a result of this difficulty? What has this situation been sent to teach you? If you had a divine force that was controlling your destiny, and this force was sending you specific learning experiences to help you to be successful, what lessons could you find in your current problem?

■ ONE THOUGHT AT A TIME

Your mind can hold only one thought at a time, positive or negative. If you are constructively looking for a solution for or a valuable lesson from every difficulty, you can't be upset or angry at the same time. If you apply the Law of Substitution and deliberately force yourself to think about the positive aspects of the situation, you will always find them. You will then be able to turn them to your advantage.

A positive mental attitude, which means a positive and constructive response to disappointments and setbacks, is largely determined by your feeling a *sense of control*. Having a sense of control means that you feel you are in control of your own life. You feel that you are in charge. You feel that you are in the driver's seat. You feel that you are on top of things.

■ THINK ABOUT YOUR GOALS

One of the most powerful ways to bounce back from failure is to put the negative situation into its proper perspective. Remember, failure is never final. Most mistakes that you make are small relative to the great scheme of things. If you think back, you will probably not even be able to remember what it was you were worrying about a year ago, much less three, four, or five years ago.

The key to your having a sense of control is for you to develop and maintain a clear sense of direction. This sense of direction comes from having clear, specific, written goals. One of the most powerful ways to keep your mind positive is to simply *think about your goals*. When something goes wrong, think about your goals. When you lose a sale, or even a job, think about your goals. When an investment fails or a business deal falls through, think about your goals.

Your long-term goals are to be financially independent, to enjoy excellent health, to have wonderful relationships, and to do work that makes a difference in the world, among others.

When you keep your mind on these goals, and on what you are doing to achieve each of these goals, you will find that it is almost impossible to feel upset or angry. Thinking about your goals empowers you and makes you a more positive and confident person.

■ THINK IN TERMS OF CYCLES AND TRENDS

Look at your life as a series of cycles and trends. Think in terms of regular ups and downs. Think in terms of summers and winters, falls and springs. When you develop this long-term perspective and you see things that happen as part of a larger pattern, you will not be too caught up in short-term fluctuations of your fortunes. You become much more capable of responding effectively to little problems and difficulties of day-to-day life. You can put things into proper perspective.

The sigmoid curve, which looks like an "S" lying on its side, explains much of human life. It has three phases. In the first phase, you are struggling and working hard to figure things out and get established. This is true for a job, a relationship, a new business start-up, or the introduction of a new product or service.

The second phase comes after you have learned the critical lessons of phase one. This is the growth phase, where you make great progress and get excellent results. Your business expands, your products and services sell well, your career takes off, and your relationships are at their best.

Then comes phase three, the decline phase, which follows phase two just as the winter follows the harvest season. In this phase, it becomes harder and harder to get the same results and satisfactions as in phase two. Sales and profitability are harder to achieve. Your job or relationship is no longer as enjoyable. Your company struggles to survive or thrive.

Which phase are you in today, in each of the important areas of your life and work? What could you do to get into or back into phase two, the growth phase? What are the cycles and trends in your life and business?

■ "DENIAL" IS NOT A RIVER IN EGYPT

Many of our problems in dealing with setbacks and disappointments come from our resisting reality. We engage in denial. We become angry and insist that this should not have happened to us or should not have happened at all. We reject it and wish that it hadn't occurred in the first place.

It is this resistance and denial that causes most of our stress. When you say, *"What can't be cured must be endured,"* you lower your flash point. You become more relaxed. You become calmer and you develop a more detached perspective. You stand back and you look at the situation as though it were happening to someone else. As a result you become more constructive about how the situation can best be resolved. You don't allow yourself to become emotionally involved in every little thing that happens to you.

Abraham Lincoln wrote, *"Most people are just about as happy as they make up their minds to be."* In the Foundation for Inner Peace's *Course in Miracles*, it says, *"You give meaning to everything you see."* Without the meaning or emotion that you attach to an event or circumstance, it has no emotional significance for you. And you can change the meaning by controlling your thinking. You can even eliminate its negative effect on you altogether by refusing to become emotionally involved in a short-term setback. It is up to you.

■ THE DECIDING FACTOR

Your ability to deal with disappointment in a positive, constructive way will do more to enable you to succeed and say more about you to other people than any other single factor. This is a learned ability, acquired by practice. Effective men and women are invariably those who have developed the ability to respond constructively to the large and small crises that occur unbidden, unexpectedly, and unavoidably. You must do the same.

Decide in advance that, no matter what happens, nothing will ever stop you. Decide in advance that, although you will have countless ups and downs in the course of your life, you will keep on persisting until you win through to your goals. When you make this decision in advance, you will be ready. When you engage in mental prepreparation, you will be fast on your feet when the inevitable problems appear, and be ready to bounce instead of break. You will be virtually *unstoppable*.

ACTION EXERCISES

1. Resolve that you will bounce rather than break. Examine your biggest disappointment in life right now and determine how you can learn or benefit from it.

2. Identify the three worst things that could happen to you in the months ahead. What is your plan to avoid or minimize their possible negative effects?

3. Select your biggest worry or problem right now and determine how you can learn and grow from this difficulty. What is the most important lesson that it contains?

4. Practice the Edison approach to life. Calmly accept that every temporary setback is merely a way of identifying a way that does not work. Therefore, it is a success.

5. No matter what happens, think about your goals and what you can do right now to achieve them. Get busy.

6. Identify the trends in your business. Which way is the market going? If things continue the way they are today, what decisions or changes will you have to make?

7. Ask two questions about your most recent important experience: What did you do right? And what would you do differently next time? Resolve to learn every possible lesson from every setback or difficulty.

Chapter 12

Live A Great Life

The only true measure of success is the ratio between
what we might have done and what we might have
been on the one hand, and the things we have done
and the things we have made of ourselves on
the other.

—H. G. Wells

The Law of Correspondence is perhaps the most important of all laws in determining your success or failure in life. As we've discussed in previous chapters, this law says that your outer world is a reflection of your inner world. It says that whatever you are on the *inside*, you will soon see the results of it on the *outside*. When you change your thinking, you change your life.

This law applies to everything you do. Your inner world of knowledge and preparation will determine your outer world of income and career success. Your inner world of personality development will determine your outer world of friendships and relationships. Your inner attitudes toward health and fitness will determine the condition of your physical body. Your inner beliefs and expectations will determine your outer attitudes and your behaviors toward other people. Your outer world will always reflect your inner world.

222

■ HAPPINESS IS THE SUPREME GOAL

Aristotle, perhaps the greatest of the philosophers, wrote more than 2,300 years ago that the ultimate aim of all human action is *happiness*. He concluded that everything a person does is to achieve happiness of some kind. Sometimes they are successful, and sometimes they are unsuccessful, but happiness is always the target each person aims at.

He concluded that every act is merely an interim step in the direction of happiness. For example, you want to get a good job. Why? So you can earn good money. Why? So you can get a comfortable home and a nice car. Why? So you can have good relationships and a nice family. Why? So that you can have a satisfying home life. Why? The final answer, the ultimate goal, is so that you can be *happy*. Everything that you or anyone else does is aimed at happiness, however you define it and however successful you are at achieving it.

■ THE ROLE OF GOODNESS

One of Aristotle's greatest insights on the subject of happiness was his conclusion that "Only the good can be happy, and only the virtuous can be good."

This is one of the most important observations in the history of human thought and experience. "Only the good can be happy, and only the virtuous can be good."

What I have found in my many years of research into philosophy and psychology is that only people who are genuinely good inside can be happy for any period of time. And in my years of study of the foundation qualities of self-confidence, I have found that only men and women with clear, positive values are able to develop the kind of unshakable self-confidence that makes it possible for them to deal effectively with anything that happens to them.

The fastest way for you to build or to regain your self-confidence is to become absolutely clear about your deepest values and convictions, and then begin to live by them. The solution to almost all human problems is a return to values. In many ways, your unhappiness and stress are caused by your drifting away from doing and saying the things that you know are right.

■ INTEGRITY IS ESSENTIAL

The most important single quality for success is the quality of *integrity*. Aristotle insisted that only a life based on values such as integrity, honesty, courage, generosity, persistence, and sincerity would lead to happiness and personal fulfillment.

I used to think of integrity as only one of the key values, equal to and separate from the others. Then one day a wise and wealthy man pointed out to me that *integrity is really the value that guarantees all the others. Integrity is the foundation value on which all of your other values are based. Having true integrity means that you always live and act consistently with your values. If you lack integrity, you will compromise your other values at the slightest temptation.*

■ CLARIFY YOUR VALUES

In our strategic planning sessions, both for corporations and for individuals, we start off by asking people to define and clarify their values. You must do the same in your own personal strategic planning. What are *your values*? What is it that you believe in? What do you stand for? What will you *not* stand for?

Your ability to clearly define your values is the starting point of your developing the kind of character that causes people to want to be associated with you and which will lead you inevitably to enjoying a good life. When you have a fine and noble character, rooted in solid, life-affirming values, you will be a genuinely good person. As a result, you will be happy inside, no matter what is going on around you.

■ ORGANIZE YOUR VALUES

Once you have defined your values, you should organize them in order of priority. To start, you need only three to five key values to create a foundation for your character and personality. These are the values that you personally consider to be more important than any others. The order in which you arrange your values is terribly important as well. This ranking of values largely determines the kind of person you are, and the kind of life you live.

Everything you do is the result of a choice. You are constantly making choices of one kind or another, to do one thing or to do something else. This ability to make choices distinguishes you from all other creatures. Each choice you make is based on your primary values at that time. Each action is based on what you consider to be the most important value at that moment of choice.

■ ACT ON YOUR VALUES

When you choose, your higher-order values always take precedence over your lower-order values. Every act you take, every decision you make, is based on your dominant value at that time. You can do only one thing at a time, and you always have to choose what it is going to be. You always choose what is most valuable to you at that particular moment.

How can you tell what your values are? It's simple. Your values are only and always expressed in your *actions*. It is what you *do* rather than what you *say* that tells you, and others, what you value most. Especially, it is what you do *under pressure*, when you are forced to choose, that reveals your true values and beliefs about yourself and the world around you.

■ THE DETERMINANT OF PERSONALITY

Both your choice of values and the order of your values are critical in determining your personality and your life. Here is an example. Imagine that two people have each been through a values clarification exercise and settled upon the same three values. Only the order is different.

Person A has decided that his top three values, in order of importance, are first, family; second, health; and third, career success. This person is saying that he puts his family ahead of his health and career, and his health ahead of his career. This means that if he has to choose between family and career, family comes first. If he has to choose between health and career, health comes first.

Person B has the same three values, except that his values are in a slightly different order. His first value is career success. His second value is his family, and his third value is health.

This means that Person B will put his career ahead of his family if he has to choose. He will put his career and his family ahead of his health if he has to choose.

■ THE BIG QUESTION

Now here are some questions for you. Will there be a difference between Person A and Person B? Will there be a *small* difference or a *large* difference? Would you prefer to be friends with Person A or with Person B? Would you be able to tell Person A from Person B if you met them socially or in business?

The answer is that Person B, who chooses career success as his primary value, will be a totally different human being from Person A, who decides that his family is most important to him. The order of family, health, and career is a life-enriching organization of values. A person who lives his life consistent with these values will be a far happier person than a person who places his career ahead of his family and especially ahead of his health. This is why you must select both your values and their order of importance with care. Your values and their order determine your whole life.

■ INTEGRITY IS A WAY OF LIVING

Once you have determined your values, your level of integrity can be measured by how rigidly you adhere to them. A value is not something that you compromise when it is convenient. Either you have it or you do not. Your choice of values and your resolution to live by those values form your character and your personality.

Throughout history, great men and women have been men and women of character. They have been people who lived on the basis of high and noble values. They have been honored and respected for the values they stood for and represented.

One of the great problems in our society today is the phenomenon of "situational values" or "situational ethics." These are the result of people changing their ideas of right and wrong depending on the situation, and often the temptation of the moment. What is even worse is when they fool themselves into believing that they are people of character when they are really only people of convenience.

■ WHAT YOU DO UNDER PRESSURE

Situational values are demonstrated when people say they believe in one thing, but they do another. They say that they believe in telling the truth, but then they lie when it is convenient, or excuse the lies of another. An individual is defined by what he or she *does*, not what he or she *says*.

Some people are confused by their emotions. They believe that if their *intentions* are sincere, their *actions* don't matter. They feel that if they wish or hope something, it is the same as actually doing it. But it is only what you actually do when you are forced to choose, especially under pressure, that tells you who you really are inside.

It is vital to your success and happiness that you are impeccably *honest* with everyone you know and deal with, both in your personal life and in your career. There is nothing that will earn you the support of people faster than for you to develop the reputation of being a person of character and integrity. At the same time, there is nothing that will damage your reputation and sabotage your career faster than for you to get the reputation of being the kind of person that others cannot trust or rely on.

■ BE TRUE TO YOURSELF

Honesty means that you are always true to the very best that is in you. As Polonius says in Shakespeare's *Hamlet*, *"To thine own self be true, and it must follow, as the night the day, thou canst not then be false to any man."*

Being true to yourself is the starting point of developing a great character. This begins with your always living in truth with yourself. You do not delude yourself or play games with your own mind. You don't try to believe things that are completely impossible. You don't hope and pray that things would be different than they are. You deal with the world as it is, not as you wish it were.

■ ALWAYS DO YOUR BEST

Every job bears the signature of the person who did it. Being true to yourself means that you always do your very best at whatever job or responsibility you take on. Honesty and integrity on the inside are expressed as quality and excellence in your work on the outside. You can tell what you are made of on the inside by the amount of time and attention that you put into doing the very best job possible at everything that is given to you to do. Don't take it on unless you are willing to do it in an excellent fashion.

Integrity means that you are always truthful, straightforward, and honest with everyone in your life. Just as you are true to yourself, you are true to others as well. You *live in truth* with others, at home and at work.

If you ask people whether they are honest, almost everyone will say that they are. Most people do not lie, cheat, steal, or engage in dishonest behaviors of any kind. But being truly honest means that you are honest with everyone in your life. This means that not only do you never lie; you never *live* a lie. You never stay in a situation that is wrong for you or in a condition that undermines your integrity or makes you unhappy. You never compromise your integrity by biting your lip and refusing to say what you truly think and feel.

■ YOUR HIGHEST GOAL

One of the hallmarks of the truly honest person is that they set *peace of mind* as their highest goal. Once you have set peace of mind as your primary aim in life, you organize your other goals and activities around it. Being truly honest means that you refuse to compromise your peace of mind for anything or anyone. You only do and say the things that you feel to be right in every situation.

Honesty and integrity mean that you listen to yourself and that you trust your *inner voice*. You listen to your intuition and you let it guide you to do and say the right things at the right time. When you are disturbed or unhappy, you sit quietly by yourself in solitude, waiting and listening for the guidance that always comes. When you get an idea or insight into the right thing to do, you put it into action. You trust your higher mind. This is the key to living in truth with yourself and others.

■ THE INTEGRITY OF YOUR OWN MIND

Ralph Waldo Emerson, in his essay "Self-Reliance," said, *"Guard your integrity as a sacred thing."* He went on to say, *"Nothing is at last sacred but the integrity of your own mind."*

Truthfulness is the indispensable requirement for the development of character, and the development of character must be a central aim of your life. Aristotle said, *"The purpose of education is the development of the character of the young."* Today, in the United States, many young people have not been brought up with a clear sense of right and wrong. Many people have been told that values are *relative*. Many people have been told, for example, that if they like to shoplift, then that particular value is just as good as a person who believes that shoplifting is wrong.

This form of value relativity leads down a blind alley. It leads to failure, frustration, and unhappiness. The fact is that values are not relative. There are values that are *life-enhancing* and there are values that are *life-destroying*. If a value is positive, living by it improves the quality of your life and your relationships with others. A negative value hurts your relationships and detracts from the quality of your life. You can easily tell the difference, because living by a positive value makes you feel happy, and practicing a negative value makes you feel unhappy.

■ FACE THE TRUTH

Living in truth means that you face the truth about yourself and the world around you. You face the truth about your work and your relationships. You look yourself directly in the eye and you live consistently with your innermost convictions. You do not play games with yourself or wish and hope that things could be different than they are.

Integrity means that you accept that your world can only get better when *you* get better. No one is going to come along and change things for you. If you want things to change, you are going to have to make the changes yourself.

Integrity means that you accept that your marriage gets better only when you become a better spouse. Your business gets better only when you become a better manager or executive. Your sales results and customers get better only when you become a better salesperson. Your financial life improves only when you become more intelligent and disciplined about money.

■ ACCEPT PEOPLE THE WAY THEY ARE

Especially, honesty means that you accept people the way they are, not demanding that they be the way you want. You do not go through life wishing, hoping, and expecting that people will change and be different so as to suit you. One of the basic principles of human life is that, with few exceptions, *people don't change*.

In fact, under pressure, people not only do not change, but they become even more of what they already are inside. If a person has a difficult personality, under pressure he will become even more difficult. If someone is stubborn or inflexible, when she is put under pressure she will become even more stubborn and inflexible. If a person is slightly dishonest, when he is subjected to pressure or temptation he will become totally dishonest. People don't change.

■ BUSINESS AND COMPETITION

Honesty in our fast-moving world also means that you see the world of business and competition as it is, not as you wish it were, especially with regard to the explosion of information and technology. Many people think that they can make a token effort to keep up with the growth of knowledge in their field and the growth of technology in their work. But this minimum effort is not acceptable to the honest person. The truly honest person realizes that today you have to *run* just to stay in the same place. The truly honest person realizes that knowledge is doubling in every field every two to three years, and this means that your knowledge has to double every two to three years as well.

Jack Welch, the past president and CEO of General Electric, once said, "If the rate of change outside your organization is greater than the rate of change inside your organization, the end is in sight." This principle applies to you as a person as well. If you are not continually learning and upgrading your skills, you are in danger of becoming obsolete.

■ WHAT ARE YOU WORTH?

All over the country today, people are being laid off or fired by the thousands, and even hundreds of thousands, each year. In many cases, these people have allowed their levels of knowledge and skill to decline to the point where their companies could no longer afford to keep them on the payroll.

Many of them were not completely honest with themselves. They did not continually upgrade their knowledge and skills so they could continue to add more and more value to their companies. They hoped that the dramatic changes taking place in the national and international economies would not affect them. And as a result, they got caught in the layoffs when the market for their products or services slowed down.

It takes the average white-collar professional two to seven months to find another job, usually taking a pay cut of 14 to 40 percent. Some people get laid off from highly paid jobs and never make that kind of money again. And if they don't get busy upgrading their knowledge and skills, it can happen again.

■ FOCUS ON ADDING VALUE

Honesty means that you accept that your income is totally determined by your ability to contribute value to your company and, through your company, to your customers. An individual must generate three dollars of bottom-line profit for every dollar of salary or income that the person earns from the company. If you are not currently generating three dollars of profit or cost savings to the bottom line for your company, your job is a prime candidate for outsourcing, downsizing, or eliminating. Honesty means that you accept this as a fact and then do everything in your power to maintain and increase your value.

True honesty means that you never expect to get out more than you put in. You never expect to get something for nothing. You don't gamble or buy lottery tickets, which in a way is an act of dishonesty. It is an attempt to get something that you have not earned. The truly honest person never attempts to get rewards without working, or to get rich quick or easy.

In the United States today, millions of people are attracted to the *quick fix*. If they are employees or executives, they want new and better jobs, and they want them immediately. They are always looking for shortcuts, and as a result they are always frustrated and unhappy.

They hope that problems that have taken many months and years to develop can be solved with a *silver bullet* of some kind. They are impatient and they want immediate results. But being an honest person requires that you resist the temptation of the quick fix in any part of your life.

■ TRUST IS THE GLUE

Relationships are central to a happy, healthy, satisfying life. All relationships are based on *trust*. Trust is the glue that holds relationships together. You can have all kinds of problems and disagreements with another person, but as long as the trust and respect are still there, the relationship can endure. But, if anything ever happens to the trust, the relationship can fall apart quickly, like a house of cards collapsing.

All business relationships are based on trust. All relationships that involve money are dependent on the word of the borrower or the creditor. All relationships with your bankers, your suppliers, your customers, your staff, and everyone else in your financial world are based on that critical element of trust.

Men and women of high integrity are fastidious about the levels of trust that they have built and maintained. They are careful about their credit, and about their financial commitments and arrangements. They always keep their word. They are careful about their banking relationships, their credit cards, their bills, and any money that they owe at any time.

■ A TALE OF TWO BANKRUPTCIES

Some years ago, two people I knew well, in two different businesses, were forced into bankruptcy because of the economic downturn. But the outcomes of their bankruptcies were completely different.

The first of my friends had been meticulously careful about all of his bills and finances throughout his career. He had always paid at least the minimum amounts on his charge cards. If ever he had a financial problem, he went to the person affected and rearranged payments and interest. When he was finally forced into bankruptcy, by a massive and unexpected financial default over which he had no control, he had no choice but to go to court, give up all his assets, and walk away penniless.

But within a week, people were approaching him and offering him money, loans, offices, credit cards, a place to live, and a new car. One of his previous business associates, quite wealthy, mailed him a blank check already signed, saying, "Just fill in the amount you need and let me know for my records; I have complete faith in you." Aside from removing a great burden of debt from him, his bankruptcy hardly affected him at all.

The second businessman, however, had a completely different experience. When he started to have financial problems, he continually misled and deceived his creditors, people who had trusted him. He neglected to make payments he had promised, and wrote checks that he couldn't cover. He avoided his creditors when they phoned, and he eventually changed his telephone number. He moved and didn't tell anyone his new address. He treated people who had trusted him by lending him money as if they were stupid. When he finally went bankrupt, no one wanted anything to do with him. It will take him years to recover, if he ever does. He can't even get a credit card; he now has to pay cash for everything.

■ THE KEY TO SALES SUCCESS

In sales, trust is the foundation of all relationships. A person will not buy from you until he or she trusts you completely. All top salespeople invest a good deal of time building high-quality, trusting relationships with their clients before they ever attempt to sell their products or services.

An association to which I belong commissioned a $50,000 survey of customers last year. Since most of our organizations sell forms of training and consulting services that are somewhat similar, they wanted to find out what caused a purchaser to buy from one company and not another.

One of the questions they asked the customers was what they were most concerned with in making a buying decision. More than 80 percent of the respondents to the survey said that the honesty and integrity of the salesperson was more important than any other factor.

When they asked them what they meant by honesty and integrity in a salesperson, the customers replied that this meant that the salesperson put their interests first. They believed that the salesperson would keep his or her word. They believed the salesperson's claims about the product. They believed that the salesperson would do what he or she promised, and that the company would fulfill any commitments that the salesperson made. They had a high level of confidence in the word of the salesperson and in everything that he or she did or said in interactions with them.

An interesting fact that came out of this survey was that the quality of the product or service was hardly mentioned. When customers were asked about their concerns over product quality, they replied that they felt that most products or services at a particular level were fairly similar and would achieve the results offered. The key to the sale was how they felt about the character of the salesperson, and through the salesperson, the company itself.

■ TRUTHFULNESS IS THE KEY TO CHARACTER

The real essence of character, and the most recognizable expression of honesty and integrity, is *truthfulness*. If you are completely truthful with yourself and others, you will almost always be viewed as a person of high character.

In our society, men and women of character seem to attract opportunities. Doors are opened for them wherever they go. They are introduced to people who can help them. Money and other resources are made available to them. This is why the most important quality you can instill in your children is a sense of honesty and the habit of truthfulness in everything they do or say.

■ PARENTS AND CHILDREN

I have four children. Each of my children has been brought up having the importance of truthfulness drummed into them from an early age. Today, all four of them are *adamant* truth tellers. They are completely honest. I can ask them any question and they will always tell me the truth.

When they were growing up, I made them each a promise. I said, "You will never get into trouble with me for telling the truth." And I kept my word. When they did something foolish, as all children do, I would listen to their stories without judging or criticizing and then ask, "Well, what did you learn?" They soon learned that they could always tell the truth and never suffer criticism or disapproval. They loved it.

Sometimes they fool around, but all I have to do is ask them for the truth and they will always give it to me, whatever it is. I'm very proud of them. It is absolutely amazing how much better relationships are between parents and children when they absolutely trust each other.

■ HUSBANDS AND WIVES

What is true for communications between parents and children is even more important for husbands and wives. One of the best definitions of love that I have ever heard is by Ayn Rand: "Love is a response to values."

You love another person because he or she represents values that you respect and cherish. The other person embodies qualities that you admire. In short, you love another person for his or her character. All else will change or fade away over time, but character remains.

Truthfulness and honesty between couples requires fidelity and straightforwardness between the two at all times. If a couple is ideally suited, they absolutely trust each other and are each other's best friends. There is no one that they would rather talk to or express themselves more honestly with than the other. Character, integrity, and honesty are the foundation qualities of a loving relationship, and are more important than anything else.

■ THE UNIVERSAL MAXIM

There is a wonderful test that you can give yourself on a regular basis to measure whether an act is good or bad, right or wrong. It is simple and you can use it throughout life. It is based on the Universal Maxim of the German philosopher Immanuel Kant, postulated more than 200 years ago. He said that *you should live your life as though your every act were to become a universal law.*

In other words, before you make a decision or take an action, imagine that everyone else was going to do exactly the same thing. Imagine that your decision was going to become a law for yourself and everyone else. This is the true test of whether your decision is a good one. It is the true test of a value or behavior. What kind of society would we have if everyone lived and behaved exactly the way you do?

Many of the problems in our society would not exist if this test were applied regularly in debates over public and social policy. Governments would be slower to approve certain actions in the areas of crime, education, welfare, and business if there was a likelihood that everyone would engage in those actions.

■ SET HIGH STANDARDS FOR YOURSELF

Here are some questions that you can ask yourself on a regular basis: First, ask yourself, *"What kind of a world would my world be if everyone in it were just like me?"* Just imagine! If everyone in the world were just like you, would this be a better world in which to live? If everyone in the world were just like you, would this be a happier, healthier, more prosperous, and more harmonious world—or not?

Then, ask yourself, *"What kind of a country would my country be if everyone in it were just like me?"* What would this country be like if everybody in it behaved exactly the way you do? If everyone did the things that you do in your daily life and work, would this be a better country? Or are there some things that you might do differently?

The third question you can ask yourself is, *"What kind of a company would my company be if everyone in it were just like me?"* Look around you in your company and ask yourself if your company would be more prosperous and harmonious if everybody in it did their work exactly the way you do your work all day long.

The final question that you can ask yourself is, *"What kind of a family would my family be if everyone in it was just like me?"*

If all the members of your family were just like you, would your family be a wonderful place to live and grow up in? Would everybody in your family thrive and be happier and more successful? Would you have the kind of family that other people would point to and admire and want to be like?

The fact is that no one can answer "yes" to all of these questions. Each of us is a *work in progress*. Each of us has a long way go. Each of us has a lot of room for improvement.

■ THE QUALITY OF COURAGE

In a review of 3,300 studies of leadership conducted by James McPherson over the years, he found a common denominator. It was the quality of courage. Winston Churchill once said, *"Courage is rightly considered the foremost of the virtues, for upon it, all others depend."*

You have heard it said that the road to hell is paved with good intentions. The world is full of people with high and lofty goals and ambitions, but there are very few people who have the courage, the discipline, and the willpower to carry them out.

The best part of practicing the quality of courage is that each time you behave courageously, you feel stronger and better about yourself. Your self-esteem increases and you like yourself more. You feel more confident and competent. You feel happier inside.

In contrast, each time you compromise yourself in the area of courage your self-esteem goes down. You feel weaker and less competent. You don't like or respect yourself as much.

■ DO THE THING YOU FEAR

A fundamental part of becoming personally powerful requires that you live consistently with the highest values you know, in every area of your life. These virtues and values not only are self-reinforcing, they also are self-rewarding. You get an immediate payoff of inner satisfaction each time you force yourself to do what you know you should do, even when you don't feel like it.

The fear of failure is the greatest single obstacle to success in adult life. The antidote to the fear of failure is the courage to take action. Courage is so important as a quality that, like physical fitness, it requires a series of exercises to build it and maintain it.

You best way to develop courage is by facing your fears. Ralph Waldo Emerson wrote, *"Do the thing you fear, and the death of fear is certain."*

When you do the thing that you are afraid of, you take control over both your emotions and your life. You shift your attitude from neutral or negative to positive and optimistic. "Do the thing you fear, and the death of fear is certain."

■ PRACTICE SYSTEMATIC DESENSITIZATION

Many people fear public speaking. But Toastmasters International has developed a powerful method of teaching public speaking even to people who are absolutely terrified of the idea of standing up and speaking in front of others. It is the process of "systematic desensitization." You can use it in every area of your life to reduce fear and build courage.

Systematic desensitization is a psychological term that refers to your doing something over and over again until it no longer holds any fear for you. In Toastmasters International, each member is required to stand up and speak, even if just for a few seconds, at every meeting. After several months of weekly meetings, people who were so terrified of speaking in front of others that they could not lead silent prayer in a phone booth become so confident about their ability to stand up and speak in front of peers that they compete for longer opportunities to talk.

■ SPEAK ON YOUR FEET

I have worked with countless executives who have taken my advice and joined Toastmasters International or taken a course from the Dale Carnegie organization. Within six months, they tell me that they are completely different people. From being shy and self-effacing at meetings and in presentations, they become calm, confident, bold, and even eloquent in expressing their points on their feet with other people. And their careers take off as well.

When you can speak on your feet, you appear to be smarter and more competent than a person who cannot. Many executives, both men and women, have seen their careers take off, their incomes increase, and their responsibilities expand as they faced their fears by speaking over and over again and until they became very good on their feet.

■ TURN TOWARD DANGER

On the Serengeti Plain of Africa, zoologists have developed a simple technique to determine which one of the animals in the herd is the leader.

When a predator—a lion or cheetah—approaches a herd of grazing animals, the members of the herd pick up the scent in the wind and begin drifting away in the opposite direction. At this time, the leader of the herd will emerge. The leader will be the animal that places himself between the predator and the herd while the herd begins to flee. The leader, risking his life facing the lion or cheetah that is moving in on the herd, will nonetheless stand his ground to buy time for the others to escape.

The leader always "turns toward danger." This is as true for human beings as it is for animals. You become a leader to the degree to which you force yourself to turn toward danger as well. You identify the areas in your life that cause you fear and stress, and instead of avoiding them and hoping that they will go away, you confront them directly.

■ DO IT ANYWAY

The actor Glenn Ford once said, *"If you do not do the thing you fear, the fear controls your life."*

It is almost as if the fear is the puppeteer and you are the puppet. If you don't deal with the fear, and cut the strings that hold you to the fear, the fear will cause you to dance emotionally and psychologically. If you let a fear go on for too long, it will tend to grow and grow and eventually come to dominate all of your thinking.

Each time you think of the fearful situation or person, your heart will beat faster and your stomach will churn. You will be unable to sleep well at night. The fear will affect your health, your happiness, your relationships, and your interactions with your customers and co-workers. Over time, you will become so preoccupied with the fear-inducing situation that you will not be able to think of anything else. This is no way to live.

■ FACE THE FEAR

The way you deal with fear is to confront the fear. You resolve to face the fear, deal with the fear, and put an end to the fear.

When I was a young man and confronted with a fearful situation, I read a quote from Mark Twain that changed my attitude forever. It said, *"Courage is not lack of fear or absence of fear. It is mastery of fear, control of fear."*

Those words had an enormous impact on me. I realized that we are all afraid of many things. To be afraid is normal and natural. In fact, the more intelligent you are, the greater number of possible fears you will have. You will have a greater sensitivity to your world and to the things it is logical for you to fear.

■ MOVE TOWARD THE FEAR

The only difference between the brave person and the coward is that the brave person confronts the fear and deals with it while the coward turns from the fear and flees from it.

And here is a great discovery. When you confront a fear and move toward it, it diminishes and grows smaller. It loses its hold over you. But if you back away from a fear, it grows larger and soon takes control of your thoughts and feelings.

When you habitually turn toward danger, do the thing you fear, face the fear, and move toward it bravely, it loses its power to affect you. Soon you dominate the fear rather than having it dominate you. You feel a tremendous sense of control. The quality that you need to face your fears, more than anything else, is the quality of self-discipline.

Wonderfully enough, when you discipline yourself to face your fears, to act courageously, even when you don't feel like it, your fear situation goes away. You will feel terrific about yourself. You will have a sense of power and control over your life.

■ LEAP AND THE NET WILL APPEAR

The first part of courage is the courage to launch in the direction of your goal. It is the ability and willingness for you to set a goal and then take the first step in the direction of achieving it.

In a 12-year study at Babson College, entrepreneurial instructor Dr. Robert Ronstadt searched for the reasons for success or failure among the graduates of the business school. Some went on to build successful businesses, but most did not. He discovered that those who built successful businesses had a special quality. It was that they had the courage to launch their businesses with *no guarantees* of success. They were willing to risk failure in the pursuit of their dreams.

Professor Ronstadt called this the "corridor principle." He said that when you launch toward your goal, however distant, you begin to move down a corridor of time. As you move down this corridor, other doors of opportunity will open up on either side of you. But you would not have been able to see these other doors of opportunity if you were not already in motion down this psychological corridor toward your goal.

Most people who succeed in life achieve their success in an area completely different from the field in which they started off. But because they were in motion, they saw opportunities and possibilities that they would not have been aware of if they had waited until everything was just right. And the fact is that everything will never be just right.

■ THE IRON QUALITY OF SUCCESS

If the first part of courage is the willingness to *begin*; the second part of courage is the willingness to *endure*. It is the courage to hang in there. It is the courage to stay the course. It is the courage to persist in the face of every setback and difficulty.

Self-discipline is the iron quality of character. It is what enables you to endure. Self-discipline is the one quality that gives you the strength that you need to take risks and to move forward in the face of danger and uncertainty. It is self-discipline, and the courage that comes from self-discipline, that develops personal power within you that enables you to overcome any obstacle in your way.

■ DIFFERENT FORMS OF COURAGE

There are several forms of courage that you can develop with practice. These forms of courage will help you to achieve the great success that is possible for you. They are all learnable with practice.

➤ Dream Big Dreams

The first form of courage is the courage to dream big dreams and to set big goals. This is where most people are stopped. The very idea of setting big, challenging, exciting, worthwhile goals is so overwhelming that they quit before they even begin. But this is not for you. Sit down, write out your goals as if anything were possible for you, and never be afraid to dream big dreams.

➤ Make a Commitment

The second type of courage is the courage to make a total commitment, throwing yourself wholeheartedly into whatever it is you decide to do. All successful people of my experience are people who are living fully engaged. They are fully involved in their lives and in their goals. They don't do things by half measures. They may have no guarantees, but they are not afraid to put their whole hearts into their activities. If they fail, they fail by trying greatly, not by playing it safe, wishing and hoping that everything will work out all right.

➤ Move out of Your Comfort Zone

The third type of courage you need is the courage to move out of your comfort zone. It is the courage to move into your zone of *discomfort*, where you feel awkward, clumsy, and alone. The comfort zone is one of the greatest enemies of human potential. When people get into a comfort zone, they strive to stay in that comfort zone. Often their whole lives pass them by while they are furnishing and reinforcing their little rut of medium performance.

You need the courage to continually move yourself in the direction of your biggest goals and ambitions. You need to be willing to face discomfort in order for you to grow.

➤ Take a Stand

The fourth type of courage you need is the courage to take a stand, especially with regard to your values, your vision, and your beliefs. You need to stand up for what you believe to be right. You need to stand up for other people who espouse those principles. You need to have the courage to stand solidly for the highest values that you know, and then refuse to compromise yourself or your character because others may disapprove.

➤ Step Out in Faith

You need the courage to launch in faith with no guarantees of success. Someone once wrote, *"If every obstacle must first be overcome, nothing will ever get done."*

Courageous people are those who have a dream and set a goal, make a plan and take the first step, with no assurances and no guarantees that their efforts will result in success. However, if you look upon every step forward as a learning experience and every setback as a valuable lesson that has been sent to you to make you stronger and better, you will not be afraid to launch in faith into the unknown.

➤ Risk Failure

You need the courage to risk failure. You need the courage to endure constant setbacks, disappointments, and temporary defeats. You need to learn to deal with failure by realizing that it is an indispensable prerequisite for success. You need the courage to treat failure as an opportunity to more intelligently begin again. You need to overcome the fear of failure by doing the things you fear over and over again, and then by resolving to bounce rather than break when things don't work out for you.

The bigger and more exciting the goals you set for yourself, the more times you will trip and fall. But as long as you have clear goals, you will always be failing and falling in a forward direction. You will always be picking yourself up a little bit closer to the goal than you were before.

➤ Face Your Fears

You need the courage to turn toward danger continuously. Identify all the fear situations in your life that cause you stress or anxiety today. Decide what the worst possible outcome of each of those situations might be. Resolve to accept the worst, should it occur. And then take action to resolve each of those situations. Refuse to allow a fear situation to remain in your life, dominating your thinking and emotions and holding you back.

➤ Practice Zero-Based Thinking

You need the courage to practice zero-based thinking continuously in your life. Ask yourself, "Is there anything in my life that, knowing what I now know, I would not get into or start up again today if I had it to do over?"

There are situations in every person's life that, knowing what they now know, they wouldn't get into again if they had to do it over. If you decide that there is something you wouldn't get into again, your next question is *how do you get out and how fast?*

You cannot make a great life for yourself if, right in the middle of your life, if there is something that you wouldn't even get into if you had it to do over again. And you always know when you are dealing with a zero-based thinking situation. It causes you a great deal of stress. It preoccupies you continually. It sometimes keeps you awake at night and dominates your conversation. You always know what it is.

➤ Admit Your Mistakes

You need the courage to admit that you might be wrong, and that you have made a mistake when you get new information on any situation. It is amazing how many people keep themselves locked into a low level of performance because they will not admit that they are not *perfect*. They will not admit that, with the passing of time, something that seemed like a good idea has proven to be a bad choice or decision.

Don't be afraid to cut your losses. Don't be afraid to admit that you were wrong and to bail out. Don't be afraid to put one course of action aside and embark upon something completely different. This is the mark of courage, personal power, and effective thinking.

➤ Be Willing to Make Mistakes

You need the courage to be willing to make mistakes and learn from them. All peak performers continually make decisions, make mistakes, learn from them, self-correct, and carry on.

Successful people are not those who necessarily make the right decisions all the time, but they make their decisions right. If they make a mistake, they accept it, learn as much as possible from it, and then continue on. Remember, you can learn to succeed only by failing and making mistakes. The more you fail and the more mistakes you make, the smarter you become and the more likely it is that you will eventually achieve your goals.

➤ Accept Complete Responsibility

You need the courage to accept complete responsibility for your life, which means to take ownership for results. You need the courage to refuse to make excuses or to defend yourself. You need the courage to say, over and over again, *"I am responsible!"*

When something goes wrong, you focus on the solution rather than the problem. You ask, *"What do we do from here? What's the next step? What is the solution?"*

You then pick yourself up and carry on, extracting the wheat from the situation and throwing away the chaff.

➤ Be Patient

You need what is called "courageous patience." This is a special kind of courage that is required after you have launched toward your goal but you have not yet seen any results. It is amazing how many people break and run in that zone between when they begin and when they start to see a payoff. Their doubts and fears overwhelm them.

But this is not for you. Once you have started toward your goal, resolve to remain calm and confident until you start to get results. Be patient and persistent, no matter what happens in the short term.

➤ Persist Longer

The final courage you need is the courage to persist longer than anyone else. Persistence is the quality that will ultimately guarantee your success. Your willingness to persist in the face of every adversity can be your greatest asset. It can be the one factor that guarantees your success.

If you refuse to quit, you must ultimately succeed. Just as in baseball, you won't ultimately hit a home run unless you keep on swinging. In 30 years of studying successful people, I have discovered one fact over and over. No one was ever defeated until they accepted defeat as a reality. No one can ever defeat you but yourself.

When you discipline yourself to do what you should do, whether you feel like it or not, and you use this inner strength to build high levels of courage and persistence within yourself, you will become an incredibly powerful person. You will soon feel that there is nothing that you cannot accomplish. You will eventually develop yourself to the point where you feel completely *unstoppable*.

■ YOU ARE ULTIMATELY SELF-MADE

Someone once said, "I'm a self-made man, but if I had to do it over, I'd bring in a little help." You and I are all self-made. We all have a lot of areas in which we could improve. We all need to set higher standards for ourselves. We all need to work continually on the development of our characters. We all need to strive to become better people. We can never allow ourselves to be complacent at any level of accomplishment. We have to keep raising the bar on ourselves.

One of the marks of superior people is that they can manage themselves. If they work for a company, they might do this by imagining their boss sitting next to them, observing them and filling out their annual performance appraisal every minute of every day. Or, by seeing themselves as role models, they might set far higher standards for themselves than anyone else could set for them.

Only the top 2 percent of people in our society can supervise and manage themselves. They can conduct themselves throughout the day as though everyone is watching, even though no one is watching.

■ THE REAL PAYOFF

When you set high standards for yourself, your self-esteem and self-respect increase. When you decide that you are going to live consistently with your highest values and your deepest convictions, you feel wonderful about yourself. When you become completely honest, you stop compromising yourself in your relationships with others. You speak sincerely to everyone with whom you live and work. You practice absolute truthfulness with yourself and others.

The more honest you are with yourself, the greater courage and self-confidence you will have. You will become more positive and enthusiastic about yourself. You will develop a tremendous feeling of inner power and personal strength. The more you live consistently with the very highest values you know, the finer your character will become. Eventually, you will reach the point where you are absolutely *unstoppable*!

ACTION EXERCISES

1. Determine your three most important values in your personal and family life. What do you believe in and care about the most?

2. Resolve to live in truth with yourself and others, without compromise. In what area of your life are you are not being perfectly honest with another person?

3. "To thine own self be true." Examine the areas of your life where you experience stress, dissatisfaction, or unhappiness and determine if you are compromising one of your values.

4. What kind of a company would your company be if everyone in it was just like you? What could you change immediately to make your company a better place?

5. What would you do and how would you spend your time if you learned today that you had only six months left to live? Your answers to this question will reveal your true values.

6. "People don't change." Since this is one of the laws of life, what changes should you make in your life and relationships, at home and at work, to accommodate this fact.

7. Practice truthfulness in all things. In what areas do you need to accept the world as it is, rather than the way you would like it to be? Be honest with yourself.

Summary and Conclusions

The world is like a great mirror. It reflects back to you what you are. If you are loving, if you are friendly, if you are helpful, the world will prove loving, friendly, and helpful to you. The world is what you are.

—Thomas Dreier

The most important principle of human life is that *you become what you think about most of the time.* This insight is the foundation of religion, philosophy, metaphysics, psychology, and all success. Your outer world is very much a reflection of your inner world. If you change your thinking, you change your life.

Your biggest challenge and your greatest responsibility are to create within yourself the *mental equivalent* of what you want to experience on the outside. By doing this, you activate all your mental powers, and put the forces of the universe to work on your behalf. You take full control over your life.

Many thousands of people have been asked what they think about most of the time. Over and over, the most successful men and women report the same things. They think about *what they want* and *how to get it* most of the time. Unsuccessful and unhappy people, in contrast, think and talk about what they *don't* want. They think and talk about their problems and worries, and about the people in their lives that they don't like. But this is not for you.

When you think and talk continuously about what you want and how to get it, this way of thinking soon becomes a habit. When you think and talk about what you want, you become more positive, purposeful, and creative. When you stay focused on where you're going, you become a more productive and effective person.

■ LEARNED OPTIMISM

Perhaps the most important quality you can develop to achieve greater success and happiness is the quality of *optimism*. You can learn the habit of optimism by thinking the way that optimists do most of the time. According to interviews with thousands of the happiest and most successful people in every field, optimists seem to have two special ways of dealing with life. These are attitudes of mind that you can develop with practice.

First, optimists *look for the good* in every situation, especially when they experience reversals and setbacks. They keep themselves positive by looking for the bright side, the silver lining, to every problem. And they always find something.

Second, optimists *seek the valuable lesson* in every problem or difficulty. They believe that each temporary failure or obstacle has been sent to teach them something. They continually ask, "What am I meant to learn from this situation?" And they always find something.

Your mind is structured in such a way that you cannot look for the good and seek the valuable lesson without taking full control over your conscious mind. When you do, you feel more positive and optimistic about yourself and your situation. You feel in complete control of your life. You perform at your best.

■ SEVEN STEPS TO HIGH-PERFORMANCE LIVING

In addition to looking for the good and seeking the valuable lesson, optimists have seven orientations, or generalized ways of thinking about themselves and their lives. These are the seven subjects that they think about most of the time.

➤ Think about the Future

First, positive, happy people are *future-oriented*. They think and talk about the future much of the time. They think and talk about where they are going, rather than about what has happened in the past. They create a clear, exciting future vision of what is possible for them. By the Law of Attraction, they find themselves attracted toward their future hopes and dreams, and their future hopes and dreams are attracted toward them.

➤ Think about Your Goals

Second, they are *goals-oriented*. They think and talk about their goals much of the time. Once they have dreamed and fantasized about their ideal future visions, they boil them down into clear, written goals and plans that they work on every day. They focus their attention and concentrate their energies. They use their goals to take control over their futures.

➤ Think about Excellence

Third, they are *excellence-oriented*. They commit to becoming excellent at what they do, to joining the top 10 percent of people in their field, whatever it is. They identify their key result areas, and set standards of excellent performance for themselves in each one. They work on themselves each day, and never stop improving.

➤ Think about the Solution

Fourth, they are *solution-oriented*. They think about the solution rather than the problem. They think about what needs to be done rather than who is to blame. They use creative thinking methods to unlock their creativity and that of the people around them. They view their goals as problems to be solved, and they believe that there is a logical solution to every difficulty just waiting to be found.

➤ Think about Results

Fifth, successful, happy people are intensely *results-oriented*. They carefully plan each day in advance. They set clear priorities on their activities. They then work on those tasks that represent the most valuable use of their time. They plow through enormous amounts of work and become known as highly productive people. Because they are so effective and efficient, they get more done, they move ahead faster, and they make a greater contribution to their work and to their worlds.

➤ Think about Growth

Sixth, high performers are *growth-oriented*. They are continually reading, listening to audio programs, and attending additional courses and seminars. They are determined to stay at the cutting edge of their fields. They know that the future belongs to the competent, to those few people who *know more* than their competitors. They know that there is a race on, and that they are in it. They are determined to win.

➤ Think about Action

Seventh, and perhaps more important than any of the others, the most successful people are intensely *action-oriented*. They think about what they can do, right now, to move faster toward their goals. They are in constant motion. They work in real time. They have a sense of urgency. They cover more ground and get a lot more done than the average person. The more they get done, the better they get, the more valuable they become, and the more they earn.

■ YOUR POSSIBILITIES ARE UNLIMITED

We are living in the golden age of mankind. There have never been more opportunities and possibilities for you to become all you are capable of becoming, and to achieve more of your goals, than there are today. You can use this book as a guide to greater success and happiness for the rest of your life. Here again are the 12 core ideas:

1. *Change Your Thinking.* The way you think about yourself, your abilities, and your potential—your *self-concept*—determines everything you are today, and everything you ever will be. Fortunately, your self-concept is learned. By taking complete control over the words, pictures, and ideas you let into your mind, you take complete control of your future.

2. *Change Your Life.* You come into the world as pure potential, with unlimited abilities in countless areas. As the result of destructive criticism in childhood, you can inadvertently develop fears of failure, loss, rejection, and criticism. You can develop self-limiting beliefs that hold you back. By getting rid of these

negative emotions, you liberate your potential and change your life.

3. ***Dream Big Dreams.*** The true starting point of living the kind of life that is possible for you is to create an exciting future vision of what you would want your life to be, in every area, if you had no limitations at all. Imagine that you could be, have, or do anything at all in your family, finances, and personal life. Then set clear, written goals, backed by detailed plans, to make your dreams come true.

4. ***Decide to Become Rich.*** Resolve today to take complete control over your financial future. Begin to do the things that others have done to become financially independent, starting from where you are today. Determine exactly how much you want to earn, keep, and acquire; set these amounts as goals; and then think about them all the time. Whatever others have done, you can do as well.

5. ***Take Charge of Your Life.*** You are the primary creative force in your own life. Everything you are or ever will be will be the result of what you do or fail to do. Resolve today to accept 100 percent responsibility, with no blaming and no excuses, for everything that happens. Exert your personal power and take control of your thoughts, words, and actions. Become the master of your own destiny.

6. ***Commit to Excellence.*** The biggest rewards and the greatest satisfactions go to those who are *very good* at what they do. Resolve to join the top 10 percent of people in your field. Determine the key skills you will have to excel at what you do, set superior performance as your goal, make a plan, and then work on getting better every day.

7. ***Put People First.*** The quality and quantity of your relationships will have more of an impact on your success and happiness than any other factors. Organize your life around building and maintaining high-quality, high-trust relationships with the most important people in your world. Network regularly to expand your range of contacts. Mastermind with other positive, success-oriented people.

8. ***Think Like a Genius.*** You are actually a mind, with a body to carry it around. You are not what you think you are; but what you *think*, you are. You have the ability to think better and more efficiently than you ever have before. When you begin to think the same way that the smartest and most successful people think, you will soon get the same results they do.

9. ***Unleash Your Mental Powers.*** Ideas are the primary sources of wealth today. The more ideas you develop to help you to achieve your goals, by the Law of Probabilities the more likely it is that you will come up with exactly the right idea for you, at exactly the right time. Your ability to generate new ideas is unlimited. Therefore, your future is unlimited as well.

10. ***Supercharge Your Thinking.*** There are several key thinking strategies and techniques practiced by top people everywhere. Any one of these methods of analyzing and assessing your situation can give you vital insights and ideas that can change your perspective, and even change your life. The more thinking tools you have, the more wonderful the life you can build for yourself.

11. ***Create Your Own Future.*** The ability to look into the future and then to take the steps today that will assure the future you desire is an essential way of thinking practiced by the most successful people in history. The most effective people plan their lives carefully, and make every effort to anticipate what might go wrong, well in advance. As a result, they think better and make better decisions than the people around them.

12. ***Live a Great Life.*** The world around you is largely determined by the world within you. The happiest, most highly paid and respected people in every area are those who are known for the quality of their character. When you organize your life around the twin qualities of *integrity* and *courage*, every door will open for you, and you will be a genuinely happy person. You will change your thinking and change your life.

■ JUST DO IT!

Mental fitness is very much like physical fitness. It takes a long time and a lot of hard work to achieve it and maintain it. But it is worth every bit of effort you put in. The payoff can be extraordinary!

When you begin the process of working on yourself, to create on the *inside* a clear picture of what you want to enjoy on the *outside*, progress may be slow at first. But when you persist, when you keep doing and saying the right things in the right way, you will before too long get results out of all proportion to the efforts you put it.

There are no real limits to what you can be, do, and have, except for the limits you place on yourself. You are a thoroughly good and extremely talented person, and there is very little that you cannot achieve if you want it intensely enough and work toward it long enough and hard enough. The key is to begin today, and then *never give up!*

Bibliography

Alexander, Bevin. *How Great Generals Win*. New York: W. W. Norton & Company, 2002.

Allen, James. *As Man Thinketh*. Marina Del Ray, CA: DeVorss & Company, 1983.

Bach, Richard. *Illusions*. New York: Dell Publishing Company, 1994.

Barker, Raymond Charles. *Power of Decision*. Marina Del Ray, CA: DeVorss & Company, 1997.

Beatty, Jack. *The World According to Peter Drucker*. New York: Bantam Books, 1999.

Bloch, Arthur. *Murphy's Law*. Kansas City, MO: Andrews McMeel Publishers, 2002.

Botton, Alain de. *The Consolations of Philosophy*. New York: Vintage Books, 2001.

Bristol, Claude. *The Magic of Believing*. New York: Pocket Books, 1994.

Brown, Les. *It's Not Over Until You Win*. New York: Fireside, 1998.

Bucke, Richard. *Cosmic Consciousness*. New York: E. P. Dutton, 1991.

Buckingham, Marcus, and Donald Clifton. *Now, Discover Your Strengths*. New York: Free Press, 2001.

Butterworth, Eric. *The Creative Life*. New York: J. P. Tarcher, 2001.

Butterworth, Eric. *Discover the Power within You*. San Franciso: HarperSanFrancisco, 1992.

Chilton, David. *The Wealthy Barber*. Roseville, CA: Prima Publishing, 1998.

Collier, Robert. *The Secret of the Ages*. Oak Harbor, WA: Robert Collier Publications, 1984.

Covey, Stephen. *The Seven Habits of Highly Effective People*. New York: Simon & Schuster, 1990.

DePorter, Bobbi, with Mike Hernacki. *Quantum Learning*. New York: DTP, 1992.

Dichter, Ernest. *Motivating Human Behavior.* New York: McGraw-Hill, 1971.

Drucker, Peter F. *Management Challenges for the 21st Century.* New York: HarperBusiness, 2001.

Drucker, Peter F. *Management: Tasks, Responsibilities, Practices.* New York: HarperBusiness, 1993.

Elkins, Dr. Dove Peretz. *Self-Concept Sourcebook.* Mystic, CT: Growth Associates, 1990.

Epictetus. *A Manual for Living.* San Francisco: HarperSanFrancisco, 1994.

Ferrucci, Piero. *What We May Be.* New York: J. P. Tarcher, 1983.

Fox, Emmet. *Alter Your Life.* San Francisco: HarperSanFrancisco, 1994.

Fox, Emmet. *Power through Constructive Thinking.* San Francisco: HarperSanFrancisco, 1989.

Fox, Emmet. *The Sermon on the Mount.* New York: HarperCollins, 1992.

Gardner, Howard. *Frames of Mind.* New York: Basic Books, 1993.

Goldsmith, Joel. *The Infinite Way.* Marina Del Ray, CA: DeVorss & Company, 1979.

Gordon, Arthur. *A Touch of Wonder.* New York: Jove Publications, 1991.

Gowain, Shakti. *Creating True Prosperity.* Novato, CA: New World Library, 2000.

Haanel, Charles F. *The Master Key System.* Wilkes-Barre, PA: Kallisti Publishing, 2000.

Hansen, Mark Victor, and Jack Canfield. *Chicken Soup for the Soul.* Deerfield Beach, FL: Health Communications, 1995.

Hansen, Mark Victor, and Robert G. Allen. *The One Minute Millionaire.* New York: Harmony Books, 2002.

Heller, Robert. *Business Masterminds: Peter Drucker.* New York: D. K. Publishing, 2001.

Hill, Napoleon. *The Master Key to Riches.* New York: Fawcett Books, 1991.

Hill, Napoleon. *Think and Grow Rich.* New York: Fawcett Books, 1990.

Holmes, Ernest. *Creative Mind and Success.* New York: J. P. Tarcher, 1997.

Holmes, Ernest. *Science of Mind.* New York: J. P. Tarcher, 1998.

James, William. *The Varieties of Religious Experience.* New York: Touchstone Books, 1997.

Keegan, John. *A History of Warfare.* New York: Vintage Books, 1994.

Leonard, George. *Mastery.* New York: Plume, 1992.

Lin, Yutang. *The Importance of Living.* New York: William Morrow & Company, 1998.

Luvaas, J. *Napoleon on the Art of War.* New York: Touchstone Books, 2001.

McClelland, David. *The Achieving Society.* New York: Free Press, 1985.

McCormick, Blaine. *At Work with Thomas Edison.* Irvine, CA: Entrepreneur Press, Inc. 2001.

McGraw, Phillip P. *Life Strategies.* New York: Hyperion, 2000.

Mises, Ludwig von. *Human Action.* San Francisco, CA: Fox & Wilkes, 1997.

Mitroff, Ian. *Smart Thinking for Crazy Times: The Art of Solving the Right Problems.* San Francisco: Berrett-Koehler Publishers, 1998.

Neville. *The Law and the Promise.* Marina Del Ray, CA: DeVorss & Company, 1984.

Neville. *Seedtime and Harvest.* Marina Del Ray, CA: DeVorss & Company, 1985.

Newman, James. *Release Your Brakes!* New York: Warner Books, 1983.

Ouspensky, P. D. *The Fourth Way.* New York: Random House, 1971.

Ouspensky, P. D. *In Search of the Miraculous.* San Diego, CA: Harvest Books, 2001.

Parkinson, C. Northcote. *Parkinson's Law.* Cutchogue, NY: Buccaneer Books, 1996.

Peale, Norman Vincent. *Power of Positive Thinking.* New York: Ballantine Books, 1996.

Ponder, Catherine. *The Dynamic Laws of Healing.* Marina Del Ray, CA: DeVorss & Company, 1989.

Qubein, Nido. *Stairway to Success.* Hoboken, NJ: John Wiley & Sons, 1997.

Rand, Ayn. *Philosophy: Who Needs It.* New York: New American Library, 1985.

Schwartz, David. *The Magic of Thinking Big*. New York: Fireside, 1987.

Slywotzky, Adrian J., and David J. Morrison. *Profit Patterns*. New York: Random House, 1999.

Smiles, Samual. *Character*. McLean, VA: IndyPublish.com, 2003.

Stanley, Thomas. *The Millionaire Mind*. Kansas City, MO: Andrews McMeel Publishing, 2000.

Stanley, Thomas, and William Danko. *The Millionaire Next Door*. New York: Simon & Schuster, 1999.

Stone, Clement W., and Napoleon Hill. *The Success System That Never Fails*. Upper Saddle River, NJ: Prentice Hall, 1962.

Templeton, John Marks. *Worldwide Laws of Life*. Radnor, PA: Templeton Foundation, 1998.

Tracy, Brian. *Create Your Own Future*. Hoboken, NJ: John Wiley & Sons, 2002.

Tracy, Brian. *Focal Point*. New York: AMACOM, 2001.

Tracy, Brian. *Goals!* San Francisco, CA: Berrett-Koehler Publishers, 2003.

Tracy, Brian. *Many Miles to Go*. Irvine, CA: Entrepreneur Press, Inc., 2003.

Tracy, Brian. *Maximum Achievement*. New York: Fireside, 1995.

Tracy, Brian. *The 100 Absolutely Unbreakable Laws of Business Success*. San Francisco: Berrett-Koehler Publishers, 2002.

Tracy, Brian. *Turbo Strategy*. New York: AMACOM, 2003.

Tracy, Brian. *The 21 Success Secrets of Self-Made Millionaires*. San Francisco: Berrett-Koehler Publishers, 2001.

Tracy, Brian. *Victory!* New York: AMACOM, 2002.

Treacy, Michael, and Fred Wiersma. *The Disciplines of Market Leaders*. Cambridge, MA: Perseus Publishing, 1997.

Walters, Dottie, and Lilly Walters. *Speak and Grow Rich*. Upper Saddle River, NJ: Prentice Hall, 1989.

Wiersma, Fred. *Customer Intimacy*. Encino, CA: Knowledge Exchange, 1996.

Williamson, Marianne. *A Return to Love*. New York: HarperCollins, 1996.

Index

Abilities, identifying, 104, 115–116
Absorption process, 119
Abstract intelligence, 168–169
Accomplishments
  limits, and life, 80
  and time, 110
Achievement
  goals, 45–49
  high achievers and, 185
  positive feeling and, 157–158
  unstoppable, 42
Achieving Society, The, 118
Acres of Diamonds, 72–73
Action(s)
  high performance living and, 252
  importance of, 173
  lack of knowledge and, 80–81
  plan and, 48–49
  positive and optimistic, 212–213
  taking in real time, 69
  taking on current situation, 73
  values and, 225
Activities, low-value, 62
Adaptive worldview, 144
Adolescence, personality problems in, 3–4
Adulthood
  fear of failure in, 4
  personality problems in, 3–4
Affirmations, positive, 186, 188–189, 191
Age of the mind, 52
Ambition, 91
Amnesia, 1–2
Anger, 21, 29–35
Apple Computer, 61, 142
Applied Imagination, 174
Aristotelian Principle of Causality, 55
Assets
  hard, *vs.* brainpower, 138–139
  most valuable, 110
Associations, benefits of, 122–123
Attachment, *see* Identification
Attitude(s)
  hardening of, 144
  positive mental, 180
Attraction, law of, 47, 49, 84–85, 86, 124, 174, 211, 212, 251
Auditory learner, 170–171

Bacon, Francis, 75, 152
Bacon, Roger, 140
Bankruptcies, 233
Belief(s)
  changing, 7–8
  and inner dialogue, 15–16
  law of, 82–83, 86
  removing negative, 42
  self-limiting, 181
  standing up for, 243
Benevolent worldview, *see* Positive worldview
Billings, Josh, 57
Bill Moyers, 106
Blame, 21, 29
Blank slate, 2–3
Brainpower
  hard assets *vs.,* 138–139
  wealth and, 137
Brainstorming, 171, 174–176
Bristol, Claude M., 52
Business, *see also* Companies
  activities of success, 112–115
  bankruptcies in, 233
  building relationships and, 132
  and competition, 230–231
  crisis anticipation and, 204–205
  and sales, 214–215
Butterworth, Eric, 108

Campbell, Joseph, 106–107
Capital, starting, 137–138
Career
  advancing, 122
  preparing for, 206
Carnegie, Dale, 105
Cause and Effect, law of, 47, 55
Chance, 116, 198
Change
  business, competition and, 230–231
  in inner world, 119
  knowledge and, 141
  life and, 79–80
  opportunities and, 54
Character
  self-discipline and, 242
  truthfulness and, 234–235

Advanced Coaching and Mentoring Program

Brian Tracy offers a personal group-coaching program in San Diego, California, for successful entrepreneurs and top sales professionals.

If you qualify for this program (you must have an income of at least $100,000 per year), you will learn how to set and achieve goals in every part of your life, develop a complete personal strategic plan, and simplify every aspect of your life.

You will be learn a step-by-step process of personal and business analysis that will change your thinking and change your life.

This is an intensive one-year program during which you meet with Brian Tracy one full day every three months. During these sessions, you will learn how to double your income and double your time off.

You will identify those things you enjoy doing the most and learn how to become better and better in your most profitable activities.

You will learn how to delegate, downsize, eliminate, and get rid of all those tasks you neither enjoy nor benefit from.

You will learn how to determine your special talents and how to use leverage and concentration to move to the top of your field.

For more information, visit www.briantracy.com and click on "Coaching," or phone 858-481-2977 and we'll send you a complete information package. Write to Brian Tracy at Brian Tracy International, 462 Stevens Avenue, Suite 202, Solana Beach, CA 92075.

About the Author

■ **BRIAN TRACY—KEYNOTE SPEAKER, CONSULTANT, SEMINAR LEADER**

Brian Tracy is a successful businessman and one of the top professional speakers in the world. He has started, built, managed, or turned around 22 different businesses. He addresses more than 250,000 people each year throughout the United States, Canada, Europe, Australia, and Asia.

Brian's keynote speeches, talks, and seminars are customized and tailored for each audience. They are described as "inspiring, entertaining, informative, and motivational." He has worked with more than 500 corporations, given more than 2,000 talks, and addressed over 2,000,000 people.

Some of his talks and seminars include:

Leadership in the New Millennium—How to be a more effective leader in every area of business life. Learn the most powerful, practical leadership strategies ever discovered to manage, motivate, and get better results than ever before.

21st Century Thinking—How to outthink, outplan, and outperform your competition. Learn how to get superior results in a fast-moving, fast-changing business environment.

The Psychology of Peak Performance—How the top people think and act in every area of personal and business life. You learn a series of practical, proven methods and strategies for maximum achievement.

Superior Selling Strategies—How to sell more, faster, and easier to demanding customers in highly competitive markets. Learn how to sell higher-priced products and services against lower-priced competitors.

Brian will carefully customize his talk for you and your audience. Call today for full information on booking Brian to speak at your next meeting or conference. Visit www.briantracy.com, phone 858-481-2977, or write Brian Tracy International, 462 Stevens Avenue, Suite 202, Solana Beach, CA 92075.